I Shall Come Forth as Gold

as Gold

by

Peter Church

Elite Books
3340 Fulton Rd., #442
Fulton, CA 954439

Cataloging-in-Publication Data

Church, William Peter.
  I shall come forth as gold / by Peter Church. – 2nd ed.
    p. cm.
  Includes bibliographical references and index.
  ISBN 978-1-60070-095-8
  1. Autobiography. 2. Theology and Religious Vocations. I. Title.

Second Edition
Typeset by Karin A. Kinsey
Cover by Victoria Valentine
Printed in USA by LightningSource

10 9 8 7 6 5 4 3 2 1

Dedication

I dedicate this book to my friends:
Through the years the good, the bad and the unfathomable, some
very special people have walked with me in the fires of life; I
acknowledge your friendship and offer this story as a tribute to
loving acceptance.

To my family: my precious wife, Suzanne,
To my dear departed wife Ada, who lives on
In our two children, Dawson and Jenny,
Who are joined by their partners Christine and Dale and
Their seven children, Jessica, Peter, Bethany Joy, Ruth;
and Lionel, Angela, and Alexander.

Contents

Part II

Acknowledgments

This edition is built on the foundation of the original published in 1980. At that time I acknowledged my debt of gratitude to those who, by their contributions of love, guidance, counsel, and prayerful support, gave birth to that book. I must now add my expressions of gratitude to a new generation of helpers.

Again, I owe more than I can express in words to my family. Only now that number has been increased. Dawson, my original inspiration and continued director-in-writing has been my mentor in the not-too-easy task of updating, rewriting, editing and producing this new edition.

My daughter Jenny, too, continues to support and strengthen me through her faithful prayers, grace and love. She is married, and with her husband, Bishop Dale F. Howard, they support and encourage me in my life's journey.

For the production of this new edition, I am indebted to the following helpers: Lyn Hawley, Harriet Taylor, and Margaret Sowell who typed and retyped the manuscript; Karin Kinsey, who typeset the book; Dawson, who guided this new edition through the labyrinth of publication; the special people who, by their love and financial support sustained us in the most recent months of our testing-times, and who, by their generosity continue to make our ministry possible.

In the original edition I expressed my thanks to: the Rand Mutual Assurance Company in Johannesburg, to the South African Chamber of Mines, the South African Consulate, New York, the South African Tourism Board, and my dear friend and colleague, Merold Stern, who so skillfully edited the very first manuscript.

I am grateful also to the late Dr. Oswald J. Smith for permission to quote his poem, *Lord Anoint Me with Thy Spirit*.

February 16, 1996

Foreword
to the First Edition

Peter Church, one of South Africa's promising young athletes, was almost crushed to death in a gold mine cave-in nearly a mile below the surface. Paralyzed, he was in a wheelchair for several months before a healing miracle put him on his feet and established him in the ministry.

As a pastor, evangelist, radio broadcaster and founder of an indigenous mission, he took the Gospel of peace to a land threatened by civil unrest and divided by racial strife.

Later, in a magnificent act of faith, Peter and Ada Church gave away all their earthly possessions and moved to the United States. Leaving behind home, family and friends, they committed themselves to a life of faith and obedience to God's call.

I Shall Come Forth as Gold is more than the miracle story of Peter Church's healing; it is an inspiring digest of faith, challenging others to step out as he has, believing God shall bring them forth as gold.

—Jamie Buckingham, Melbourne, Florida, 1980

Preface

The scripture verse from which the title of this book is taken says it all:

"He knows the way that I take, and when He has tried me, I shall come forth as gold."

This book is the story of a man in relationship with God, the God who has revealed Himself on the pages of the Hebrew and Christian scriptures.

He is a God who knows all things so it is not surprising that He knows and understands the ways that we take. He is a God who not only allows trials, but actually sends them. Listen to the word of the Apostle James:

"Consider it pure joy, my brothers, when you face trials of many kinds, because you know the testing of your faith develops perseverance."

Why would God want us to develop perseverance? The Apostle responds, "So that you may become mature and complete, not lacking anything."

And now you can understand the faith of the author expressed in the title of this book: "I shall come forth as gold." This is a story about frustration and faith, testing and triumph. It will instruct, it will encourage, and it will inspire.

—Dr. Everett L. "Terry" Fullam

Introduction

From the dawn of time we humans have wrestled with the question, "Why do people suffer?" The purpose of this book is not to explore the mysteries of suffering, nor to delve into the reason why. Rather, my desire is to share some of the experiences which have molded my life and to show that a loving God, in infinite grace and kindness, has a special purpose for every person whom He has placed upon this earth. It is best expressed in the words of Job: "He knoweth the way that I take; when he hath tried (tested) me, I shall come forth as gold." [Job 23:10]

On February 15, 1978, twenty-eight years after a near-fatal accident in a South African gold mine, I underwent a major surgical operation at the Baptist Hospital in Memphis, Tennessee. Dr. Marcus Stewart of the Campbell Clinic performed a bone graft in which five of the vertebrae in my spine were fused together. For three months I was in a plaster cast from my chest to my left knee. For six months I was unable to sit up.

In April 1988 a second and more radical procedure was performed at the University Hospital in Cleveland, Ohio. In that ordeal, I looked death in the eye, yet lived to bear testimony to the sustaining love of family, friends and "the God of all mercy." [II Cor. 1:3,4]

I have had a glimpse into the meaning of the words of the apostle Paul who wrote, "For this thing I besought the Lord three times, that it might depart from me. And he said unto me, My grace is sufficient for thee; for my strength is made perfect in weakness. Most gladly, therefore, will I rather glory in my infirmities, that the power of Christ may rest upon me. Therefore, I take pleasure in infirmities;...for when I am weak, then am I strong." [II Cor. 12:8-10].

The apostle Peter wrote to his dear friends, "Don't be bewildered or surprised when you go through fiery trials ahead...instead, be really glad because these trials will make you partners with Christ in his suffering, and afterwards you will have the wonderful joy of sharing his glory." [I Pet. 4:12, 13 (TLB)]

And there is the key! Joy. Joy in spite of testing; triumph in the face of trials!

I am humbled, yet grateful, at the reception which the first edition of *I Shall Come Forth as Gold* received. A great number of people have borne witness to its effect on their lives. Others who have endured serious trauma have written to me, called me, stopped to talk to me and told me how much my own story has done to encourage, strengthen and give hope.

All this makes the pain, the disability and the limitations seem more understandable, because the One who is Ultimate Wisdom, Infinite Grace and Eternal Comfort has given us this word of assurance, "Blessed be God, even the Father of our Lord Jesus Christ, the Father of Mercies, and the God of all comfort; who comforts us in all our tribulation...." [II Cor. 1: 3, 4]

I offer this revised and enlarged version of my personal pilgrimage through the valley with the hope and prayer that it will make your burden a little lighter and enable you, the reader, to discover the joy of the Lord which is our strength. [Neh. 6:10]

Part I

Chapter One

emories are stored like flood waters in the hidden reservoirs of the mind. Sometimes it takes only a chance incident to open the gates and let the tide rush out.

In March 1968 I was at the Washington, D.C. airport. Blowing on my finger nails to keep them warm, I looked forward with enthusiastic anticipation to my appointment with Senator Mark Hatfield that morning. It was my introduction to the capital of the United States. I had spent the previous night in a housing development in a Philadelphia ghetto and had come away sobered by the glimpse of how America's underprivileged people lived. Now I stood on the curb of the airport looking forward to seeing the gleaming city of Washington. What a contrast! The section I was viewing seemed sparkling in comparison to the depressing poverty of the night before.

As I debated my next move, a distinguished looking gentleman came through the swinging doors behind me and stepped into a waiting limousine. I awakened to who he was when a bystander said, "There goes the greatest man in the world and nobody recognizes him."

I walked around the side of the car, tapped on the window and, when the genial man within rolled the window down, I extended my hand to him. He responded, and as I shook his hand I said, "Dr. Barnard, I am a fellow South African. My name is The Rev. Peter Church. I have seen your appearances on television in England and in the United States. You have conducted yourself with distinction. Congratulations." He thanked me. He had indeed given a good account of himself in some harrowing experiences before highly critical audiences which had accused him of conducting experiments on humans, "because South Africans place such a low value on human life!"

In December of the previous year, Dr. Christian Barnard had awed the world by announcing the first human heart transplant in medical history. It had been performed at the Groote Schuur Hospital in Cape Town, South Africa. That single pioneer operation catapulted Dr. Barnard to international fame and brought Groote Schuur to the attention of the world. It was ironic that we should meet here in Washington. Later that morning I met the eminent physician again in one of the elevators in the Senate Building. Those two encounters took me back in memory to the beginnings of my own life because Groote Schuur and I have much in common — our age and our origin.

It was in the shadow of Table Mountain at the Cape of Good Hope, that I was born. Groote Schuur Hospital lies on the western slope of Table Mountain, at the point where it sweeps down to the sandy plain called the Cape Flats. Behind the stately white building the mountain rises steeply till, at almost 3,000 feet, it levels off abruptly to form the huge Table of grey rock which, from the distant bay, appears flat and even. Majestic and awesome, yet serene, Table Mountain is one of the wonders of creation. Unique in the world, it is a symbol of the old city below it, yet its grandeur is more stunning than any creation which human ingenuity could fashion.

When the colossus is shrouded in a table cloth of rolling mist, legend tells that the Devil is smoking with an ancient sailor. Then when the sun breaks through the billows of white cloud, the rugged grey rocks stand like ancient sentinels guarding Table Bay—the gateway to Southern Africa. Between the wide sweep of the bay and the foot of the mountain, the city nestles beneath its trees, a checkerboard of brick-red roofs, and white buildings. Some of the buildings date from the days of the first Dutch Settlement. With their sturdy walls, high gables and thatched roofs they stand as gracious and tranquil monuments to their solid ancestry.

The early settlers named this paradise the Cape of Good Hope. It was into the rich heritage of this Eden of the South that I was born on February 16, 1932. Unhappily, the circumstances surrounding my birth formed a sharp contrast to the beauty of this "Fairest Cape."

My mother was an Afrikaans lass, descended from the Cape Dutch settlers. My father, in some mysterious connection never made clear to me, was linked with the maritime tradition of the Cape. Is it possible that a boy could know nothing certain about his father? It was rumored that he was an engineer who helped build a famed pavilion on the Bay. It was rumored, too, that he was from Austria; or Scandinavia. I do not know. He deserted my mother the year I was born. The circumstances must have been most traumatic for my poor mother, for she remained tight-lipped on the issue to her life's end. She divorced my vagabond father soon after my birth, and was left to fend for herself, burdened with the responsibility of her other son, my brother, Theo, three years older than myself, and me.

My memory was born in the days when my brother Theo and I romped and scrambled around a very large playing area just over the sand dunes which separated my grandfather's house from the sea. We spent our hours sliding down the dunes and running along the white sands of the beach. More than once an older child or an adult would remark about the towering concrete pavilion and remind me that my father had helped to build it.

How well I remember the awe with which we viewed the huge steel ball which lay abandoned on the sand above the high tide mark. With the ignorance of childhood I did not grasp the significance of the words, but I knew instinctively that the fearsome looking, spiked, giant sized sphere with protruding rods was something ominous. It had washed up on our beach after the First World War. It was a mine. Though we treated the giant orb with an unspoken respect, we nevertheless clambered over its rusting surface with great glee.

These were the years of the Great Depression and times were hard. Families struggled to make ends meet in a harsh world and Mother found it desperately difficult to support us. To compound her miseries, she was exposed to the social ostracism meted out to divorcees by a harsh and intolerant society. Guilt weighed her down. Alone, she had to cope with the shock of rejection; to return to her parents or relatives was out of the question. Perhaps she had married against their wishes; I was never told. The whole matter was so upsetting that memories were hustled into the family closet, never to be opened. The subject was forbidden.

Cruel prejudice made her a stranger, even in her own family.

In an attempt to escape the morass of disillusionment that had turned "the Fairest Cape" into a place of perpetual bitterness and defeat, Mother packed our bags and headed for Johannesburg, 1,000 miles to the north. Founded on the wealth of its gold mines, Johannesburg lured people with its promise of prosperity. Mom intended to establish a fine new life for herself, but this ideal crumbled before the onslaught of harsh material facts. She eventually found work in Springs, a sprawling town 40 miles east of

Johannesburg. We found lodging in a rooming house. Our "home" was one, single room.

I have a phantom-like recollection of being spirited away to the local hospital soon after our arrival. Immediately after my birth the doctors had performed a major operation on my abdomen and I now was suffering from a complication which in turn required further surgery. An adult patient in the hospital took sadistic delight in tormenting me; he would stand at the foot of my bed and terrorize me by contorting his face and threatening to pull off his head and spill the blood all over me. Scared out of my wits, I would pull the sheets over my head to the accompaniment of his amused laughter.

It snowed that year. From my hospital room I marveled at the beauty, the wonder of something so new.

They let me sit on the veranda wall as people rolled around in the white powder, and I became so excited, I slid off my perch and fell among the rose bushes at the bottom of the wall. I don't recall suffering any harm, but I did remember the snow!

The year was 1934 and I was happy to be released from the hospital.

The most pressing problem now was to find some place to leave Theo and me while Mother was at work. Theo was old enough to attend school, but I was too young to join him. We became part of the traditional South African white culture. Mother hired a black "nanny" to watch me during the day and to be at the rooming house when Theo returned from school.

One morning the nanny did not show up. My mother could not stay home for fear of losing her job. She had no friends with whom to leave me and there was no one else to take care of me. To prevent my straying, she had no alternative but to lock me in the bedroom of the shoddy rooming house where we lived. Through the long hours of that day my mind darted between loneliness and fear.

There were no distractions; no TV, no radio and very few toys. I lay most of the day staring at the ornate, old-fashioned pressed metal ceiling and the green walls, wondering when Mother would return. I had no way of telling the time, and the longer I waited the more fearful I became.

Unfamiliar noises, real and imagined, penetrated the room to unnerve and menace me. In the afternoon I heard the first low rumble of an approaching thunderstorm. These violent electrical storms are a common occurrence throughout the gold mining area, which lies on a continental plateau 6,000 feet above sea level. They may last only a few hours but produce torrents of rain, high-velocity winds and wild flashes of brilliant lightning that illuminate the landscape like a million neon lights.

The ear-splitting crash of the thunder is like the roar of cannons; it scares uninitiated strangers, rattles the windows, shakes the walls, and terrifies the children. Four years old and locked alone in the bedroom, I was overwhelmed by panic as the building trembled with each crash of thunder. There was no one I could turn to in my terror and no other human being to whom I could run for comfort; just the bare walls and the cheerless, unresponsive furnishings. When I at last heard the key turn in the door, my terror exploded in a paroxysm of wild sobbing.

Mother somehow managed to win a meager living to meet our needs and eventually earned enough to allow us to move into a small rented house in a mining community named Geduld ("Patience"), which adjoins Springs.

That shadowy figure, Father, here, briefly, and for the last time, entered my life. He would arrive at the house at night when Theo and I were already stowed away in our rooms. Inevitably he and my mother would fight, always verbally, sometimes physically. Fearful, I would creep under the bed to hide from the shouting and banging in my mother's bedroom. I feared for her safety, but never dared emerge from hiding. I never saw this shadow called "father," but his irregular, nocturnal visits always caused strife, a further contribution to the insecurity of our troubled lives.

I developed another physical problem; a blockage in my nose that prevented me from breathing except through my mouth. I underwent several operations and came to fear and hate the doctor who would chloroform me and scrape out my nasal passages. My nose was then plugged with hard rubber corks. The chloroform made me retch and I would wake up after the operation, sick, dazed and struggling to breathe. I would instinctively clutch the irritating tubes and wrench them from my nose. After several such episodes I came to dread the experience. The operations produced no lasting relief, so eventually, the doctor gave up. Exasperated by my frantic efforts to remove the wedges he resignedly cut the bandages, took out the plugs and stalked away, telling my mother, "He will have to have the operation done when he is older." That prospect added to my growing store of fears.

At one time, a faith healer had passed through our town. I was little then, but I remember so well. Mother must have felt this held out some hope, because she dressed me in my finest and we set off to the large hall where the great healer was to appear. A crowd of curiosity seekers jostled for the best seats amidst an almost carnival atmosphere. I sensed I was due to witness a spectacle well out of the ordinary. My childish curiosity was roused.

The service began with much vociferous singing, accompanied by the stomping of feet and the clapping of hands. Eventually, the healer presented himself to the enthusiastic crowd and called a man on crutches onto the platform. In a loud, booming voice, he began to work up his audience into a lather of expectation. At the climax of his harangue, he boldly commanded the man to toss away his crutches. The prospect stood shakily for a few moments, till the healer, riding the crest of a wave of anticipation, demanded that the man walk across the stage: "Come, walk to me!" he yelled. The man made an unsteady move forward, lost his balance, hovered uncertainly for one more moment and went crashing spectacularly to the floor.

Pandemonium broke loose in the auditorium and amid the shrieking and hollering, mother grabbed me by the hand and bolted for the door.

Chapter Two

In 1938, following a stint in nursery school, I officially began my student days at Springs Central Primary School. As the "new boy," I was soon put to the test. Within a few days, a race was set up between me and the school "champion runner," a title given by the other children to a wiry, supple boy called Richey.

On the appointed day, a group gathered at the playground oval to watch the "new boy" race the champ. We set off down the straight; then, suddenly, I heard yells behind me. I looked back to see that Richey had veered off; there was another turn on the unmarked track that I had missed. I swerved back into the race and caught up with Richey once again, passing him by the time we had reached the finish line. The crowd was reluctant to hail a new champion, and Richey was truculent in defeat. From that day on, he eyed me with hatred and would stand on the curb and shout taunts at me across the street; always from a safe distance. I detested him thoroughly, from his impudent face to the soles of the feet attached to his spindly legs.

One day, I set off to the store with my mother. I had nagged her into buying me canned spinach, after seeing Popeye's dramatic transfiguration in cartoons at the local cinema. I was sure the wonder-working green leaves could do the same for me.

Walking beside my mother down the narrow street I saw the provoking presence waiting on the opposite corner. In the same instant, Richey spied me; "Naa-na-na-naa! Naa-na-na-naa! Mommy's boy, Mommy's boy," he chanted from across the street. I pretended to ignore him, but Richey only hooted the louder, smug in the belief that I would not dare retaliate while in my mother's restraining presence. Suddenly, breakpoint was reached. Casting aside caution and without a thought for the consequences, I broke free of my mother's hand and shot across the street. Richey, pragmatically choosing discretion above valor, bolted off like a startled hare. He raced down the block with me fuming in pursuit. Poor Richey; he ought to have remembered the outcome of our race. Fate and I caught up with him in a few blocks. I dragged him to the ground and beat the tar out of him.

That was the end of my trouble with Richey.

That year I also won my first trophy for running. Elementary school sporting events in South Africa are a mixture of chaos, noise and color. The wildly excited kids are only brought to order when a race is being contested on the track, otherwise the miniature athletes and their excited, cheering compatriots are, well, just noisy, highly active kids. That day was no different.

Each school sports its banners and rowdily supports its runners with shrieks, yells and school songs.

My mother had decked me out in my running shorts and shirt, and pinned a huge school rosette on my chest.

I ran, and I won. And the school cheered. My reward was a gleaming silver cup.

It would be a long time before I would experience that thrilling sensation again.

Without explanation, Theo and I were suddenly shunted off to a boarding school in Middleburg, in the north-eastern district of our

Province. Perhaps my mother simply could not make ends meet in Springs, but whatever the case, she consigned the responsibility of caring for us to the institution. Attached to it was a State-operated home for unruly and incorrigible boys where once again we were the "new boys," forced to defend our right to exist in the harsh atmosphere of the "home."

The official regimen had a military tone to it. Each day followed a routine: rise early, line up for the washroom, queue for breakfast, answer the roll-call and march in file to the school. The matron was a hefty Dutch woman who enforced discipline with a will of iron and a rod of hickory.

Saturday was always looked forward to eagerly, if only because the ritual was changed: clean the dormitories, change the linen, wash the windows, tidy the grounds and line up. Next came the weekly dose of castor oil or Epsom salts. This was administered with no ghost of a chance to question or protest. Breakfast followed. The rule was, "no dose, no breakfast." We then changed into our "town clothes."

If we passed inspection we were handed our weekly allowance; one shilling for the small kids; one and sixpence for the middle-sized and two shillings and sixpence for the big ones. In those days a shilling would buy admission to the bioscope (movie theater), a bar of candy, and still leave you with change. Some boys had more money than others because their parents sent additional allowances which were distributed on Saturdays along with the regular minimum. You signed a book to affirm you had received your allowance.

But Theo and I did not have a dad who would see to it that we had a little extra. I remember the embarrassment, the feeling of shame and the dejection which followed on a few occasions when there was nothing in the account for Theo and I. On those terrible Saturdays we had lined up at the table of exchange only to hear the crushing words, "There is no pocket money for you today." My eyes stung, but little as I was, I knew that in a boarding school, one tear could get you the epithet and scorn of being a "sissy."

The shadowy figure who had earlier drifted in and out of Mother's life had by now completely disappeared. We were never to see or hear from him again. He was as phantom-like as one of the shadows drifting across the screen at the bio where we invested the larger portion of our allowance in the hope of a thrill. Horror movies were standard matinee fare. Werewolves, Frankenstein, wailing mummies, grotesque monsters and other dreadful creatures were highest on the entertainment scale. When the flickering figures appeared too real I would duck and hide under the seat!

Where did illusion end and reality begin? These fictional characters mingled with the more palpable disturbances already bewildering my impressionable mind, to produce vague, yet real fears. I was the youngest boy in the school—low man on the totem pole— and the obvious target for jests and worse. In the rough atmosphere of the boarding school, never certain from which quarter to expect the next attack, sensitivity and tenderness had to be suppressed. In a place like that, "Boys don't cry." You fight back the tears. They may sting your eyes, but if you break, you are the laughing stock of peer cruelty. I withdrew into mistrust, eyeing everyone with suspicion. There was not a soul on whom I could rely for friendship. Recurring nightmares filled my sleeping hours with dread.

One night I awoke suddenly to find myself cold, clad in my pajamas, in some strange, eerie place. I had walked in my sleep, wandering from my own dormitory. The night was black as pitch. The room I found myself in was completely dark. I spread my hands out all around me but could feel nothing. Transfixed by fear, I dared not cry out but sank slowly to the floor and, trying vainly to pierce the gloom around me, began to reason. I knew I was in a room and that the room must have a door. I reasoned that if I set out in any direction I would find a wall and following that would inevitably reach the door. I inched forward on all fours till my hand touched the cold steel frame of a metal bed. I groped again and recoiled swiftly as my hand touched a face! There was a momentary halt in the heavy breathing and I crouched low on the floor, terrified almost out of my wits. The unknown sleeper drifted off once more and I resumed my search for the familiar. To add to my misery, I was attacked by a disorder common to all small boys in a panic: I had to go!

I worked my way around the bed, around a closet, another bed. I realized I was not in my own dormitory. I was lost in the dark. I was desperate! Stark panic added to my physical problem.

I was lost. I was in the grip of a cold terror. And I could no longer hold it in!

I slid my hand along the floor. I fumbled under a bed, found a shoe, and relieved myself. That over, some of the panic subsided, and I resumed my methodical circuit of the room. Weaving my way cautiously around each bed, stealthily crawling on hands and knees, my fingers finally slipped into the space between the floor and the bottom of a door. Feeling my way up the wall I discovered the light switch. Bracing myself for action, I threw the switch, took a swift look around, turned the light out, flung the door open, and bolted down the hall.

The next day the school buzzed with the report of a break-in attempt by an audacious burglar in the senior boys' dormitory. I offered no opinion. One lesson I had learned very well: "There is a time to talk and a time to keep silent."

A furious senior produced a now-ruined shoe, threatening murder on the culprit if ever he could catch the joker who had peed in his shoe!

On hot summer days most of the boys would take off for the local dam, a small man-made lake with a stream trickling in at one end and a compacted earth wall at the other. Besides the bio, there were no sophisticated attractions in that little Transvaal town and so we provided our own amusement.

One Saturday we were treated to a dramatic diversion. A knot of boys watched in silence as men from the village dived from the wall at the deep end of the dam. They were searching for one of our number, a boy who had been reported missing during the course of the afternoon. The atmosphere was alive with question marks. After several hours without success, the men decided to drain the dam. An enormous metal pipe ran through the dam wall, through which the water could be released. We watched as the valve was opened and water gushed from the pipe. It seemed to my active imagination to be a huge open mouth, disgorging mud. As the water level dropped, a shout went up from the men standing inside the dam.

The boy's body was found wedged in a pitiful heap against the grille at the entrance to the pipe. When the gruesome task of removing the corpse had been completed, the boys surged forward onto the muddy floor with a thrill of horror to inspect the great iron throat that had swallowed their companion. The iron "teeth" on the front of the pipe leered grotesquely. My stomach still contracts at any sight which bears resemblance to that gaping drain.

Another pastime (which in retrospect seems bizarre) was the occasional Saturday when we found time to sally forth to the local abbatoire—the slaughterhouse. Of all our excursions in search of a thrill this made the pulse beat faster and the feeling of awe more palpable than any other.

But it was not mere curiosity which made a small band of boys brace this spectacle.

There was the natural urge to "discover," but there was also the reward at the end!

We would help herd the cattle from the pens into the long boarded runways which led to the place where the ghastly deeds were done. I would stand spell-bound as each steer was hooked around the horns with a heavy rope and then dragged to the hitching post.

This was not the movies. I had seen buffalo hunts on the screen, and an occasional make-believe execution of a mortally-wounded horse. But this was for real.

As the hefty pistol in the hand of the "executioner" boomed out, each steer would drop with a mighty crash as the bullet brought instant death.

Why were we so fascinated?

Perhaps it was the stark reality of life and death.

We continued our wide-eyed scrutiny as the carcasses were cleaned, skinned and hung to cure.

The reward was a choice slice of beef steak at the end of the day's work.

In the gathering twilight we would make a wood fire, huddle around the sweet, smoking aroma of our barbecue, and grill our steaks on the end of a stick cut from a nearby tree limb.

I learned many of the lessons of life at the Boarding School. Some were good, some questionable, but they were all there, hung out in the show-and-tell real world of a life without a father, and a very distant mother.

Visits from Mother were rare, but she would appear on major holidays.

During the Easter weekend of 1942, she was accompanied by a slightly familiar face, one that was to change the direction of our lives forever.

Theo and I called him Uncle Sam.

I recalled that on an earlier occasion, when we lived in the rooming house, my mother had rushed in the front door one night, breathless and in a panic. Sam was there, waiting for her. She blurted out that a strange man had accosted her in the darkness as she was walking home from work. At that moment the man appeared at the head of the steps on the front porch. My mother yelled, "That's him!" Sam was quick as lightning. He leaped over the threshold, onto the porch, and threw a punch to the man's jaw that propelled him off the top step and sent him rolling down the flight and sprawling onto the sidewalk. He sprang to his feet and bolted down the street.

Enter, Sam Church!

That Saturday afternoon they collected us and took us for a drive. As we bumped along one of the rural roads in Sam's Hudson Terraplane with my mother in the passenger seat next to Sam, Mom turned to Theo and me as we sat in the back seat and inquired casually, "How would you like to have Uncle Sam for your father?"

The question was casual enough, but the answer would produce undreamed of changes. Mom had made her choice; she had already married Samuel Montague Church. I had no appreciation of the implications of my answer, but with little hesitation I answered, "Yes! I would like to have Uncle Sam as my father." What could possibly be worse than a life of continuing fatherlessness in the stark, competitive, hateful atmosphere of that boarding school?

I was soon to find out.

Chapter Three

The father of Sam Church, Samuel Montague Church Esq., was one of the English pioneers who settled in the Transvaal Republic. In 1887 he established himself in Alberton, a rural community south of the spot on which Johannesburg burgeoned after the great gold rush of 1886. An educated man, respected in the community, he practiced as a frontier lawyer and school master. He married a woman much younger than himself, who bore him two children, Samuel Montague, Jr. and Ethel Hermione. He died when Sam was twelve and Ethel but a baby. Unable to maintain the family, Sam's mother abdicated responsibility for her children, so at fourteen, Sam dropped out of school to support himself and Ethel. He delivered newspapers and worked as a messenger boy in the booming city of Johannesburg, finding his way inevitably to the gold mines.

He married my mother, Johanna (Jo) Margarita van Niekerk. She was thirty-three, divorced, with two young sons. My brother Theo was already thirteen, only twelve years younger than Sam. A bonny baby daughter had been born to them in 1940. They named her Hilda Ethel.

Theo and I were formally adopted by Sam and Jo Church in June 1942. Now I had a father figure to fill a long-standing void and Sam plunged into the role with enthusiasm and sincerity. He began to discipline us, instituting a morning exercise program and a system for taking care of household chores. He dealt out responsibility for the garden, the yard and cleaning the car. He really did try and slowly Uncle Sam gave way to Dad. That year, a son was born, Edward Montague Church.

In retrospect, I see how heavily stacked the cards were against the family's succeeding. Sam's own background gave him little experience of a stable family; ours had no precedent of consistent fatherhood. Theo and I were not of his flesh and blood. Family relationships at best are a testing ground, but our peculiar circumstances created problems which seemed insurmountable.

Sam and Jo ran into conflict almost immediately, and in asserting his newly assumed authority, Sam began to punish Theo and me out of all proportion to our shortcomings. We became fearful of his unpredictability. He had a violent temper which he found difficult to restrain. One day he thrashed me with a leather belt because I forgot to polish my school shoes! I was incensed because my omission was purely a lapse of memory and not an act of defiance or disobedience.

Our fledgling family began to feel the pinch of a war time economy. In 1939 Britain had declared itself at war with Germany over the invasion of Poland. One day later, amid strenuous controversy and the threat of Afrikaner rebellion, the South African Prime Minister, Jan Smuts, hurled South Africa into the conflict as an ally of Great Britain.

At first, the war seemed distant, but as the years dragged on, its dark presence cast long shadows of despair that reached as far as South Africa, and filled our homes with an uneasy gloom. We were called upon to make personal sacrifices for "the war effort."

Certain items, usually taken for granted, became scarce. Even as children, we felt the ominous threat of an unseen enemy. We joined the crowds who gave up their pots and pans to be melted down for guns and tanks.

Store-bought toys were a rare luxury. I was fortunate enough to have the skill and ingenuity to manufacture" my own play things. With friends, I scavenged scrap yards, retrieved the lead from abandoned car batteries and, by trial and error, learned to melt the lead and make my own toy soldiers.

We carved make-believe six shooters from boxwood, fashioned the hammers from lead molds and relived the famous battles of the American West which we had seen on the movie screens. It was a time to improvise, and some of us did it well.

Tumblers for drinking were scarce. We made goblets from empty bottles. The secret was to place old motor oil in the bottle, then plunge a red hot poker into the oil. It caused a clean break, and we smoothed the rough edges with fine sand paper.

The pressure on South African men to enlist increased and in 1943, shortly after the birth of Edward Montague (Eddie), Sam joined the South African Corps of Engineers.

Once again we became a family without a father. With Dad away and Mother working long hours in a munitions factory, Theo and I were left to our own devices. I began to roam the streets.

A singular episode, with religious overtones, fills a particular niche in my memory of those days. I don't know how it came about, or by whose engineering, but I was asked to audition for a particular role in what must have been a concert of sorts.

I can not recall any other feature on the program, but I was asked to "read" for the part of reciting a poem to be performed at a rather "swanky" concert in the Presbyterian church in the center of our town. With the nonchalance associated with 10-year old boys, I took the challenge, and was selected to recite *A Psalm of Life*, by Longfellow. For weeks, I was drilled by an elocution teacher, and on the night of the performance I must have acquitted myself well. I received accolades and warm words of appreciation.

However, I instantly sunk back into the anonymity of a lonesome boy who's parent's were very absent from social life.

One special love filled my life: A loft of homing pigeons!

From small beginnings, I had built up a fine flock of racing birds. Their streamlined bodies, their powerful wings, their grace, beauty and the sureness of their homing instinct, all struck a chord of admiration in my heart. I had acquired considerable knowledge of racing and looked forward to the day when I would enter my own birds in a race. Before he had enlisted, my new Dad and I had built a pigeon loft out of some scrap-iron sheets and pigeon wire.

My young world was bleak, but I treasured these graceful warm creatures which cooed so softly and felt so warm to my touch.

One of our neighbors, also a pigeon lover, hearing of my interest in the birds, and knowing that my father was away on active service, invited me to visit his home sometime to see his flock. One afternoon, after school, I strolled to his place and knocked on the front door.

I stood at the door for several minutes, then knocked again, but no one answered. I sauntered around to the back of the house and rapped loudly on the back door; again there was no response. As I stood on the porch surveying the yard, my eyes were drawn toward the pigeon loft. Warily, I walked across to the large, solidly built loft with its handsome stock where birds cooed, pranced and flew in flurries from perch to perch across the magnificent structure. I was awed. I had never seen such birds, and in such profusion. I thought of my few birds, caged in that makeshift bird house in our yard. My efforts seemed puny beside this grand array. Interest became avarice; desire turned to covetousness. An overwhelming compulsion to take two of those homers set my heart thumping in my chest.

"There is no one at home," I told myself. "If I take just two of those birds they will never be missed." I hesitated, shifting uncertainly from one foot to another. My mouth went dry with tension, then desire spilled over into action. I quickly slid into the loft, cornered two of the best looking specimens, a chocolate and a blue-bar, and deftly slipped them inside my shirt. Lying against my skin, the birds brought comfort and exhilaration. I slunk out of the loft, out into the street and hurried home.

In my own shabby loft, the two birds looked magnificent, like royalty in the slums. Carefully my mind concocted the story I would tell my mother if she ever found out that there were two extra birds. I practiced the nonchalant tone I would adopt as I told her I had traded them, or, better still, received them as a gift, or, the ultimate fiction, had caught them in a trap. I returned to the house, far from confident, my uneasiness mushrooming as I pondered possible reprisals. I hid myself in my bedroom after carefully locking both the front and back doors. The house seemed alive with threats and, as the minutes ticked by, I became more and more edgy. I began sweating with the realization of my wrong-doing, chills running up and down my spine. Guilt brought foreboding of serious trouble.

Righteousness appeared suddenly in the form of a blue-clad policeman. He strode up the front pathway and rapped officiously on the door. As I was alone in the house, I took a leaf out of my neighbor's book and attempted the trick that had just been played on me. I did not answer the door.

From a corner of the kitchen window, I watched, breathing quickly. My mouth was dry with fear, as the policeman, accompanied by the indignant neighbor, strode round to the back of the house where the man pointed out his two birds sitting peacefully in my loft. I knew that my number was up, but I considered that, since they did not know I was at home, the best thing to do was to sit tight and be as quiet as a mouse. My plan was no sooner hatched than it failed: I heard my mother at the front door. The neighbor, girded with outraged righteousness, had telephoned my mother at work, reported my crime and informed her that he would shortly be at our house to meet her, with the police. She cycled hurriedly back from the factory and stormed into the house, her bearing expressing anguish and fury. I was flushed out to stand trial before the three angry adults. Close to tears, I could not understand the perfidy of a neighbor who would allow me to think there was no one at home when there was. Why had he let me go into the loft to look at those birds? Why had he let me sneak out and then followed me home and called the police?

My mute inquiry brought no replies. The only sure thing was the inevitable retribution. I was guilty. The policeman offered my mother two alternatives: the neighbor was "willing to forgive" if I was given a good beating (usually six cuts with a rod) and if I promised never again to steal. Otherwise he would formally charge me and I would appear in juvenile court which might mean probation or a reformatory. I chose the rod, but over the next few days, with the stripes smarting on my buttocks and the wounds of what I believed to be the neighbor's betrayal rankling in my soul, I looked for a way to protest. I found it: I ran away.

It was a hurried departure, with nothing to go on but a little money and a few provisions. I had no intention of going far, so the first night I spent out in the veld on the outskirts of the town where I discovered how bitterly cold nights on the Transvaal high veld can be. The second night out was so miserable that I stealthily made my way back to the house, hoping to grab the blankets on my bed. I quietly levered open my bedroom window, crept over the sill and dropped to the floor. Without warning a heavy hand gripped my shoulder firmly. I was caught again.

But the hand this time belonged to a man cut from a different cloth. He was gentle, soft-spoken and persuasively reasonable. I found myself responding warmly to these unfamiliar qualities. He explained my mother's feelings, telling me she felt as unhappy about the neighbor's conduct as had I and convincing me that she had had the same sense of being helplessly trapped. She knew I had been set up and was grieved and concerned for me. Sadly, she had been unable to convey her own feelings; to reach out from her own misery and touch me with consolation. Instead, she had appealed to this strange man and asked him to help her. She had not dared to go to the police. The man was a friend of my father and his gentle manner convinced me that the comfort of my bed was far better than the bitter cold of the veld. I stayed!

When I was twelve, Sam Church was discharged from the army. To my confused mind he seemed to appear from nowhere. Powerful, handsome and distinguished in his uniform, he towered heroically above me. His return from active duty marked the beginning of years of shifting; from mine to mine, job to job, town to town and house to house. The post-war economy made the business of living precarious, so we kept on the move, following now this star, now that. Tantalizing visions of a better life for him and his family drew Sam on, leaving a trail of unfulfilled dreams and inarticulate longings in his wake. He had started his mining career in the ranks of the lowliest white laborers, but his dauntless, fiery spirit would not long tolerate that mean position. In a rare display of intelligence and sheer doggedness, he became one of the few miners of his time to write and pass the demanding Mine Captain's examination at the first attempt.

Our new Dad was also struggling with his unaccustomed role as father, provider and protector. He did things which we, as children could only appreciate in the later years of our lives. His efforts were valiant. They were often sporadic. He was groping for answers, but in the process he added many invaluable lessons to my life.

Tangible evidence of our Dad's desire to be a good father was the adventure in which he led us when we decided to add a brood of ducklings to our menagerie. Every kid must surely love those tiny, yellow, downy balls of fluff that come, miraculously, out of the eggs.

We had a pair of ducks; the hen laid eggs; they hatched. But what were we to do to give them a good life?

Well, we dug, scooped and carried sand, then lined the hole with concrete which we mixed ourselves. Dad taught us; so many parts river sand, so many parts stone, and the right amount of concrete.

I learned that you could fill the pond before the concrete was completely dry, because concrete cures, even under water.

In one weekend, we had a duck pond, and a bunch of happy ducklings. But we also had added another set of lessons to our practical education.

Dad was good at doing things like that.

We always had pets around the house. At various times, a dog, cats, often chickens, the ducks, and even once a small pig. It was good training and discipline as I learned to care for the creatures!

In a genuine effort to make up what Theo and I had missed by not having a Dad, our new father introduced us to another unaccustomed facet of childhood — family outings. Most memorable for me was the day we went to the races. Not the horses, but the regional motor speedway track. It was the thrill of my young life. I was smitten. It was love at first sight and sound.

The star of the show was "Put" Marsman. I remember it well. I was enthralled by the speed, the dare devil stunts and the deep throated roar of the motorcycles as they sped around the oval in hot pursuit of I knew not what. But who cared? The derring-do and the sheer marvel of the mean looking machines captivated my imagination.

The aroma of the exhaust fumes, the flying dirt and thrill of an occasional spill simply stole my heart. All these ignited a spark in me that was to find fulfillment in days yet to come.

The allure would one day almost cost me my life!

Chapter Four

n 1886, a wandering prospector had stumbled by chance on the outcrop of rock which led to the discovery of the richest gold vein in the world. When the cry went up, "Gold!," men rushed to the Transvaal like vultures to the kill: prospectors, treasure hunters, financiers, adventurers, miners and all the human flotsam that churns along in the wake of a gold rush. A mining camp sprang up on the site of the bonanza and, shortly after, there arose the city of Johannesburg. Within fifty brief years, the city was a bustling metropolis with towering buildings and a population of over one million people.

As its furnaces glowed and refined the gold, people from many nations poured into the melting pot of its political and social life. But greed for the glittering gold blinded white eyes to the suffering of the black laborers who swarmed to the city. Appalling slums proliferated on its fringes. These sons and daughters of the tribes of Africa were the cheap labor force upon which the prosperity of the city and the nation were built. Our family moved to this Golden City in 1944.

We made our home in Mayfair, a run-down suburb of small houses on tiny lots. It was like a no-man's land between the stately homes of the rich and the outer fringes of the poor. Each day Dad would wheel his bicycle into the road in front of our postage-stamp sized home and begin the 10 mile pedal to the mine where he worked. Between them, my parents scraped together a living amid post-war economic woes. Because they were away all day, I was subject to little parental control. Mayfair teemed with kids, who, like me, found its streets a spawning ground for mischief and worse.

The older boys who gathered around my brother Theo were skilled in the arts of wrong-doing. Their daring left me wide-eyed and their casual attitude to their crimes astounded me but soon I began mimicking their behavior, their habits and their speech until I was accepted by them. I accompanied the small gang of sorties as they pilfered little things from shops, heaved rocks through the windows of old buildings, smoked cigarettes, sipped brandy, drank beer and swaggered through the streets in search of mischief. Unfortunately, pranks, like tipping over fruit stands outside stores gave way to more serious acts like the night we slipped over a factory wall and stole candies and chocolates.

Old mine shafts and abandoned diggings stood in silent invitation to adventure on the fringes of Mayfair's dingy streets. On balmy days, I would stay in school just long enough to be registered; then, when an unsuspecting teacher had her back turned to the class, I would drop my school satchel out the window. The next move would be an innocent sounding request for permission to go to the cloakroom. I would walk out of the classroom, steal around the building, collect my bag and saunter off to the beckoning excitement of the streets or the eerie challenge of the old mine workings. I forged my Dad's signature on letters of excuse and on my school reports. I often skipped doing my homework, and produced the perennial excuses.

"The dog ate it."

"I've left it at home."

"I lost it on the way to school."

"Somebody stole it."

I had a companion in all this: my best friend was a lanky blond boy we called Zoes.

There were constant fights between the "foreign" kids who lived in the area and ourselves. Tension between the ethnic groups was high and would often manifest itself in street and playground brawls. One thing is certain; we were never bored. We had a standing invitation to devilment as the excitement kept us keyed up, always on our toes.

My only diversion from Mayfair was a weekly excursion into the fantasy world of down-town Johannesburg. Every Saturday morning found me wandering the streets, sauntering in and out of the department stores or taking in the movies. I returned again and again to the fascination of the soaring buildings, restless crowds of unfamiliar faces and stores awash with all that gold could buy.

Two odors gripped my fertile and awakening senses. The one was the smell that wafted from a bakery shop where they sold fresh-baked Cornish pasties and ground beef pies. It was a ritual. I bought one every Saturday morning.

The other smell which captivated me was that of books. New books. Their crisp pages and fresh print began to capture my heart. I could close my eyes and imagine myself wandering between the rows of fascinating novels, and yes! even comic books.

I was there when Superman was born.

I was part of the exciting, fantasy world of all the American dream characters. I lived momentarily in the fleeting escapades of Captain Marvel, Captain America, Submariner, Wonder Woman, and Mickey Mouse.

Such visits seemed all too brief, and I would have to return to the sordid streets of Mayfair and the cauldron of frustration and resentment heating up in the heart of our family.

Once, because of a train delay, Theo returned from visiting a friend an hour later than Sam had stipulated. Nevertheless, Sam thrashed him mercilessly. Every stroke of the cane resounded like a whip lash through the tiny house.

Mom and Dad gave in to short tempers and irritable exchanges with each other, adding to the clinging frustration of the menial circumstances in which we lived.

One afternoon Sam arrived home from a typically tiring day: rise at 5:00 a.m., a long cycle ride to work, back breaking hours in the mine, the ride back, returning home at 5:00 p.m. As he came up the front steps of the little brick house in which we were living, I was sitting on one of the steps and noticed that the brim of his hat was turned down at the back. I reached out to turn it up, but he misread my intention and, as my hand neared his head, he half-turned, struck my rising arm with all the force of his pent-up anger and growled, "Don't you touch me!"

Through many such incidents, bewildered resentment toward this unpredictable, unloving "father" grew in me. Theo, always silent, often morose, must have suffered more than I did.

One evening a power failure plunged us into darkness. Candles were lit. While Theo and I were taking our bath the curtain in our bedroom blew across the flame and caught fire. By the time an alarm was sounded, the bedroom was dense with black smoke; the curtains, window frame and wall were all burning fiercely. Dad rushed into the room, grabbed a blanket off the bed and smothered the flames. His hands were burned and the room badly damaged, but the danger to the house was over. When we were alone after the incident, Theo, by now a young man of sixteen, said to me, "I wish the house had burned down." Such was the atmosphere of melancholy and bitterness that hung over our home.

We never did attend church, either as a family or individually, but we did experience one "brush with God." Sometimes Mom and Dad would take us four kids, Theo, Hilda, Eddie and me, to the local municipal pool for a Sunday picnic. The trip, made on foot, took us past the Mayfair Presbyterian church. Mom and Dad had been married in a church, but, like so many others, they looked on the church as a social convenience maintained only for births, deaths and marriages. As we walked by in our swimsuits, the Sunday school superintendent was entering the gate and seeing us, he summoned his courage and spoke to Dad.

"Good morning," he said. "Beautiful day."

Dad stopped in stony silence; I stopped beside him. The rest of the family moved on slowly down the street.

"Mr. Church," he said, "Don't you think your children should come to Sunday school before going to the swimming pool for the day?"

Dad looked the grey-haired gentleman square in the eye and replied coldly, "You mind your own damned business and I'll mind mine."

We spent the day at the pool.

Once in a while there was a happy relief. In early 1945, when I was just 13 years of age, I was in the Mayfair Junior High School. The Provincial Education Department "made a decree" that every child should be tested. Unknown to us, the entire student body sat down to a single aptitude test. I was dumfounded weeks later when I was awarded the prize for the second highest score attained in the whole school. It was a book!

One bright prospect threw a dazzling beam across the dismal shadow of our lives. The family was to spend a vacation on a farm.

Dad, Theo and I made the more than one hundred mile journey by bicycle, because Dad could not afford train fare for all of us and in our financial pinch we had long since bid farewell to the car. After planning the trip eagerly, we set off long before dawn on a crisp, cold July morning. The exhilaration was short lived, however, as I realized I was in for the most physically grueling experience of my life. For one thing, I had not realized just how cold it would be. I was wearing short trousers and my legs were exposed to the chill wind. My fingers grew numb on the freezing handlebars.

We were heavily loaded, as Sam thought we might have to spend the night camping out in the open. Between my knees, strapped to the crossbar of the bike, was my sleeping roll. My legs chafed against the rough blanket as I pumped the pedals mile after mile. The skin soon began to burn and itch. I was riding an old racing bike with narrow tires that sank deep into the thick sand as we left the urban streets for the rutted, unpaved roads of rural South Africa. Three years younger than Theo and unaccustomed to long bicycle rides like my Dad, I often lagged behind in solitary, sometimes tearful, frustration. Mile after mile after unmarked mile, the road stretched on. If I fell behind, I simply had to catch up. There was no alternative and no understanding smile or word of encouragement to help. The stark fact remained: "You've got to keep moving."

By midday, I had been pedaling for eight hours and I thought I was at the end of my physical endurance. The night had brought intense cold; now the day brought the baking sun. The sky was cloudless and the world hung silently suspended in the shimmering heat. I pedaled on in this nightmare, flinging my store of curses at the uncaring universe. At noon we stopped to eat some of the food in our packs and to mull over the sour fact that we had the same journey ahead of us coming back. After a short sleep, stretched out on the offending blanket by the side of the road, Sam decided to press on without a night's break. We arrived at the farm around eight o'clock that night.

The four weeks that followed were like a dream. On the farm I discovered a new world, one of unending novelty and fascination. I learned to milk the cows, tend the sheep, harness the oxen, plow the fields and drive the tractor. Riding horses was the most exciting adventure of all and we grew daring to the point of foolhardiness around the horses, considering ourselves experts after three weeks!

The farm was the largest learning arena I had known to that point in my life. The days and nights gave opportunity for gathering information just by being in that new environment. There was work, and there was play. There were also pranks and practical jokes.

I well remember the frustration of chasing selected chickens from the huge flock which roamed the vast territory around the old stone house and surrounding buildings. We had been assigned the task of catching and dressing a few choice birds for Sunday's dinner. Those chickens were smart, and quick. Even if we cornered one, the bird would somehow regain its lost power of flight and go soaring over our heads, the hedge or the fence.

I had a solution; combine work and pleasure! I persuaded the elder member of our party to fetch our .22 caliber rifles, and we simply "picked off" our quarries with a few well-aimed shots!

One of the most lurid spectacles came with preparations for a festive Saturday night gathering of friends and farmers from the surrounding area. It was to be a traditional Afrikaner cook-out. Replete with the always-served cornmeal treat called "pap" (pronounced with a long, open vowel sound) and "wors" (sausage), we were also featuring pig-on-a-spit.

Slaughtering the pig was an education. I thought I had seen it all at the abbatoire in Boarding School! This was a step beyond bizarre. The black farm workers first had to catch the pig. Everything on the farm roamed free. What a chase. We all joined in, and eventually, with a diving tackle, one of the black men caught the squealing pig by a back leg. That creature, driven by fright (and perhaps premonition) dragged the man across the yard to the loud yells, hooting and random directions of all the other "hunters and gatherers."

The end for the hog came in a crude fashion. Wedged between the legs of the black captor, the pig was struck a mighty blow on the head with a huge hammer, then, quickly its throat was slit. When I asked "Why?" The reply was, "Unlike other animals, the pig must bleed to death."

I reveled in the tantalizing aroma of fresh farm-baked bread that wafted through the old stone house every morning and relished the wholesome meals cooked on the huge iron stove in the enormous kitchen. We butchered a steer for fresh meat, and made our own farm sausage — "borewors." I learned skills as diverse as drying beef jerky (biltong) and cracking a whip to sound like a rifle shot.

I also had my introduction to party politics. A burly Afrikaans youth swaggered around the farm and he would confront Theo and me with an adversarial attitude and the proclamation:

"Ek is 'n Nat!" ("I am a Nationalist!")

The statement made no sense, but I instinctively knew a couple of things: He did not like us; he considered himself superior, and he planned to do something about it. The year was 1945, and the Nationalists were rising inexorably to power.

One day we took the horses out further than usual. The jaunt passed without incident until, returning, the horses sensed their nearness to home. We had been keeping a steady walk along the road towards the farm gates when, without warning, the horses which my father and Theo were riding broke into a gallop. My horse, hearing them coming, bolted for home and this in turn spurred on the others. They thundered toward me and as the three frenzied animals, with their helpless cursing riders, galloped abreast (with Dad and me on the outside), Theo's horse missed a step, stumbled and threw him into the path of the flying hooves. He struck the ground with a horrible thud and the horses went pounding over him.

Desperation gave us new power to get the horses under control. We dismounted and ran back to where Theo lay. He was absolutely still, with not a vestige of color in his face. I was terrified, certain that he was dead. Dad, using first-aid skills learned in the mine, worked skillfully with Theo till the color began to return to his face and he drew a few shuddering breaths.

Amazingly, he had survived the fall without major injury. After a few days in bed and treatment with home remedies, he was once again not only on his feet, but on horseback.

A wild horse was almost the death of me too.

On a rugged, open range, a herd of unbroken horses roamed the veld. The leader was a huge white stallion with mean, crimson eyes. One fine day we decided to corner the animal, and endeavor to ride him. We succeeded in separating the beast from the herd, but once cut off, the monster simply put his head down and charged. I was directly in its line of escape. I was frozen to immobility as the monstrous hulk charged directly at me. I knew I was doomed!

In a flash, one of the expert African horsemen threw himself against me, and we were both sent sprawling in the sand as the hooves of the white stallion went thundering by.

We never tried again.

My savior's name was "Moketsi." In Afrikaans, he was called Petrus; Peter!

I developed a deep admiration for Petrus. He belonged to the Sotho tribe and dressed in typical garments: a conical grass hat with an intricately woven crest and a brilliant blanket worn over the shoulders. Petrus was about thirty years old and lived with his family on the farm.

The laborers were each allocated a small piece of land, in a remote area of the farm, on which to build a mud hut and attempt to grow maize and perhaps a few vegetables. In that dusty soil it was difficult to coax any crop into existence. The women had to farm as best they could, for their husbands were away from dawn to sunset, working the farmer's land. Each laborer might have one or two head of cattle, a few scrawny goats and even scrawnier chickens. Each man received a pitiful wage each month. For them, life was a perpetual struggle to keep body and soul together.

I became Petrus' shadow, watching as he herded the cattle or horses, tended the sheep or milked the cows. He taught me to catch and ride the wild Basotholand ponies native to the area and I spent many wonderful hours acquiring these new skills under his tutelage. Petrus was usually at work by the time I got up in the morning and left again at dusk. I used to wonder how much sleep he got! After leaving the old farmhouse he still had the long, lonely walk to his hut ahead of him and his own family responsibilities to attend to.

One Saturday night, after all the guests and the family had eaten supper, Petrus appeared at the farmhouse. Earlier in the day some of the sheep under his care had strayed into the garden and played havoc with the vegetables and flowers the farmer's wife had planted. To make matters worse, several of the sheep had died from eating poisonous plants. Petrus was pale, and fearful. The angry farmer took him to an outside room and gave him a merciless beating with his "sjambok" (rhinoceros-hide whip).

I was sick with revulsion because Petrus was so badly beaten that he could not walk home that night, but lay huddled painfully in his incongruously gay blanket. Not even his seemingly innate fear of the "Tokolosh" or bogeyman could motivate his broken spirit and beaten body to tramp the weary miles to his desolate hut.

The farmer was absolute master within his domain and he ruled with a rod of iron, often punishing the blacks harshly for the mildest offenses. I heard him say, "Blacks are just like children; you have to beat them to show them who is 'baas' (boss)." My own sensitive spirit, wounded by callous acts of unkindness, cried in sympathy for the pitiful laborers.

There were several other young Nationalist Afrikaners on the surrounding farms and besides holding the blacks in sneering contempt, they derided the English. There was continuous friction between them and the English speaking boys which often erupted in fights. Although I could speak Afrikaans and my mother was an Afrikaner, my English name was sufficient to involve me in constant conflict.

Chapter Five

In 1886, we moved again. Ever Westward. This time we settled in a fresh, new housing development in the town of Florida. I became part of an educational experiment in a sparkling new facility—Florida High School. The Education Department of the Province conceived the idea of "integrating" the white school children, placing both English and Afrikaans high schoolers in the same complex. These dual-medium high schools were intended to foster harmony between the two white language groups, but the innovation was a dismal failure. The two cultural groups clashed head-on.

As each dream failed to bring the hoped-for pot of gold relations worsened between my parents. One night, after a bitter argument, Mother locked herself in the bathroom. Theo and I did not understand what was happening, even when Sam broke down the bathroom door to reveal her lying in a pool of blood. She had slashed her wrists. She was taken from the house in an ambulance and we did not see her for a several weeks.

Shortly after she returned, Theo and I were introduced to an immigrant couple, who, we were told, would be taking care of the house for a while. With that, Dad and Mom mysteriously disappeared. I began asking questions about the date of their return, but the couple were strangely uncommunicative on the point. After two months of awkward co-existence with this English pair, the truth dawned on us: Mom and Dad were not coming back. They had moved out, taking Hilda and Eddie with them, after arranging with the immigrant couple to take care of us in exchange for the use of the house. It seemed a convenient arrangement for all the adults involved. However, the two principal players, Theo and I, had not been informed of the transaction. We were oblivious to a postwar economy which wrestled with the problems of housing shortages, displaced peoples and immigrants.

One lonely Friday night, as I lay in my bed, I came to a decision: the following morning I would set out on my bicycle and, come what may, I would find my parents. Before the household stirred that Saturday morning, I set out on my old bicycle. I had made no preparation; I had no money and no idea of where I was going, but mile after mile, with a bundle tied on the back of my bike, I worked my way westward, remembering that my father had talked about opportunities in the gold mines which were opening along the far-west reaches of the Witwatersrand.

The "headgear" of a gold mine is the tall, stick-like, steel structure which stands like a towering guard over the gaping hole in the ground where the seekers for gold have sunk their shafts. Above the steel framework is the gigantic wheel and cable which lowers the men and materials into the dark and dangerous nether world where the glittering temptation is locked in the harsh, unyielding rock.

I followed these spindly-looking steel sentinels, mile after mile, asking at every opportunity, "Do you know, or have you heard of, a Sam Church?"

Following the Westward trail, never taking the negative shake of a head as a final answer, I arrived on the fringe of a new development on the Far West Rand. It was a tiny village called Venterspost.

Weary, hungry and penniless, I stood at nightfall outside a small farmhouse at the entrance to a long, low valley. I asked the farmer if he knew where I could find a Mr. and Mrs. Church. In a slow, heavy accent he told me that a family by that name had rented a rondavel—or "round house"—on another farm down the road. Could it be Mom and Dad? I followed the man's directions to the distant light.

It was! There was mutual shock when they opened the door, but the awkward silence was followed by a tearful reunion. The air was soon heavy with emotional resolutions to change, to patch things up. Theo followed shortly afterwards but dropped out of school and took a job in a local store.

Venterspost was a mining community with a few stores and a recreation area, but no high school. I was enrolled for the next term in the Witwatersrand Technical College, 15 miles away in the nearest large town, Randfontein. I traveled the distance each day by bus, along with all the other high school students from the area.

Once again I was the new boy, the stranger, an object of hostile scrutiny in an unfamiliar setting. By now the experience was becoming a regular part of each year's routine. Things were made difficult by the fact that the trade school attracted many drop-outs from the academic high schools; boys who wanted only to sit out the time till they reached sixteen and the law allowed them to leave school. My English name again drew hostile attention.

However, the workshops, with their array of electric machines, fascinated me. The lathes and other machine tools fired my interest and I studied hard, gaining an academic distinction at the end of that first year.

Community life in Venterspost differed vastly from the crowded, crime-ridden streets of Mayfair. There were wide open fields in which to ride bicycles; playing fields for tennis and rugby, and a large public swimming pool. The friends I made in Venterspost were different from the gangs in Mayfair.

I met two boys who were to change the course and destiny of my life. They were Johnny Buchler and Archie Muller. They invited me to play tennis. Tennis? I had never seen a game of tennis in my life. I had never held a racket in my hand, but I accepted the challenge and took to it like the proverbial "duck to water." It came to me naturally, and soon I was playing an excellent game. This instant success sparked my interest in other sports.

The energies previously directed into the mischievous pursuits of Mayfair's sleazy streets were now redirected into exciting activities. I joined the school cadet band of which Johnny Buchler was the drum major. I lugged my side drum back and forth to school each day amid the taunts of the Afrikaans boys. But I wanted more than anything else to master the drum, to play in that band. And I did!

It wasn't long before Johnny and Archie invited me to the Buchler's home where Johnny's older brother, Freddy, held a young people's Bible study every Friday night. I went because I felt obliged to go, but I found myself a stranger in an unfamiliar environment.

I had known the words "God" and "Jesus Christ" only as curse words and although I held myself aloof and felt embarrassed, I went back each Friday night for several months.

I was drawn by the social contact, the fellowship with other young people and the friendliness of Freddy Buchler. Besides, there was nothing else to do in that town; no cinemas, no theater, no entertainment, no cafes, nothing. Not even a church!

In November, when I had been attending the Bible study for about four months, Freddy announced he was leaving Venterspost to enter a Bible School and, as a parting gift, he presented me with a

Bible, bound in leather and shining with newness. I had seen a Bible only occasionally before. My mother possessed a small Dutch Bible which I had never seen her open; now, to own one was a novelty.

This book was to change the destiny of my life!

Chapter Six

In every community, there are two sides of the track. However, in South Africa the distinctions which divide people were deeper and more entrenched than simple stations of poverty or riches. People were born into ethnic categories. They were classified by the government as European, Non-European, Colored, Asian or Black. White South Africans could climb the ladders of success and achieve their dreams if they possessed the will or if fortune smiled on them.

Not so the Black, Asian, or mixed-race "Colored" people. Race and color determined one's station for life. The so-called European people could live by the dictum, "Whatever you can conceive and believe you can achieve."

The Non-Europeans, all those classified as non-whites, were locked into a legal cage of prejudice which prevented them by law from rising above the limits fixed for them in where they could live, what work they could perform, or how high they could rise above the mire of poverty.

The most significant influence which the white settlers brought to the shores of South Africa with their pioneer spirit was the heritage of a strong Christian ethic.

Consequently, South Africa was a deeply religious country by tradition and many of its leaders had been dedicated Christian men. In the preamble to the Act which had constituted the Republic of South Africa, the proclamation declares:

IN HUMBLE SUBMISSION to Almighty God,
Who controls the destinies of nations and the history of peoples;
Who gathered our forebears together
    from many lands and gave them their own;
Who has guided them from generation to generation;
Who has wondrously delivered them from the dangers
    that beset them;
We, who are here in Parliament assembled,
DECLARE that whereas we are conscious of our
    responsibility towards God and man....

Bible lessons were part of the curriculum in all South African schools. Strong religious conviction led to the passing of laws requiring observation of the Sabbath by commerce and industry. Cinemas and theaters were closed on Sundays and it was unlawful to hold any public entertainment at which an admission was charged on the Lord's Day. The Bible was read at state functions and prayer was an integral part of all State occasions.

Through the years I had listened to the Bible lessons in school. Homework involved memorizing portions of the Psalms, but when, on occasion, I asked a teacher what these verses meant, the reply was usually, "Don't ask questions, just learn the passages."

But now, as I took this Book in my hand, a new emotion stirred within me. I was curious and I began to read. I soon became engrossed and read by day and by night. I carried the Bible in my school satchel reading it on trains and on the bus. Within the year, I had read it from cover to cover and without suggestions from anyone, I marked the passages which seemed specially relevant to me and my life.

Social patterns underwent a change too, during the year of 1947. I started participating in several sports. I grew several inches, attended military cadet camps and worked hard at my studies. Playing truant was a thing of the past. I was growing up, yet more important, the light of God's Word was scattering the darkness in my soul.

That year I was treated to another visit from the police.

On arriving home to find the law waiting, I took a hasty inventory of my conscience. Memories of my previous encounter almost unmanned me. However, the police had come to seek aid in tracking down one of my former associates in Mayfair. The petty crimes there had blossomed into something worse and the situation had become alarming. Happily, I was out of it.

God, who is so rich in mercy, was drawing me gently to Himself.

As I hungrily read my Bible, a rising tide of awareness crept over me. In my reading, I closely identified with God's indignation against the disobedience and waywardness of the Old Testament characters. In my imagination, I sided with the Creator in sending the flood; I found myself approving His judgments on Sodom and Gomorrah; I condoned His wrath in punishing the people of Israel for their fickleness. But gradually, under the brilliant light of God's truth, I saw myself mirrored in the sinful rebellion of these ancient people. It was as though the prophet pointed a finger at me and said, "You are the man!"(1)

Slowly, but surely, I realized that my own life was a great empty void. I saw the wrong actions of my childhood and teenage years in their proper light.

I became increasingly aware of my antagonistic attitude toward my parents and Theo. The memory of specific wrongs confronted me: the school reports I had forged, skipping school, things which had seemed so inconsequential but which now seemed so wrong. The unthinking abuse of the names of God and Jesus shamed me. In the light of God's Word I saw myself for what I truly was: a sinner far away from God, lost in darkness.

I now knew God was displeased with my actions. If He so severely judged the people of the Bible for their wrongdoings, I knew that I could hardly hope to be spared. The words of Jesus pursued me, "Unless you repent, you will all likewise perish."(2) I had read the words of the prophets, I had marked their calls to the children of Israel, "Seek the Lord while He may be found, call upon Him while He is near,"(3) and I had been constantly amazed, in reading the Bible, that the people to whom the message came were so stubborn and unwilling to respond. I would think, "If only they would turn to God; if only they would listen to these prophets." In reading the story of the deliverance of the children of Israel from Egypt and their subsequent failures in the desert, I felt bemused, angered, by these complaining, ungrateful and stiff-necked people. The truth now came to me: You are just as they were! The message is for you!

The Word of God had penetrated my heart. The witness and prayers of Fred, Johnny and Archie had eternally affected me.

It was a sobering journey. I did not understand then that a deep, Spiritual transformation was taking place in the center of my being. On a special day in the Bible class, Freddie Buchler prayed with me. It was the opening of my heart to the Gospel which the three "musketeers of the faith" had demonstrated by life and by lip.

One night as I lay on the bed in my starkly furnished room, conviction deepened. I went down on my knees beside my bed and unashamedly wept as I saw my condition. The tear stains are still on that Bible, but repentance and sorrow for sin was accompanied by hope, for I had also seen the glorious light of the Gospel shine from the pages of the New Testament.

The story of Jesus of Nazareth, as it unfolded, had captivated me. Horrified by His crucifixion, but gladdened by the victorious account of His resurrection, I wanted to follow Him. As I waited upon my knees that night, I saw that Jesus was crucified for my sins.

The words of the angel from Matthew's Gospel thrilled me, "You shall call his name Jesus, for it is He who will shall save His people from their sins."(4) Paul's words to the Philippian jailer spoke to me, "Believe on the Lord Jesus Christ, and you will be saved."(5)

Peter's boldness reached across the centuries and confronted me, "Neither is there salvation in any other: for there is none other name under heaven given among men, whereby we must be saved."(6)

In reading my Bible, I had eagerly marked many glowing statements. Isaiah, Chapter 53, moved me deeply. I saw that Jesus was the one of whom the prophet spoke. The words became personal, "He has borne our griefs, and carried our sorrows:...He was wounded for our transgressions, He was bruised for our iniquities; the chastisement of our peace was upon Him; and with His stripes we are healed."(7)

I saw myself in another compelling verse, "All we like sheep have gone astray; we have turned every one to his own way; and the Lord has laid on Him the iniquity of us all."(8)

The tender words of the Lord Jesus in the upper room on the last night with His disciples; the agony of Gethsemane and the injustice of the mock trial before the self-righteous Pharisees; the washing of Pilate's hands; the scourging by the soldiers; the crown of thorns and the sheer cruelty of the Crucifixion touched me and drew from the depths of my soul the confession, "Jesus, I believe. I believe you suffered and died for me. I know you were dead, but now you are alive. I receive you as my Savior."

I rose from my knees and lay again on my bed, staring at the ceiling. There was a new tranquility in my heart as the lost feeling of the years rolled away. I knew something of great significance had taken place. Softly, the words of St. John echoed in my soul, He came unto his own, and his own received him not. But as many as received him, to them gave he power to become the sons of God. (9) For God so loved the world, that He gave His only begotten Son, that whosoever believes in Him should not perish, but have everlasting life.(10)

I sensed the great love of God for me. I dimly saw that I had become a child of God.

I had found my Father.

Chapter Seven

In the harsh dry deserts of Mexico grows a cactus plant which produces the fiber used in the manufacture of high quality rope. Some years back, a group of American businessmen saw the potential of growing this plant in the United States, where it would be closer to the factories for processing. At great cost, the cactus was cultivated in the more favorable and benign climate. After devoting special care, adequate water and controlled conditions to its development, the speculators anticipated an abundant harvest and a large return on their investment. Harvest time came; the leaves were cut and processed to extract the fiber. The result: failure! Under the favorable conditions of the milder climate, the fibers of the leaves were soft and turned to pulp. The cactus plant needed the burning sun, the driving wind and the harsh conditions of the Mexican desert in order to develop its strong, tough, fibrous core.

Right at the outset of my new life in Christ I ran into the persecutions, trials and testings of which the New Testament writers warned. As I continued to read the New Testament, the call to devotion, discipline and steadfast faith was clear.

Jesus said, "In the world you shall have tribulation; but be of good cheer; I have overcome the world."(1) Paul warned, "Unto you it is given in the behalf of Christ, not only to believe on Him, but also to suffer for His sake."(2) "We must through much tribulation enter the kingdom of God."(3)

Whereas my parents had previously been indifferent to the point of neglect concerning my behavior, they now began to run a campaign of interference. Restrictions were handed out wholesale whenever I asked permission to attend meetings or engage in other Christian activities.

Formerly, my brother Theo and I had had the usual petty sibling differences. Now, he took delight in pointing out any failure on my part to display Christian grace. "You are supposed to be a Christian," he would taunt. "Christians don't do things like that!" Where had he got hold of the rules anyway?

In the face of their criticism I often came close to despair. I had years of bad habits to unlearn. Years of self-imposed silence and repression made it difficult for me to communicate with my family. But while silence dominated my domestic relationships, I could speak my heart to God in prayer. I would go for walks at night under the stars and feel the freedom to lift my voice in prayer, talking unrestrainedly to my new-found Friend, my Heavenly Father.

I learned a few simple hymns. As I rode my bicycle across the open veld, I would lift my voice, singing to God with thanksgiving. The first hymn I learned was The Old Rugged Cross. I had discovered an old 78 rpm phonograph record with the beautiful words:

On a hill far away stood an old rugged cross,
The emblem of suffering and shame;
And I love that old cross, where the dearest and best,
For a world of lost sinners was slain.

Refrain

So I'll cherish the old rugged cross,
Till my trophies at last I lay down;
I will cling to the old rugged cross,
And exchange it some day for a crown.

In the old rugged cross,
So despised by the world,
A wondrous attraction I see;
For the dear Lamb of God,
Left His glory on High,
To bear it to dark Calvary.

To the old rugged cross,
I will ever be true,
Its shame and reproach gladly bear;
And He'll take me someday,
To His home far away,
Where His glory forever I'll share.

My face was sometimes wet with the tears that welled up from deep inside me.

Though I was changing on the inside, in my heart and soul, I was still myself, with my old nature ever present. I was living in the same unhappy, trouble-torn home. Outwardly, I was still an adopted child with the attendant tensions and the legacy of a turbulent childhood. But inside I was new. With a bold assurance of faith I knew that, "old things are passed away...all things are become new."(4) I was, "...born again."(5)

Sam Church, independent and aggressive, was constantly reaching toward new heights of achievement. He was advancing in the gold mining industry, where, from common miner, through shift boss (underground supervisor), he had steadily worked his way up the ladder. His spirit, however, was restless. The quest for a better life meant one upheaval after another and constantly stirred the waters of our co-existence into turbulence and muddied uncertainty as we were constantly on the move.

It was 1948 and we were moving to the large mining town of Randfontein. The relocation was a bitter experience for me. I had entered a tennis tournament. I was excited, "pumped up," ready to do combat on the court, and eager to prove my prowess in the sport which had captured my imagination and earned me a sizeable measure of admiration because of my "game."

My hopes were dashed the night before the tournament. I was coldly told I would have to stay at home and be present to attend to the move and direct the packers. Just like that! No choice!

I was crestfallen. Hurt. Bitter. Angry.

The movers were due at 8:00 a.m. I was to remain at the house, see the packing done, and ride in the huge truck with the handlers. The whole day I waited; restless, alternating between near-tears, frustration, and sheer helplessness.

The movers did not arrive until that evening. Mom and Dad were already home. I had lost a day, a day which I had anticipated so eagerly. It should have been a gala occasion with friends and "friendly foes" in competition, but it was lost. Without understanding, without apology. That's the way it was!

The house was now a silent place. There was seldom anyone there during the day to fill it with the common sounds of home.

Mom worked. Hilda and Eddie spent their days in school. There were cold barriers between Mom and Dad, so that when any exchange occurred, it would usually be gruff and sullen. Laughter was a stranger and we rarely talked together as a family or did things of common interest. For all that flowed between us, we might have been animated waxworks with the house as our crypt.

A problem common to adopted children kept presenting itself. Dad's sister Ethel was a frequent visitor and she would often treat the children to outings. On several occasions a well-meaning adult would say, "You look so much alike; just like aunt and nephew should!" The situation always made me feel awkward and a silent shrug was my only answer.

At school my athletic bent flourished. At the start of 1948 I was appointed to succeed Johnny Buchler as the drum major of our cadet band and though a country-wide threat of polio curtailed many group activities, before the year's end I had achieved distinction in rugby, swimming, tennis and track and was awarded honors for these sporting accomplishments.

As marks of sporting distinction, athletes would be presented with small embroidered scrolls called "colors" which were sewn onto their school blazers. My list of colors became longer and longer as I mastered one athletic achievement after another. I reveled in the newfound joy of physical accomplishment and the prestige of having the longest list of colors in the school by far. In July, the head prefect of the school (appointed head of the student body) died suddenly and, because I was still in my semi-final year, I was awed when the headmaster called me to his office and appointed me as successor to the position of honor.

The unruly element at the Trade School had always poked fun at my name, but after the news of my conversion experience began to circulate, they took special delight in taunting me about my new "religion." I bore it all as patiently as I could throughout 1948. But the months of goading gradually came to a climax. The situation became more and more tense, till the lid blew off.

As drum major, I led our cadet band in the annual inter-school competition, which only cadets in the band were permitted to attend. The school forbade other boys to go, but a good number played truant and took in the show. The day following the competition, the teacher in the classroom asked me point-blank if a particular boy had been at the stadium. I was suddenly confronted with a situation that was beyond me. Faced at that moment with a straight question, I gave a straight answer. I said, "Yes, he was there."

The atmosphere in the classroom iced over immediately. To the boys of the school, I had become a traitor. I had "split" on one of their heroes and from then on, relations plunged rapidly downhill. Without malice I had evoked the animosity of the rough and tough guys.

Trying to show a genuinely Christian attitude, I bottled up the angry reactions which rose inside me. Finally, the malcontents selected a champion and to him they assigned the pleasure of a physical confrontation with me. On a Friday afternoon, as I came out of the school gate, they were waiting for me: a crowd of about fifty.

The elected representative walked up to me and snarled, "I want to see you at the railroad station." I knew what that meant!

Fighting had been outlawed, since a few years before a boy had died following a fight. Also, I was the school head prefect and a professing Christian. I was in a dilemma. However, the mob quickly resolved it for me as they surrounded me and marched me to the vacant lot behind the railroad station. As we trooped down the road, they taunted, jeered and threw stones, relishing my predicament. They wanted my blood!

Out of the entire crowd, one boy alone walked by my side. I shall never forget him. He was an Afrikaner: van der Westhuizen was his name. He encouraged and supported me.

On arriving at the secret battleground where the school fights took place, my accuser stepped out of the crowd. The mob formed a ring around us and, as is customary, my opponent confronted me.

In that moment, I saw no way out, but I decided to talk, for I had no idea what his grievance was.

"Tell me what's wrong," I said, "and I'll make it right."

"I never meant it, honest! I didn't know the teacher was after you guys. I'm really sorry," I countered.

The crowd booed and shouted me down.

"Donder hom" (smash him), they yelled.

The final accusation flabbergasted me, "You took my girl friend from me," he almost yelled.

I knew he was angry and serious in his accusation.

I almost pleaded, "I don't know what you're talking about. I don't even know who your girlfriend is."

But the situation had gone beyond reasoning. The mob was yelling, urging him on.

Van der Westhuizen stepped up to me and said, "You'd better take your blazer off."

In the act of slipping my jacket over my shoulders, while my arms were pinned behind me, my opponent hit me. The blow caught me square over the left ear.

First, a deafening roar, then a ringing went through my head. I saw bright dancing lights before my eyes. Stars! Then the old self in me took over. Neither my assailant nor the school rough-necks knew my past.

Van der Westhuizen pushed the other boy aside, gave me time to get my blazer off, and said, "Pieter, kneuk hom op." ("Peter, beat him up.")

I did! Once roused, I drew on all the skills of the streets and the lessons learned in Dolph du Plessis' boxing club in Mayfair. I was in good physical shape and I fought with fury and skill, till the battered "champion" sank at my feet. Since the first foul blow, he had not been able to land another punch. However, there was nothing to be proud of. I felt I had broken school rules, disgraced my office of prefect and ruined my testimony as a Christian. But, strangely, God makes even "the wrath of men to praise Him." That single contest and victory won for me the respect of the entire school!

When I most needed support and confirmation, God gave me a spiritual father or, more accurately, a grandfather, who taught me the basic truths of the Christian life. His name was Mr. Kirk (as he was respectfully known by all who knew him). He was only about 5 feet 2 inches tall and often himself joked about his small stature.

However, he was a giant of a man in the Scriptures. He introduced me to the world of Christian books. From the dim reaches of history he brought to life for me great men like Martin Luther, John Calvin, John and Charles Wesley and George Whitefield. He channeled the inspiration of the great preachers of bygone years to me: Spurgeon and Moody, Finney and G. Campbell Morgan. He opened his library to me and encouraged me to read from his storehouse of Christian literature.

He was selfless in his devotion to Jesus Christ. No chore was too menial and no sacrifice too great for this miniature saint. He drove his car countless thousands of miles as he ferried people to meetings in the city of Johannesburg so that they could enjoy the benefit of Christian fellowship and sound teaching from the Word of God.

He opened the song books of the Christian faith and taught me the value and the beauty of Christian songs and hymns. In his home he had an antique pump organ. He would pull up the bench in front of the ornately carved instrument, begin to pump the bellows with his feet, and as the old masterpiece would wheeze and grunt, Mr. Kirk would move his fingers across the keys and coax the old instrument into producing the melodies of the grand hymns of the faith.

Often, with tears streaming down his face as he sang those beautiful hymns, he would explain to me the origins and the deep significance of the lyrics. Through his tutelage, I learned the great doctrines of Christianity.

Fearless in his stand, he accepted the Bible as the inspired, infallible Word of God and stressed the importance of the fundamental theological truths. In detail, he expounded for me the great doctrines of salvation, redemption, atonement, sanctification and the second coming of Christ. I understood, through his teaching, the meaning of conversion, repentance, reconciliation, grace, faith, perseverance and holiness. He tried to explain the nature of God and the Trinity. He expertly defended the deity of Jesus Christ and warned me against error and heresy. He would say repeatedly, "You judge a teacher not by what he says but by what he does not say."

With misty eyes, he would talk about heaven. He loved the Lord Jesus and he looked for His appearing. The coming again of Christ Jesus was one of the themes upon which he often dwelt.

Patiently, he told me of the Holy Spirit. He urged me to walk in the Spirit, be filled with the Spirit and made me aware of the power by which I could live a victorious life and be a faithful witness. In my infant state of Christian experience I could not fully appreciate the depth of his wisdom, but he would often say, "It is possible to know about Jesus and not know Jesus. It is possible to know about God and not know God."

He knew Jesus in such a personal way. He stressed the importance of witnessing. By the challenge of his example he set the pace for me to follow. He worked as a locomotive engineer in the gold mines but devoted every waking hour to the service of the One whom he loved: Jesus.

His abiding influence in my life can be summed up in a principle which he continually underscored, "Read many books, but be a man of one book: the Bible."

I was only sixteen, but the conversion experience of receiving Christ was manifesting itself in dimensions other than those of my home life.

One night I was visiting friends in a cafe, when I saw a slightly built black boy enter with darting eyes and a furtive manner. His large brown eyes and thin limbs were so typical of the black children who moved warily through the streets of my home town. He slipped into the store with an inbred caution and tried to move inconspicuously up to the counter.

The stillness of the night air was shattered by the entrance of a rowdy band of white youths. They, too, were typical of the gangs which roamed the streets by night in search of mischief. We caught the scent of trouble.

Without warning the youngest of the white boys stepped up to the shabbily dressed little African and with a vicious swing smashed his fist into his face. The blow sent the black boy sprawling across the floor. He crashed into a newsstand which sent books and magazines flying, but with flashing eyes and the desperate spirit of a trapped animal, he sprang to his feet.

Bloodied but brave, if doom should require it, he was ready to exchange blow for blow with his assailant. But even as he came erect and squared off to meet his tormentor, the other white youths advanced menacingly toward him. Seeing the hopelessness of his situation, eyes wide with terror, the black youngster fled, leaving a trail of blood. The jeers and laughter of the "heroes" followed him into the night.

I was trembling with indignation. Anger choked me. I rose from my seat to intervene, but my two Greek friends, Costa and Apostle, who owned the cafe, laid restraining hands on my shoulder and said, "Peter, stay out of it." With a sense of outrage and seething fury squeezing my chest, I realized that I, too, was helpless against these brutal young Afrikaans thugs.

Inside a conscience told me there would be a day of reckoning. An inner warning told me there would be a harvest day for all such seeds sown in hatred.

Chapter Eight

he sand in the hour glass of 1948 had almost run out, and the magical season of Christmas was upon us.

There is a uniqueness to Christmas which can only be understood by the children of the white employees of the gold mines. About a week before the "big day" every mine put on a jamboree that made us children dream of that day with tingling excitement for more than 360 days each year. To us it was simply the "Mine Christmas Tree."

Each employee paid money into a fund, which the company would match. The mine would contract with toy manufacturers, and every kid in each age bracket would receive one major present, with accompanying treats like soft drink, candy, cake, and ice cream. It was a carnival. The atmosphere was always electric. There were clowns, pony rides, side shows, and the gay-colored tents with music filling the air made it a children's paradise.

Kids were everywhere, unwrapping gifts, squealing with delight, and even some wailing with fatigue, or perhaps discontent!

For most of the men, it was an occasion to consume as much alcohol as they could to brace themselves for the ordeal. Our Dad was numbered among them.

By the time we arrived at the gaily decorated community hall for the festivities of 1948, Dad was already dangerously drunk. It took only a minor incident for him to turn on Mom in fury. To avoid a public scene, I persuaded them to leave the party. Hilda and Eddie, too young to comprehend the behavior of their parents, were crestfallen. Tearful and afraid, they had to forego the fair, the free rides and the happy Christmas spirit.

In the car, the atmosphere was frigid, but underneath, the tensions between Mom and Dad were reaching explosion point. Once home, they stalked inside, while I parked the car.

When I walked in, all hell had broken loose. Mom and Dad were in fearful physical combat. Dad was a powerfully built, strong man, and he had begun to beat my mother with his fists.

In self-defense she had grabbed a steel iron from the stove and was lashing back with frightening success.

I was sick to my stomach.

Hilda and Eddie were screaming for me to intervene. I rushed up to Dad, shouting and yelling at him to stop but he turned on me and, with a mighty swinging blow to the side of the head, knocked me out cold.

It was some time before I regained consciousness, still feeling stunned and shaken. The house was strangely quiet, except for heavy breathing in the front bedroom. I cautiously made my way to the sound and there, lying distraught on the floor, was Sam. His face and head were bruised and bloodied from the blows Mom had struck with the fire iron.

With a love that only God's Holy Spirit could have poured into my heart I fell down on the floor beside him, took him in my arms and began to weep at his distress. I gathered that Mom had walked out of the house with Hilda and Eddie, vowing never to return. Sam pleaded pitifully, asking me to go after them and bring them back.

Mom could not drive, so I knew she would have started walking towards the nearest railroad station. I left Sam lying on the floor and hurried after her and the children. I found them walking slowly and disconsolately down the road. Mom was sobbing; Hilda and Eddie were confused and their tear-reddened eyes showed a pitiful incomprehension of it all. I felt overwhelming compassion as, gently pleading, I persuaded Mom to return to the house. I promised her that with God's help everything would be different.

It wasn't.

For weeks they both bore the marks of that awful confrontation but when the crisis had passed they were their same, unhappy selves. Nothing had changed.

But I had changed; and I was changing. There grew in my heart a deep, tender spiritual love for those precious people. Oh, how I loved them. I longed to see them come to know the Savior. I was especially consumed with tender compassion for Hilda and Eddie.

1949 dawned with the usual good resolutions. At a New Year's party I saw several adults make solemn vows to reform. One friend of the family, a jolly, sandy-haired Englishman named Mr. Hopkins, promised, as the clock struck twelve, that he would never again smoke another cigarette. With a hoarse cough he threw his pack of cigarettes out the window and manfully declared, "Never again!" At twelve-thirty I came across the gentleman groping in the flower bed under the window looking for his pack. To round out his performance, this affable, alcohol soaked Englishman sat on a collection of my prized gramophone records.

What a beginning to 1949!

I was learning that good resolutions are powerless to change human nature. I had witnessed the plight of my stepfather; I had seen this man of strength and determination, at his lowest point, making personal resolves that things would be different. But they weren't. God was teaching me in the crucible that it is, "Not by might, nor by power, but by my Spirit, says the Lord of hosts."(1)

Through this exposure to constant human defeat I was to learn that people are born again, "not of blood, nor of the will of the flesh, nor of the will of man, but of God."(2)

Only the Father can bring His children to birth. Only God can make a Christian.

In 1949, I witnessed the miracle of the new birth in my brother Theo's life. The delivery room was a huge open air stadium. For many months I had prayed for my brother, then one day the opportunity came to take him with me to a great Youth for Christ evangelistic meeting in Johannesburg. At the close of the service I turned to him and said, "Theo, would you like to accept Jesus as your Savior?"

His answer was a quiet, "Yes!" and he knelt on the hard concrete floor next to a wooden seat and became the first of my family to make that decision. There was joy in heaven, and on earth.

I did not grasp the significance of that moment, but I rejoiced with a surge of gladness and praise to God. It was the turning point of my relationship with Theo. We were instantly drawn into a new friendship.

The fact of our adoption was a sensitive family secret.

Because of my age at the time of adoption, it never presented a problem to me, but Hilda and Eddie were not to find out until they were teenagers. Although I was only half blood brother to them, a deep love developed between the three of us. Whenever Ed was asked, as little boys are, "What do you want to be when you grow up?" he would reply, "I want to be big like Peter."

I plunged into numerous sporting activities, some legitimate and others hazardous; such as the period I served as mechanic and novice rider in a motorcycle racing club. It nearly cost me my life!

My latent talents and exuberance for life and excitement drew me into the hazardous sport of motorcycle racing. At one of the athletic gatherings, in which I competed in the track and field events, the day closed with the spectacle of an evening of "dirt-track' racing. Something stirred in me as the lean, but loud, motorbikes screamed around the ash-covered oval. I recalled the time, years before, when our new "Dad" had taken us to the "Speedway," and I decided now that I would participate in the thrills.

I joined the West Rand Lions racing team, first as a mechanic, then graduated to novice rider.

What a sensation! I thrilled to the roar of the mean-looking machines and thrived on the atmosphere of excitement. The exhaust fumes, spiked by additives to the gasoline, were like a stimulant. The smell of the race track, the cheers of the crowds, mixed with the roar of the bikes was magnetic.

Once each year the Motor Club sponsored a Rally which drew drivers, mechanics and a large entourage of racing enthusiasts together for a festive end-of-the-season extravaganza. Abandoning their motorbikes, the drivers now competed in automobiles. Each driver has a navigator and each car is equipped with a special clock.

As a time trial event, the route planned for this Rally was to cover a large portion of the Eastern Transvaal, taking in rugged mountain routes as well as the expansive dusty, flat-lands. The race requires, not speed, but skill, timing, and dependability of man and machine.

I was assigned the role of a time keeper. Stationed at undisclosed checkpoints along the route, the time keepers are transported to their stations well ahead of the competing drivers. After all the cars have passed through every check point (where their arrival time is clocked), the time keepers are then picked up and taken to the finish point. The 12-hour trial ends with a dinner party and awards ceremony.

It was a long, tiring, thirsty day.

The van which was to pick me up after the last car passed my checkpoint did not appear. Toward evening, as the sun was dipping in the West, a car came gliding through the shimmering haze. The driver told me a sobering story.

The van which was assigned to my detail had missed my checkpoint, and a few miles further along had missed a turn in the mountains. The van had crashed down a ravine, and the passenger space had been crushed. The consensus at the hotel that night was, had I been in the van I surely would have been killed!

Without adequate coaching and direction, many of my athletic adventures were ill-executed. Some were humorous and showed the lack of direction in my development. Though no laughing matter at the time, one of my more pathetic misadventures occurred during the Southern Transvaal Junior Athletic Championships in 1949.

I had qualified to run in the final of the half-mile race on Saturday afternoon. The stadium in which the championships were being held was about 20 miles from our home in Randfontein and, with several hours to spare between the morning events and the final, I decided to make the journey home for lunch. It was a gross miscalculation. Depending on the local train service for transportation, I failed to take into account that the South African Railways run trains very infrequently on weekends. I set out from the stadium on the long walk to the nearest railroad station.

The train finally arrived and only when I was halfway to my destination did I realize that there would be a similar one or two hour delay in waiting for a return train. I made a hurried decision. At the next station I jumped off the train, crossed the railroad tracks and waited for the train going in the opposite direction which would take me back to the stadium. My wait was almost in vain. I spent anxious, solitary hours on the platform until finally the same train which I had abandoned reappeared making its return run.

To make the start of the race I had to run the distance from the station back to the track. I arrived back at the stadium tired, agitated, and breathless, having neither eaten nor rested the whole day. There was only time to hurriedly throw off my street clothes and don my running shorts and shoes. I presented myself to the starter with barely seconds in hand. The race was called, the starter's gun sounded and the athletes sprang into their stride. Already keyed up and limber from my run to the stadium I set a cracking pace for the first lap.

That Saturday was a memorable one because the race produced a new South African half-mile record. But not for me. After the strident pace which I had set in the first lap, I was forced to abandon the race coming out of the first turn on the second lap. I sank to my knees with my heart pounding as though it would burst; my throat burned like fire as I gasped agonizingly for breath.

The winner of that race was proudly hailed as a worthy champion. He sought me out and thanked me most profusely for setting the pace in the first lap which ensured a record time. It did not help when he asked me where I had placed in the race! The winner went on to become a hero, a household name in South Africa.

In December 1949, I graduated from the Trade School in Randfontein and at my Dad's insistence I went to work as a Learner Official on the Randfontein Estates Gold Mine.

I pursued my athletic career with undiminished enthusiasm as a member of the Krugersdorp Wanderers Athletic Club, in company with numerous other young men. I trained during the week and participated with dedication in league and championship track meetings on Saturdays.

By the commencement of the 1950 track season I was taller and stronger and had switched my main participation to the hurdling events. Representing our Club, with four of my friends, we entered the Southern Transvaal Junior Athletic Championships in March. Numerically the other teams were far superior; some had over thirty athletes. Our team of five simply divided the total number of events between us and we each entered about seven. My responsibilities were the mile, the half-mile, the hurdles and the field events; discuss, shot, and javelin.

The outcome of the competition was a rout—for every other team! The five of us carried the championship with a huge margin. At the end of the grueling weekend, we were the Southern Transvaal Junior Athletic champions!

My four friends eventually ranked among South Africa's great young athletes.

Barris van Houten, one of the four, held South Africa's long jump and triple jump records for many years. He also became the South African decathlon champion.

Vivian Cooper was South Africa's junior high jump champion, setting breath-taking records which stood for almost a decade.

Stanley Trapedo was the third; he gained recognition as one of the country's finest sprinters, holding the record for the 220-yards.

Dereck Laiety was the other, an all-round athlete who excelled in the middle distances; he was a Victor Ludorum athlete of outstanding ability.

A greater triumph came for me just a few weeks later, when, still a junior having just reached eighteen years of age, I participated in the Senior Club Championships at the Johannesburg Wanderers' Stadium. In the final of the 220 yard hurdles I placed fourth. The three who beat me to the tape that day, Ron Wilke, Harold Rall and Des Beaumont, were among the country's top national athletes, men who had won distinction for South Africa at home and abroad. A new record was set that day; 24.2 seconds. There was no glory in placing fourth, but I had no reason to be ashamed in their company.

Chapter Nine

A mong my fellow athletes information circulated about American universities and colleges where promising young stars could obtain scholarships and professional coaching unheard of in our country.

The Olympic Games were a matter for cautious discussion. No one was willing to betray his hopes or make bold predictions and we assumed an air of nonchalance about our personal athletic goals. Yet, in the hearts of all was the dream. I was no exception. I cherished ambitions too sacred to risk sharing with another.

Prompted, if not propelled, by my diminutive mentor, Mr. Kirk, I had become involved in active Christian service in a local church as Sunday school teacher, then as superintendent of a branch Sunday school. I was also leading the Friday night youth fellowship in Venterspost. I made the weekly journey by bus, returning home in the early hours of Saturday morning in order to work the early shift in the mine so that I could be free to participate in athletic meetings on Saturday afternoons.

I experienced the thrill of helping numbers of young people discover Life in Jesus Christ. The hours of preparation required for the Bible study drove me to an earnest searching of the Word of God and constant prayer. If an opportunity presented itself to preach or share my faith in Christ, I was always eager.

Uncertain at first, I was timid, but as confidence grew I began searching for occasions to proclaim the good news. As I did not possess a suit, whenever I spoke I wore my official high school uniform. By the time I graduated in December, 1949, my black blazer bearing the school crest was adorned with scrolls which listed the sports in which I had obtained distinction. Decked out in this sartorial wonder I attended a Child Evangelism Fellowship meeting in March 1950 and was introduced to Mr. Ralph Amm, a layman from the neighboring town of Roodepoort.

Mr. Amm was a senior member of the board of deacons at a Baptist church where the youth fellowship was languishing under a common complaint; a lack of young men. He went home and described me to his four girls. I am not sure whether it was I who had impressed him or my honors blazer with its shameless array of scrolls! I was blissfully unaware of the intrigue which developed, but as providence decreed, the leaders of the youth group were an immigrant couple from England, Ted and Betty Follows. Ted also happened to work on the same mine where I was employed. Mr. Amm's eldest daughter, Ada, asked Ted if he knew Peter Church. He did.

Unknown to me, and only recently disclosed (by the chief architect), another "conspiracy" was at work to link my love-life with that particular girl—Ada Amm. My closest friends in my home town were the Rodd family; and most notably Wally and his two sisters Yvonne and Lynette. I was reserved in the presence of the two girls, but Yvonne, even then a consummate match-maker, was suggesting to my mentor, Mr. Kirk, that this certain Ada Amm would be the ideal match for me. The Rodd and Amm families were distantly related—I was the unknowing piece in an intriguing game of chess! Mr. Kirk, Yvonne, and the others, all collaborating together, though none knowing what the other was doing, conspired to get me to a rendezvous.

A month later, accompanied by my Randfontein friends, I found myself at a barbecue on a small farm outside Roodepoort, the guest of no less than twenty girls! Mr. Amm introduced me to Ada and invited me to attend services at the Baptist church in Roodepoort. Across the dancing flames of the barbecue fire I watched and listened as Ada bore testimony to her warm devotion to Jesus. Drawn by her fresh, sparkling personality and infectious gaiety, I knew I wanted to know her better. Another feature attracted me: this group of people obviously believed and were committed to following the teachings of the Bible.

I became a regular caller at the Amm home and in May 1950 I was baptized by their pastor, Thomas Nosworthy. Rev. and Mrs. Nosworthy had been missionaries in the Congo and with that same dedication had been instrumental in starting new Baptist witnesses on the West Rand. I participated with them in the founding of a church in my home town, Randfontein. Ada came with her father to attend the meeting and this gave me an opportunity to introduce her to my Mom and Dad. They were as charmed as I was. She brought a sparkle into our home with her bubbling humor and vivacious personality. On May 31, I accompanied her to an all-day Baptist youth rally. It was our first official "date." A gala occasion of the year for Christian youth, the rally attracted young people by the hundreds from across the Witwatersrand. It was a wildly happy day for me. We laughed and talked and scarcely noticed the time as the hours of fun and fellowship ebbed away.

My job as a Learner Official in the gold mines had been chosen by my father. Sam Church was a dyed-in-the-wool gold miner and he wanted me to follow in his footsteps. After six months in the course, I had come to my last day and my last shift in the underground Sampling Department.

It was 7:00 a.m. on Friday, June 2, 1950.

Three days before I had purchased a sleek new motorcycle, flashing with polish and chrome. I was elated as I rode it that Friday morning in the sharp winter's air and parked it with pride outside the "change house" at the head of the shaft. I exchanged my street clothes for the protective clothing worn underground–heavy hob nailed boots, thick linen trousers, an undershirt, a work shirt, a heavy leather jacket and a helmet with a lamp clipped to its front. Strapped around my waist was the battery which supplied the lamp with power. I was happy to be alive. I was elated with my new motorcycle. Memories of my fabulous day with Ada whirled like a carousel in my mind. I had another date with her for that evening.

By 7:00 am I was with the other miners at the head of the Number 3 North shaft waiting for the "cage," a large steel elevator suspended by a 2-inch steel cable which drops miners into the darkness of the "underworld." The massive steel "cage" sounds woefully insecure as it rattles downward, away from the light of the sun and the sweet, fresh air. Accidents, through broken cables and errors on the part of the men who drive the huge winches which pull the elevators up and down the shafts, are rare, but the horrible specter hangs over every miner. Hundreds of terror-stricken men have been sent screaming to their deaths at the bottom of these shafts.

From the central, vertical elevator shaft, horizontal tunnels branch off at various levels and shoot off in different directions following the vein of the reef in search of the rich ore deposits. Men daily say good-bye to the sunlight and the comparative safety of the surface to extend the tunnels, seek new caches and lift the gold-bearing quartzite to the surface, where it is crushed and the gold extracted.

My assignment that day was on a level about 3,000 feet below the surface. The ride is always accompanied by a mixture of noise and uneasy silence. The noise of the clattering cage emphasizes the stillness of the men fighting the hollow feeling brought on by the plunging descent. It seems to take forever. A barb of insecurity pursues every miner into the pit. Many die each year and many more are injured by subterranean explosions, falling rock and mechanical accidents.

On this day, my companions in the cage occasionally laugh or jest coarsely in an effort to quell the whispering anxiety within.

By eight o'clock the cage has reached the end of its run. We are on Level 32. The last to leave the cage, we are deposited at the lowest working level of the mine and the cage closes and starts the long haul back to the surface. We are alone!

The sampler's task is to chip samples from the "face" that is being worked. These will be sent to the surface and assayed (tested) to determine the quality of the ore.

We are in a remote area and I and my crew of four black men are isolated, far away from any other miners. Alexander, the "boss boy" or leader, directs my crew of helpers. The language we use is Fanagalo, an amalgam of several native languages which originated in the mines. It is a working language only, used for orders and instructions, and has no terms for emotions, intellectual concepts or abstract ideas. As we walk along, however, I do my best to talk to Alexander. He is a good "boss-boy," with a broad smile and a pleasant disposition. We have been working together for several months. Each day he sees to it that my boots are cleaned, my lamp is trim and the battery charged. He also makes sure the other men report each day to the correct shaft and there he assembles the team. For this he receives about three shillings a day,* while the others get two shillings and sixpence.

These black miners leave their wives and families in their homelands to seek their fortune in the gold mines. They come from neighboring territories and countries, sometimes more than 1,000 miles away, to work in the mines. The pay is meager, but if saved over a period of a year, it is many, many times more than the men can hope to make in their distant homelands. The men live in compounds: bleak, smelly, communal quarters. After working for eleven months they may return home for thirty days. If they fail to report back within the prescribed period, they lose all benefits and salary advances and start at the bottom once again. Life is brutally hard for these men, I reflect, as I walk along in the stillness, our hobnailed boots striking an uneven tattoo on the cold rock floor.

We get to work at a faster pace than usual, because it is Friday and we will be able to return to the sunlight once we have collected the required number of samples; we want to take the first available cage going up.

While I chip the samples from the rock with my tools, my helpers collect them in canvas bags. Each sample is labeled and then recorded on a special chart. The small canvas bags are carried in larger shoulder bags by Alexander's team.

Most of the working area (stope) is no more than 3 feet high. We crawl on hands and knees or slide around on padded seats, remaining doubled over for several hours on end.

I look at my watch. It is almost noon. I decide that we will cut the last sample for the day from a nearby fault and head for the tunnel which leads to the shaft.

I strike the rock with my chisel, but it is iron-hard and unyielding. I decide the only way to dislodge a piece of the rock is to strike the face with my four-pound hammer.

To command more striking power I ease myself off my seat and kneel before the rock face. I am turned slightly to the left and I give the word to Alexander to come round to my left side. Because of a fault (a rift in the rock face) I have to kneel at the bottom of an

18-inch step in the floor. I raise the hammer and bring it down on the stubborn rock with all my strength.

There is an ear-splitting crash; a micro-second of incomprehension, then the roof gives way, and the rock comes crashing down on me. The breaking roof smashes me to the floor as tons of rock cascade down with a grinding roar. I am crushed like an insect under a gigantic boot.

There is a split-second of stunned silence and total darkness.

Then the screams.

I hear blood-curdling cries from throats torn by fear and panic! But the settling rock muffles the sound and the frantic yelling for help is stifled by the cascading rockfall.

I am stunned from the initial blow on my head.

The rocks above me shift again and the increased mass settling on my shattered body drives fresh agonies to my brain.

I try desperately to squirm my way out from under the mountain of rock.

I cannot comprehend what has happened.

Dazed and confused, my thoughts refuse to be regimented into a plan for action. The blow on my head has stunned me, but my hard hat has kept me from being knocked unconscious.

The pain intensifies. It does not issue from any one member, but surges through my whole body. I cannot figure out the position of my limbs, but I know that I am unnaturally forced forward, bent double at the waist.

My face is crushed against the stone floor between my knees. I cannot move a foot or a finger and my lungs are tightly constricted. I cannot breathe properly but only gasp for small quantities of air.

I am alone.

It is dark. Darker than any night I have known.

I am cold.

I have no awareness of time. I am conscious, but only in the sense that I know, vaguely, that I am alive. I hold on to that, as the measureless time crawls by. Breathing is becoming more difficult.

All around me now is deathly silence. The blackness of a tomb has engulfed me.

Some inborn sense warns me not to struggle. I remain still, concentrating on the little gasps that are drawing air into my lungs.

Slowly it dawns on me that we are trapped in a cave-in, although I don't know how long it has been.

Panic grips me with its icy fingers.

I want to thrash about and hurl the killing mass of rock away from me, but the mad urge acknowledges defeat and subsides. My mind races while my body tries to fight the pain. Although the mine air is warm and clammy, I am cold and start to shiver.

I cannot move any part of my body. I am transfixed, pinned to the floor, nailed to the black, unyielding rock.

I talk to God.

My every thought is a prayer.

I recall the people, the places, the events, that have brought me to this moment. My mind returns repeatedly to the plans I have made for that night. It is my weekly rendezvous with Ada. How will I let her know that I am trapped down here, nearly 3,000 feet below the surface of the earth, in the cold belly of a caved-in, deserted mine shaft?

I try not to dwell on the fact that there is little chance of survival.

It is Friday afternoon and miners habitually vacate the mine as soon as they can before the weekend. I am not due at the office until Monday morning and nobody works in the mine office on Saturdays.

It will be days before we are missed! How long can I survive, trapped as I am, beneath this rock fall?

Not long! Not long for sure. Time is dragging to a standstill.

Yet I know that my heavenly Father is with me. The words of Jesus are very real to me; "I will never leave you nor forsake you."(1)I wonder about my four assistants. I remember that three had been seated on the rock floor immediately behind me. I think of Alexander, whom I had sent around to my left towards the open side of the work area. But I am doubled over. I cannot draw enough breath to shout or call to them.

"Oh, Father."

Shadowy thoughts flit through my mind. Vague recollections pass across my consciousness. I think of the wide open spaces I love so well, of the races I have run, the games I have played, of the tennis courts and the swimming pools, of many, many pleasant hours.

I think of the farm. My imagination carries me to the land, the horses, the hunting, the fishing and the native people. And my family; Dad and Mom, Theo, Hilda, Eddie.

I think of Ada. Constantly I think of Ada.

And I am cold, so cold. Surely the agony cannot get worse?

Claustrophobia is pressing me towards panic. I feel blood trickling from my mouth as the breathing becomes more difficult. I cannot cry, I cannot speak, I can only wait for the end to come. But, again, I think of my heavenly Father and, in my spirit, I appeal to Jesus, my friend. I know that the Comforter, the Holy Spirit, is with me.

The will to struggle and fight ebbs away and I begin to sink down into the swallowing blackness.

Suddenly I am alert. There is a faint ringing sound.

I hear the clink of metal on stone, then the grinding of rocks being cleared away.

There is a faint sound of voices. It is like the chorus of angels. I cannot call out or draw attention to where I am, but I know it is a rescue party. They are getting closer and finally their cap lamps begin to dance like fireflies in the blackness. The beams of light fall across me.

I feel the relief as the cruel, crushing rock is being lifted off my compressed frame. I feel warm hands reach down into my tomb as the men begin to pry me out from the rubble and lift me from my stone prison.

But suddenly, pains begins to rush through me like an electric shock.

I scream out in agony. I cannot bear to be touched. My body is possessed by pain. I begin to wish I had died. I hear kind words as they lift my twisted frame from the rubble, but my only thought is, "Leave me! Leave me!" I pray, "Oh, God, don't let them move me. I can't stand it. Please God, let me die or let them leave me here."

Gently, one of the mine workers speaks to me and says, "We can't leave you here. There is going to be another rockfall and if we don't get out, we'll all be killed."

I am strapped face down on a stretcher. My arms are placed alongside my torso, but there is a strangeness; where are my legs? Have I been cut off at the waist?

The stretcher is dragged as gently as possible down the working slope to a waiting emergency trolley which is pushed along the narrow gauge tracks in the tunnel. Each time the flatbed car hits a joint in the rails the wrench sends a shudder through my body. I know now that I am injured, seriously injured.

Then, vague awareness begins to dawn.

I cannot feel the lower part of my body! Through the suffocating fog of pain and shock the awful truth strikes home. I AM PARALYZED!

As the cart rolls across the tracks and the pain tears through my body, the words of a hymn pass through my mind:

There is a green hill far away,
Outside a city wall,
Where the dear Lord was crucified,
Who died to save us all.
We may not know, we cannot tell
What pain He had to bear,
But we believe it was for us
He hung and suffered there.

I cannot reason clearly, but deep inside an awareness fills my heart. In some mysterious way, I think of the agony of God's beloved Son, Jesus. A vision of the Lamb of God rises in my inner being. The words of Isaiah, read so many times, come to my clouded mind:

Surely he hath borne our griefs,
And carried our sorrows.
Yet we did esteem him stricken,
Smitten of God, and afflicted.

But he was wounded for our transgressions,
The chastisement of our peace was upon him;
And with his stripes we are healed.

He was oppressed, and he was afflicted,
Yet he opened not his mouth.

He is brought as a lamb to the slaughter,
As a sheep before her shearer is dumb,
So he opens not his mouth.(2)

The mine is on emergency alert. The cage is waiting at the end of the tunnel to pull me directly to the surface. A crowd has gathered at the shaft head. There is a hubbub of voices. Commands ring out, and I am whisked off to the emergency station.

In the first aid room I am still conscious and I vaguely sense the ambulance driver examining me. First aid regulations require that patients with back injuries be strapped face down on a stretcher, supported under the stomach with a pillow or a folded blanket.

This has not been done.

The rescue team has overlooked a vital procedure.

The ambulance driver, a skilled first aid man, loosens the straps on the stretcher and takes me gently by the hips. I hear him say to an attendant, "When I lift him up, slide the pillow under his stomach." As he lifts my broken body by the hips the agony is so unbearable that nausea sweeps over me and I lapse into a merciful unconsciousness.

Chapter Ten

t is Friday evening; dusk is yielding to the darkness of night as I regain consciousness in the Randfontein Hospital.

I open my eyes. Every detail of the ward stands out sharply after the engulfing darkness of the silent, clammy mine shaft. I taste blood in my mouth and there is grit between my teeth. To my right is our family doctor. He is speaking to my mother and father.

I open my eyes. Every detail of the ward stands out sharply after the engulfing darkness of the silent, clammy mine shaft. I taste blood in my mouth and there is grit between my teeth. To my right is our family doctor. He is speaking to my mother and father.

Dad is ashen gray with shock. Mom is sobbing uncontrollably.

Dr. Eidelman says, "Mr. Church, there is nothing we can do for your boy. His spine is fractured, he is paralyzed and he has multiple injuries. The best we can do is to rush him to the Chamber of Mines Hospital in Johannesburg."

The nurse begins preparing me for the ambulance ride. So many of my bones are broken that they cannot lift me or turn me, so the nurse begins cutting my clothing away, first the heavy khaki trousers, then the thick khaki shirt.

Seeing I am conscious, the nurse gives me a shot of morphine and I slip back into the darkness.

In the ambulance I regain consciousness. I begin to retch violently and cough up blood.

My mother is with me, distraught and almost hysterical, demanding that the attendant do something for me. He tries to explain that there is nothing to be done.

We reach the hospital and there is a whirl of activity; people and rooms pass by in a blur before I drift once more into the mist of pain and shock.

Now it is Saturday morning. I rally briefly.

There are two visitors at my bedside: Pastor Nosworthy and Maurice, the son of Mr. Kirk. They read the Scriptures and pray with me; they assure me of the prayers and concern of the young people in the youth fellowship. Maurice promises to visit me regularly and help me in every way he can. Shortly after they leave, I lapse into semi-consciousness.

The fog clears again briefly that evening and I see Mr. and Mrs. Amm standing beside my bed. Serenity flows from their presence like a soothing balm to my spirit, although every nerve in my body shrieks with pain. With an effort I muster the strength to open my eyes once again and catch sight of Ada. A tenderness and concern I have never seen before seems to shine through her. They cannot stay more than a few minutes, but before she turns to go, Ada pauses for a moment, bends and kisses me gently on the forehead. My eyes follow her as she tip-toes from the room and passes out of sight. Despite the agony of my body and the dullness of my mind there is a feeling for her somewhere deep inside me, a glowing warmth which I have never experienced before.

I did not regain full consciousness for many days. The silver cord of life was badly frayed and the breath in my body was held by only the most slender of threads.

Then, one morning, I awakened suddenly. I saw the sun streaming in through the French windows separating the ward from the balcony. I could see the tops of the trees growing outside and the distant green of the rolling hills. The puzzle came together piece by piece, the hospital ward, with its typical sounds and distinctive colors, a white-clad nurse sitting at my bedside, the forest of tubes, bottles of all sizes and metal paraphernalia suspended around the bed. These all told their grim story. I had been under intensive care, a "special," attended by two nurses who kept watch over me night and day.

The nurse, spotting my wakefulness, chirped a cheerful "Hello!" and followed it with, "Time to brush your teeth." Her remark struck me as being ludicrous; to be welcomed back from the grave with so trivial a ritual as brushing one's teeth seemed ridiculous and I smiled weakly.

I could move my arms and turn my head, but a cautious exploration of the rest of my body gave some idea of the extent of my injuries. My fingers touched a thick plaster cast encasing my torso. I reached for my thighs and became alarmed: I could not see my legs and I could not feel them. They seemed not to be there, as though I had been cut in two and the lower half merely happened to be lying there, severed. I could not move my toes, not even the tiniest twitch.

The whole mine-shaft nightmare came back to me. I recalled the cave-in, the fearful screaming, the unearthly silence that followed, the unending hours with my face smashed hard against the granite-hard floor between my knees, the agonizing jolting of the flatbed trolley on the journey to the vertical shaft and the awful consciousness that my back was broken.

Now, I lay in a clean, sparkling ward of a sterile hospital, paralyzed from the waist down. My body, or the parts of it that were still capable of sensation, ached. I began to weep, not from the pain, but from a delayed reaction and emotion which rose from somewhere deep within me till it squeezed tightly at my eyelids. The tears rolled down my cheeks. My spirit ached, even as my body ached. The horror of physical brokenness rolled over me like a stifling wave.

The hours merged and became nameless days and nights. I was unable to do anything but think and brood. My mood vacillated between hope and despair. In the first days of brooding, I nursed the optimistic hope that, somehow, I would awaken to find it had all been a nightmare, as had happened with bad dreams before. I remembered the dream I had had in the boarding school; the waking to find myself in a strange dormitory room. All that had been needed then, was a little while to work out a solution and the will to apply it.

I was in the Chamber of Mines Hospital, a medical institution famed in the mining community for its medical staff, facilities, and successes in the care and rehabilitation of seriously injured workers. I was under the care of one of the nation's premiere orthopedic surgeons, a Doctor du Toit.

In my fantasy-land of reveries and wishful thinking, I somehow fancied that one morning Dr. du Toit would breeze into my hospital ward, remove the bulky cast, and tell me cheerfully to get up and walk.

In a spaced-out, illogical maze, I thought that, after a little season of convalescence, I would be back on my feet, outside in the glorious sunlight that came streaming through the expansive glass doors.

But the days passed by and no such cheerful order was issued. Day succeeded day. Days passed into weeks. And there was no change.

Maurice Kirk kept his promise.

He was the opposite of his father in stature. Rugged, tall and strong, he brought an invigorating sense of solidity into my life. Almost every weekday he came by to see me. He was preparing for an engineering career at the University of the Witwatersrand not far away. His faithful companionship sustained me through the otherwise long, tedious afternoons; he brought books, fruit and other small things for my comfort. In touch by telephone with numerous people, he brought messages to me day by day.

The evenings were brightened by visits from my friends; Mr. Kirk, with Mrs. Rodd and Yvonne and Lyn in tow, and from my new friends from the Roodepoort Baptist Church. They would come, bringing not only books and flowers, but moral uplift and spiritual encouragement too.

Several times a week Mr. Kirk would round up young people from distant Randfontein or Roodepoort and bring these energetic dispensers of cheer to my bedside. He also supervised my reading. He brought me books on biblical archaeology, Christian doctrine, Bible study, Christian biography and theology. With gentle prodding and wise suggestions he added profit to days which might otherwise have been wasted in idleness.

The high point in any day was those moments when Ada came to visit. I would often ask her to linger when everyone else had left. Those moments witnessed the first timid expression of our mutual attraction. Neither of us could as yet overcome our shyness and comfortably express the gentle surging emotions of love.

Johnny Buchler remained a steadfast friend and bulwark. Later he would tour England with a South African Springbok Rugby team and gain international recognition as one of the nation's all-time great players. During one of his visits to the hospital, he cautiously elevated the blanket over the "cradle," a wire arch designed to keep the weight of the blankets off my legs. I raised my head to watch as Johnny took my right leg in his hands and gently lifted my heel off the bed. There was a strange look on his face, as he said softly, "They are so thin!" As I continued to watch, he placed his thumb and index finger around my leg above the ankle. As though measuring a normal healthy wrist, his fingers met. My legs were wasted away. Like branches from which the sap had been drained, they lay limp and useless on the bed. The legs which had carried me to so many athletic triumphs were now like useless spindles!

Although the truth stared me in the face, I was unable to grasp it.

I constantly encouraged myself: "It's not permanent. The weakness will go away. Sure it will. Soon I'll be better, be up and about, strong as I was before, running, jumping, playing tennis and rugby. Just a little longer and I'll build up my muscles again, exercise, work-out, get myself into shape, it won't be long now!"

Three months had passed since the accident; three months in a heavy cast; three months of discomfort and pain; three months of alternating hope and despair.

My parents visited about twice a week.

Deep compassion for these two lonely people was maturing in me, a love which the Holy Spirit alone had brought to birth and was now nourishing. But it was still unexpressed. The walls of reserve which years of insensitivity and mistrust had raised between us would take time to dismantle.

Secretly, I prayed that through this shattering disaster they would turn to God and find peace and fulfillment in Jesus. I felt that all the hurt, all the pain and all the broken hopes I had suffered would be worthwhile if Mom and Dad would turn round and become aware of their need for the forgiveness, love and life-changing power of Christ.

One day they seemed more somber than usual. I noticed, with surprise, that Dad had grown decidedly older. His hair, quite suddenly, had turned gray. Mother sat at the bottom of my bed, tears rolling down her cheeks. To encourage her, I affected cheerfulness and said, "I'll soon be out. Be sure you keep my rugby boots polished and my running shoes ready." I sensed an awkward tension in the air. Dad turned abruptly and walked out of the hospital room. Mother refused to be comforted. They evidently knew something about my prognosis that I did not.

The revelation was soon in coming.

Standing by my bedside one Thursday morning, after concluding his usual examination, Dr. du Toit said in his frank and forthright manner, "Young man, I don't think you will ever walk again, unless I perform a major surgical operation on your spine."

The news fell like a thunderbolt.

He continued, "However, I cannot guarantee success. I can only offer you a fifty-fifty chance." He paused a moment, then went on, "I am going to be away for two weeks. Think about it, make your decision and, when I return, let me know."

The words were like the uttering of the death sentence. "You may never walk again!"

When he moved away from my bed I lay there too stunned to think. This was no passing nightmare. Everything was for real. All my chirpy optimism about running shoes, football boots and tennis rackets were the stuff of which pipe dreams are made.

I was paralyzed, more seriously injured than I had understood. I might never walk again!

That evening, Mr. Amm and Ada were my visitors. When they were about to leave, I shared the news with them. Many people had been praying for me. In the first few days, when my life had been hanging in the balance, a skeptic attending one of the churches in

Johannesburg had heard the minister speak of my plight and had heard the prayers offered on my behalf.

As Peter Kent sat in that church, he had said, "I don't believe in God. I don't believe in prayer, but if there is a God I will put Him to the test. If He hears this prayer, and if this boy lives, I will know that God is real. I will surrender my life to Him and become a Christian." I lived! Confronted with this evidence of answered prayer, Peter Kent believed and received Christ as his Savior. We met later and became friends.

But now the slender hope offered by Dr. du Toit was a new challenge to our faith. I asked Mr. Amm that Thursday night to pray that God would perform a miracle for me. I wanted more than anything in the world to walk again. I asked him to pray that God would touch me and restore the use of my legs. In simple faith we asked our heavenly Father to do just that. They left and I was made ready for the long night.

Since the accident I had been troubled by nightmares. In every horrifying dream I would be struggling to pull myself clear from an onrushing train or a speeding car, while lying across a track or some other thoroughfare. I would dream I was struggling furiously, trying to claw my way helplessly out of the way of the onrushing vehicle. In these chilling night terrors, I was always trying to drag my limbs out of the way before the wheels bore down on me, threatening to crush my legs or sever my body at the hips. When these nightmares reached the split-second before impact I would wake up dripping with sweat, to find myself frantically tugging at my legs in a futile struggle to move them.

That night I grappled with the recurring nightmare, but when I was jarred awake I felt a burning, stabbing pain shooting down my left leg. As I lay there sweating profusely, dizzy from the harrowing nightmare, the thought flashed through my mind, "O God, are you going to do it? Lord, are you going to work a miracle for me?"

He was!

When Dr. du Toit returned at the end of his two week absence, during a close examination of my condition, he discovered a twitching in the toes of my left foot. A minor sensation stirred among the group around my bed. Excitement mounted as word flew from person to person until the entire floor was buzzing with the news.

God was answering our prayers. A flicker of life had returned to my paralyzed legs. A long and arduous journey lay ahead of me, but through an unmistakable intervention by God, impulses were again being transmitted from my brain to my feet. Normally, if this does not occur in two or three weeks, there is no hope of the paraplegic walking again.

A miracle was happening to me, before my eyes.

Chapter Eleven

A s sensation and control of movement slowly returned to my wasted legs, hope rallied.

Often my mind returned to the exploits of the track, the rugby field and the tennis courts on which I had excelled. But my horizon now was this world of white sterility; long corridors that led to the physical therapy section. I traveled them twice each day in a wheelchair!

The rehabilitation program was demanding. Two therapists were assigned to my case. Mrs. Tobin was a diminutive, elderly practitioner, whose quaint idiosyncrasies nevertheless inspired my enthusiasm. Robbie was an ex-miner. A charge of dynamite in a mine shaft had detonated in his face and left him blind, but with courage and determination he had studied and persevered till he qualified as a therapist. It was an inspiration to see him feel his way along the corridors as he went diligently about his hospital duties.

As I battled with the childish tasks of throwing balls from a wheelchair and playing darts on the terrace with other disabled men, the world outside rolled on. Johnny Buchler was selected to play rugby for South Africa. Friends and team members of the Krugersdorp Athletic Club gained international status. Young athletes who had been my rivals went on to become stars.

The tide had left me washed up on a beach of disappointment, brokenness and pain. My domain was the territory I could cover in my wheelchair and from the therapy terrace I watched wistfully as the off-duty nurses played tennis on the hospital courts.

My days were filled with following simple routines and exercises designed to help me walk again. Dr. du Toit ordered that I be measured for orthopedic appliances essential to the program of rehabilitation. When the technicians arrived to take my measurements, I was aghast.

Legs which had been pillars of iron were reduced to skin and bones.

About a week later the technicians appeared suddenly one morning with an awesome array of contraptions which clanked ominously as they were carried into the ward. My fellow patients in the large general ward filed past and peered with curiosity as the men worked at fitting, altering and adjusting the appliances. It seemed to me that I was being fitted out like a medieval knight for battle. All I lacked was a lance and a plumed helmet.

My "armor" was comprised of an evil smelling cast designed to keep my spine rigid when the time came to stand me up. There was something obscene about the fleshy pink substance of the brace they called a "celastic jacket." It encased me from my neck to the top of my legs and laced up the back.

Even more menacing were the two sets of leg irons. With heavy leather straps placed strategically at the top of my thighs, around the knees and ankles, these metal rods were locked in position and served to keep the leg joints rigid. Then, to complete my wardrobe were the specifically designed and made-to-order boots into which the leg-irons were clipped. A finishing touch was provided by four springs, two for each ankle, which pulled the feet upwards to avoid dragging, which might produce permanent damage to the tendons which support the arches and ankles.

When the outfit had been measured, marked and noted for adjustment, the technicians gathered up the whole disgusting heap and hurried from the room. No friendly chatter had accompanied the ordeal, so I was not able to determine when they would return with the finished suit of armor.

I said nothing about these fittings to friends and family, as I planned to surprise them. I kept "mum" about my new "legs" because I had decided that, when I was ready to don them, and at an appropriate evening hour, I would stun my callers by standing at the head of the stairs to welcome them.

I relished the sensation it would cause! After the past months of seeing me helpless and bed-ridden they would now see me walking—yes, walking! I could hardly wait.

The day came.

The preliminary fittings had been completed; the "valets" delivered my array. I watched misty-eyed as they carried my rig into the ward. Methodically, they fitted, tested and adjusted each piece.

I entertained fantasies of myself "on parade" the coming weekend. I could picture myself walking tall and straight into the youth meeting on Friday night. I imagined everyone's surprise. In my mind I planned a date with Ada for the Saturday night. I knew she would be free, because she wasn't seeing any one else. Sunday I'd be in church, worshipping the Lord.

The delivery was beautifully timed; Thursday afternoon.

Most of my friends attended Wednesday night Bible study. Friday was youth night, so Thursday night was usually a "bumper" visiting hour.

It had taken nearly an hour to dress me up. It seemed almost like a royal ceremony—lacing the jacket, lacing the leather straps and finally the boots. I had never seen so many laces in my life.

Springs had to be clipped, the leg irons fitted into the slots in the heels of the boots and all the joints securely fastened on the metal struts.

Finally it was all over. King Arthur's gallants had nothing on me! But there was one vital difference.

Once strapped into the irons, the boots and the jacket, I was totally helpless.

My wasted limbs felt like wicks without a candle. They were so weighed down by the boots and irons that I was utterly inert. I could not raise my shoulders from the bed or move a muscle in my lower body. I was exhausted by the ordeal. Trapped in my "armor."

The technicians left and the nurse in charge of the ward came to "behold and see this thing which has come to pass." She looked as proud as Punch. After a careful examination she nodded her head (which she always did when pleased or annoyed) and said, "Now you just lie there and get the feel of it." With that, she hurried out of the room.

I lay there, weary with effort and feeling terribly alone.

The "aids" designed to help me walk had become, instead, a ball and chain. I was frustrated and angry and saw my dreams of instant independence dissolve before my eyes.

To struggle was useless. As the disappointment rushed in, I felt the tears sting my eyes. They ran from the corners of my eyes, into my ears, down my neck and onto the pillow.

Pinned on my back by the weight of these encumbrances, there was nothing else to do. Too beaten to fight, I fell asleep.

Evening found me too dispirited to eat or talk. At visiting hour my friends came. Ada was among them. My leg irons, with their huge boots and the revolting jacket, stood mutely mocking me from a corner. As each friend ogled the display, they realized, too, that this was going to be no breeze. It was to be a long drawn-out business.

For several days the physiotherapy team rigged me out in my irons and left me lying on the bed, to get acquainted, they said. Then the big day came when I was to be stood up in my outfit next to the bed.

I can never forget it.

The operation seemed to be going smoothly; lots of jests, puns and fun. This kind of thing didn't happen there every day! Paraplegics don't usually get back on their feet. Mostly, they die, some sooner, some later. At best they live out their days confined to a wheelchair. And here I was with new life coursing through my legs and strength gradually returning to my limbs.

I was standing next to the bed like a wooden soldier, hinged at the hips. Each leg dangled from my pelvis like a broken branch of a tree.

Several nurses were needed to prop me up.

To support me, the therapists wheeled in the oddest perambulating contraption I had ever set eyes on.

A "walking machine" they called it!

It looked like a giant bird cage of sorts. With two crutch-like armpit supports the stainless steel monster-on-wheels was designed to provide a frame on which to lean one's weight, while enabling the "driver" to lunge forward and simulate the act of walking.

My head spun. I was dizzy, weak and scared.

I stood shakily for a short while, and then it was time to end the experiment. The attendants marshalled their wits, joined forces and tried to heave me back onto the bed.

I grasped the "monkey chain" which hung just above my head in the bed and tried to haul my upper body into the normal reclining position. The attendants were supposed to lift and swing my heavily weighed but useless legs in one harmonious movement onto the bed.

The entire operation was intended to be an exercise in fluid motion.

Instead it was an inglorious fiasco. They swung my legs too high, too far, too fast. The result was a jarring, twisting movement which wrenched my arms, legs and back and forced a scream from my lips.

I let go of the chain and crashed onto the edge of the bed, causing a jack-knifing effect which sent shock waves of pain and nausea through my entire body.

I was eighteen, going on nineteen, but I shouted, half pleaded, "Don't you ever come near me again. Don't ever try to make me walk again. I don't ever want to walk. I never want to see these leg irons or you people again. I'll never let you touch me. Do you understand? I don't want to ever walk again!"

But the next day they were back. We tried again.

After several cautious attempts I began to shuffle clumsily around the ward in the "walking machine": the weird combination of crutches and wheelchair. The whole contrivance rolled on three wheels. I was being taught to walk like a baby.

I, the athlete, the miler, the hurdler, the rugby player, the tennis player, now a baby learning to toddle.

Somehow, the innate ability to master physical and mechanical challenges gave me a natural edge. I was quick to grasp the mechanics of the walking machine.

You raise the left side of your body, and that lifts your left leg and, consequently, your left foot off the ground. You lean forward in the machine and the leg just swings from the hip.

You have taken a "step"!

Now, you do the same with the right! You're walking!

Once over the initial "breaking-in" period, I became adept and I determined to make rapid progress.

I graduated from the walking machine to crutches in astonishing, "record" time.

"Suiting up" for each day was a major performance, and it took a team of two to get me ready for my daily excursion.

Each day my small world expanded. I was able to use the elevators, visit the other wards and, draped over my crutches, I could stand by the bedside of fellow patients and talk to them about Jesus. I carried my Bible in the pocket of my robe. I prayed with other patients and witnessed to the hard-boiled mine workers about the Lord.

The hospital became my mission field.

Chapter Twelve

powerful and molding influence began to shape my life: preaching!

The Rev. Ivor Powell, an eloquent Welshman and one of the most successful evangelists ever to visit South Africa, was preaching in the Baptist Church. I wanted to hear him.

God gave me an idea. I asked my Dad if he would take me to hear Ivor Powell one Saturday night. The doctor gave me permission to go home for the weekend, so, wheelchair, leg-irons, boots and celastic jacket were loaded into the ambulance and we set out for Randfontein—40 miles away.

Mom was wonderful. What a welcome she gave me! It was an occasion replete with my favorite dishes plus a chocolate cake.

Dad bundled me up in the red hospital blanket on Saturday night and carried me into the little church where a special chair had been reserved for me. I now only weighed about 100 lbs. so Dad, who was tough and strong, was able to carry me like a child. Throughout the service he stood behind my chair. Finally an invitation was given and Mr. Powell asked all who would repent and receive Jesus as Savior to leave their seats and come to the front of the church. I looked up at Dad. He was in the toils of a raging battle. The sweat stood out in great drops on his forehead and his knuckles were white as he gripped the back of my chair.

I prayed, "Dear God, please let him go forward. Let him come to You tonight and be saved."

He stayed fixed to the spot. He didn't go forward. More than anything in the world, I wanted him to find what I had found. But the moment had passed. He carried me out to the car and we drove home in silence.

When Mom had put me to bed, Dad came into the room. He stood by my bed, looked intently at me, and said, "You are wondering why I didn't go to the front of that church tonight. I'll tell you why. I know I could never live up to your standards. Your Christianity is okay for you, but it's not for me. I know myself, I could never keep it up."

This was the most direct and personal face-to-face opportunity I'd ever had to be a witness to my father. I took the moment, and found a boldness to tell him the Good News.

I pleaded with him, "Dad, you don't have to live up to anything. You don't have to keep it up. If you let Jesus come into your life, He will give you the power to live the Christian life." I pressed my point home with the words of Christ, "I am the vine, you are the branches. He that abides in me, and I in him, that person will bring forth much fruit, without me you can do nothing."(1) I showed him Philippians 2:13, "For it is God who works in you both to will and to do His good pleasure." I stressed the point that the Christian life is a walk of faith, trusting Christ to save you and to keep you. My well-worn Bible came to my aid and I read to him from its pages.

He listened, then with characteristic abruptness said, "You don't understand. I just couldn't live up to it. I'd be a hypocrite." He turned and walked from my room.

Chapter Twelve

Sunday brought a happy surprise. Mom came to my bedroom door and announced that I had a visitor. She stepped aside and, there, in the doorway, was the smiling face of Alexander, the man to whom I owed my rescue and my life.

He had heard that I was home and had walked many miles to see me. We talked about the accident. He showed me a badly injured arm. When the roof had caved in on us, he had been hurled aside by the blast of air and falling rock. A razor-sharp fragment had gashed his arm but he, alone, had not been pinned by the cave-in. Though bleeding profusely, he had stumbled through the darkness to find help. His presence of mind and concern raised the alarm and brought the rescue team to where the others and I had been buried.

The other men had fared badly. The oldest, a reed-thin man, already weakened from years in the mines, died in the black miner's hospital. The others had suffered broken legs and other injuries, but after hospitalization, they had recovered. However, explained Alexander, they had left the mines to return to their families in the distant homelands.

Perhaps, when the fear was past, they might return. Or, perhaps, never.

I never saw Alexander again.

I heard rumors that he had lost his arm by amputation. But I shall never forget his devotion to duty—or was it more? To him I owe an eternal debt.

When I had gained sufficient confidence to use my leg-irons with crutches, the doctor gave me permission to go on a Sunday afternoon outing with Ada. Maurice took care of the details and Mr. Kirk let him use the large family car. With a couple of other young people, we decided to drive to the beautiful lake adjoining the Johannesburg Zoo.

I was strapped into my "gear" and ready almost an hour before they arrived. Like a kid let loose in a candy store, I was more excited than I could remember. They arrived, and on a wave of laughter and high spirits, we set out.

We arrived at Zoo Lake in time for the South African ritual of "afternoon tea." I was helped out of the car while people stared. I walked with an awkward gait, swinging my legs and lower body between the two crutches.

It was tedious, hard work.

The "celastic" jacket keeps one erect but leaning back, so that one needs to compensate by bending forward at the hips. It feels much more clumsy than it sounds—but, you're walking! You're on your feet, out in God's open air. The grass is green, the flowers are in bloom, the birds are singing and your heart leaps up to join them. And you're with the girl you know you love.

It's all so new—so brand new. And you praise God. You say, "Thank you, Father. Thank you, Jesus." This is not a track meeting or a ball game with cheering spectators. You're just shuffling along while people stare, but you're smiling and you're grateful. The legs are walking you back into life.

Someone said, "Ice cream" and we headed for the tearoom on the terrace.

It seemed like a great idea until we got to the steps. I could not climb them.

Maurice was an engineer and applied his wits to the problem but neither of us could figure out a way to get me up those steps. I was happy to settle for an ice-cream cone seated on a bench by the water's edge.

Next day back at the hospital, when I was all "strapped in," I headed for the stairs. I was determined to master the art of getting up and down, and I did! I discovered I could unlock the hinge on my right leg iron, bend that knee, place my foot on a step, and pull myself up to the next step. Painfully, patiently, I negotiated an entire level of stairs.

But neither grit nor determination could eliminate all the difficulties. My left leg remained thin and weak. On one occasion, when a couple of my fellow patients were helping me up out of the bathtub, one of them, standing behind me, let out a soft exclamation. After a slight pause, he asked, "Have you seen how crooked your back is?"

Of course I hadn't seen my back! I had noticed, though, that I was somehow lop-sided.

It was not till then that I realized how badly twisted my spine was. The doctor called it scoliosis. My mother was furious when she heard about it and blamed the doctors for not taking sufficient time or exercising enough care when I had been first admitted.

Now it was too late.

The bones were set. The damage would be permanent.

Mrs. Tobin affectionately called me her "walking miracle."

To demonstrate what was being accomplished in the field of rehabilitation, a film crew from the prestigious *African Mirror*, a movie newsreel, came to the hospital to take pictures of my progress.

They filmed me in my wheelchair, in the games room and in the heated swimming pool.

The documentary film was screened in cinemas across the land.

There were days bright with fun and laughter and days of bleak, dismal despair.

One of the jovial patients was a lanky Irish immigrant miner named Pat. He loved his regular shot of whiskey and soda. Of course, drinking was rigidly forbidden by the martial discipline of the hospital. Pat had a severely injured leg which had barely been saved following a rock fall, and he walked with a comical gait as he moved his 6 foot 6 inch, pole-like frame around the ward and hospital corridors. After many weeks of confinement, Pat requested, and was granted, permission to take a bus ride into the city.

He returned in high spirits, well lubricated with alcohol. He stood by my bed in an effusive mood and told of his carefree jaunt into the wide world. As he turned to go, I playfully tugged the cord of his robe. The ensuing moments were like a comedy enacted in slow motion.

A bottle of Irish whiskey slid from his robe and shattered on the hardwood floor with a muffled thud.

Pat was transfixed with horror.

After a dazed moment's pause, he grabbed every snowy-white hospital towel in sight and threw himself on the floor in a frenzy of mopping the whiskey. The reeking liquor was powerful stuff. The towels picked up the whiskey, but also picked up the floor polish and the wood stain. Poor Pat gazed at the ruined towels and the huge tell-tale bare patch at my bedside. He lunged for the lockers where the floor polish was stored, grabbed anything he could use as a rag and frenziedly began to polish the wooden blocks. The bizarre sight brought howls of laughter from the patients. It was genuine mirth, but fueled by anxiety. The matron was a tyrant and this breach of rules could get Pat expelled from the hospital–and that was serious because it could affect his workmen's compensation.

When the mess was cleared, my end of the ward smelled like a distillery, so Pat raided my locker and emptied a couple of bottles of cologne and aftershave lotion all around my bed. The final move was to hide the tell-tale towels. I didn't know where he stacked them, but he seemed to have pulled it off.

He was granted leave of absence for the weekend, making his departure on Friday evening. On Saturday morning a dragon-like matron descended upon me. The towels had been found stuffed into an opening under a bath tub. Monday morning was designated for the confrontation and I was nervous.

When Pat sailed in, beaming from ear to ear, he announced that he had become a father over the weekend. In the congratulations and hilarity, the offense was forgotten. Such Irish charm!

My moods were a mixture of fierce determination, optimism and uncertainty. I wanted so desperately to be my old athletic self. I sometimes joked about my return to normal life, but deep within was the haunting suspicion that I was destined to be different.

Yet, in my heart, I knew that God was working in my life in a special way. Gradually, He unveiled to me a precious secret.

Like the sun breaking on the horizon at the dawn of a new day, His light slowly pierced the questioning gloom of my soul with promise and hope. Many, many times I had asked, "Why? Why, God? Why me?" He had saved me from my life of lonely despair, but for what? Was there more to life than this sterile environment, this infirm body and its dying-ember dreams?

One day, as I sat in my wheelchair in the shaded garden of the hospital with my open Bible on my lap, God spoke to me.

Ada's mother, lovingly concerned, had asked a pastor friend to visit me. The Rev. Tom Wilson came that very day and I tentatively shared a growing sense of calling with him. His advice was simple, but sound.

"Ask God to speak to you through His Word. If He is calling you to full-time Christian service, He will confirm it to you in the Bible."

God did. With startling clarity, verses of Scripture began to impress themselves upon me with peculiar insistence. The mists began to clear. The purpose of God ceased to be a riddle.

God was calling me to the ministry! The burden of the Apostle Paul became mine.

"I am compelled to preach, woe to me, if I do not preach the Gospel!"(2)

"I thank Christ Jesus our Lord who has enabled me...putting me into the ministry."(3)

From the pages of Isaiah, the Holy Spirit tenderly witnessed with my spirit as I read, "But now this is what the Lord says—He who created you,...He who formed you,...Fear not: for I have redeemed you, I have called you by name; you are mine...Behold, I will do a new thing;...you are my witness, says the Lord, and my servant whom I have chosen: that you may know and believe me, and understand that I am he...."(4)

Chapter Thirteen

ay followed day with a regimen that seemed to vary but little. At five o'clock each morning the coffee wagon rattled into the ward and the attendant noisily proceeded to rouse the patients with jest and coarse talk.

My days revolved around two sessions in the physical therapy department. The morning routine was filled with personal attention in the hot whirlpool, supervised exercises, massage and walking with my leg-irons, brace and crutches. The afternoons were supposed to be passed in playing games; darts and other innocuous diversions.

The passing weeks saw a gradual strengthening of my muscles, although my left leg remained wasted. My spine was twisted, my pelvis out of line. The left side of my body was almost totally numb but my shuffling gait gradually gave way to a more confident walk.

One day I stepped on the scale in the physical therapy room. Clad in all my finery I tipped the scale at little over 120 lbs. I was the proverbial shadow of my former self. Wan and pale from months of confinement, with my hair cut short for easy care, I looked like a scarecrow and my appearance reflected the uncertainty within.

By April, 1951, the orthopedic surgeon attending me decided the time had come for me to leave the supervision of the hospital and be re-introduced to the working world. I had been a patient in the Chamber of Mines Hospital for almost one year.

The world to which I returned had changed. I was wary and cautious. Gone was my fierce independence. Almost all my companions of former years were gone also. I emerged from my hospital cocoon to find that relationships that had been based merely on physical respect were flimsy at the last and had collapsed. On the other hand, the new friendships, built upon a mutual faith and eternal values, had taken the trauma in stride and survived.

The eleven months I spent in the hospital had seen a deepening of my relationship with Ada, her family and the people of the church. Mr. Kirk had made innumerable trips to bring young people to visit me. Maurice had kept a self-appointed vigil over me throughout my hospitalization. I was discovering the true meaning of the "body of Christ." The family of God formed the heart of my new social life.

It was now time for occupational therapy.

The staff at the Therapy Center gave me some choices; knitting, basket weaving or some similar activity. I was mortified. The thought of my being reduced to such a helpless level of activity fired my indignation and galvanized my resolve.

I appealed to the surgeon who was directing my rehabilitation. He consulted with the directors of the hospital, as well as the management of the Mining Company, and reported another option to me.

I accepted with alacrity. I was eager to start life anew!

I was assigned to work in the personnel department of the Randfontein Estates Gold Mining Company. Little bits of information leaked out to me, revealing the extent of my disability. I had been classified: "permanently unfit for underground service."

Shortly afterwards I discovered that my status on the mine had been changed accordingly. No longer was I designated "Learner Official." I was merely a surface employee.

Payday brought home to me what that meant. I was relegated to the ranks of those who could no longer enjoy the greater financial benefits of underground workers.

My new duties were to assist in the testing and classifying of the thousands who came from the tribal homelands to the mines in Randfontein. Initially, my duties were elementary and I could work for only a brief spell each day.

I yearned to be physically free again; to ride my motorcycle, to run and jump and play. Inside, I was still me; but my body was now classified: "Fifty-five percent totally, permanently disabled."

Later in the year, I was walking in a park where a group of young men were playing rugby. The ball flew wide and came bouncing unevenly towards me. Instinctively I picked it up and tried to kick it back to them. It should have gone soaring gracefully through the air to the waiting players.

No dice! It struck my shoe with a thud which nearly tore my foot from my leg. The ball trickled off my limp foot and rolled only a few yards. It was several minutes before I could place my throbbing member on the ground. The pain caused by the impact of my foot on the ball flashed through my leg, but was nothing compared to the chagrin in my soul.

I limped severely for nearly two weeks.

I was often embarrassed in this way. It was humbling to have to cope with this new image. I couldn't help with physical tasks. Excuses had to be found whenever I could not do my share of manual labor.

Yet, through it all, I was conscious of the tender love flowing from God my heavenly Father. In a mysterious yet real exchange, I was drawing an inner strength from the Power of Christ within me.

My emotions swung like a pendulum from bright, carefree hope and optimism to a dejected longing for my former freedom. There were still times when it all seemed like a bad dream.

I imagined that, like Samson, I would awaken to simply shrug off the disabling, confining weakness and leap into action. I prayed and in faith I asked God to remove this "thorn in my flesh." Instead, He gave me the assurance He had given to the apostle Paul, "My grace is sufficient for thee."(1)

Now in my dreams at night I was always trying to run in a race. But my feet were made of lead. They would not respond to the urgent appeals of my mind. But this was no mere nocturnal illusion. It was real—too real.

Also, I could see, with a sinking heart, that I was moving towards a confrontation with my Dad. There was no question in my mind that at the right time God would open the door for me to enter the path of Christian service. It was only a question of waiting for Him to reveal that moment. The Lord was continually confirming His call to me through His Word. Through the encouragement of our pastor, Rev. Nosworthy, Mr. and Mrs. Amm, Mr. Kirk and other Christian friends, God also confirmed His call. I received numerous invitations to preach and joyfully accepted whenever I could.

The opportunity to talk to my father never seemed to arise until one day late in 1951 when he had taken me from Randfontein to Johannesburg for a checkup at the hospital. I was finally walking without mechanical aids.

On the way home, Dad was speaking glowingly of the future ahead of me in the gold mines. The management, he said, was delighted with my natural aptitude for personnel work. He himself had been promoted to a senior position in the personnel department. He predicted that in spite of the accident, my disability and weakness, I had a marvelous career in front of me.

It was a tense moment because I did not want to hurt him. I wanted more than anything to show him respect. He was subject to violent outbursts of temper and I wanted to avoid that at all costs.

A struggle began inside me. I prayed, "O God, help me." Then, as the car purred along the country road, I said quietly, "Dad, I'm going to leave the mine. I want to go to college to study and become a minister. God has called me and I must obey Him."

I longed for him then to stop the car, reach out, embrace me and tell me he understood, that he loved me and would support me. The car sped on.

His face became set and hard. His complexion paled as he replied, "If that's your decision—do it! But don't expect any help from me."

Crushed and hurt, I turned my head to stare at the landscape rushing by. Tears of disappointment filled my eyes and we drove the rest of the way in silence.

The ugly presence of a deep and desperate unhappiness hung like a pall over the house. There was a dark brooding discontent which cast its ugly shadow over every room.

Mom and Dad were living in a war zone; the territory was like a field of land mines. It could explode at any time.

And it did! I never knew what caused the detonation, but one Friday night I brought Ada to our home. Some incident had caused Dad's fragile temper to break and he had vented his anger on our defenseless young brother Eddie.

In a fury he had whipped the little boy with a cane so brutally that Ed could neither sit down nor lie on his back. Hilda, broken and sobbing, was sitting beside him on the bed with ice cubes in damp towels over the welts, cuts, and bruises. I stood beside my precious brother, and between my sobs of grief, I prayed for Eddie. My heart was breaking.

I applied to the newly established Baptist Theological College in Johannesburg and was accepted for the academic year beginning in January, 1952. There were many obstacles which stood like mountains in my way; my disability, lack of finances, Sam's truculent attitude. Once more the Holy Spirit ministered to me as the Comforter and I experienced a new tranquility as God spoke to me through His Word, "When my father and my mother forsake me, then the Lord will take me up."(2)

I was strengthened by the words of the prophet Isaiah, "When you pass through the waters, I will be with you; when you pass through the rivers, they will not sweep over you. When you walk through the fire, you will not be burned. For I am the Lord your God, the Holy One of Israel, your Savior."(3) Almost unknowingly, I was learning the deep secrets of the Christian life, proving that we experience the grace of God in the arena where we face the adversary, and in the fire where "the Son of God" walks with us.(4)

Like the Shepherd of promise in Psalm 23, the Lord was guiding me with His promises and guarding me with His power. He was not only allowing me to be proved in the crucible, but He was providing for me in my hours of need. I treasured the image of the God who cared for me as a loving "Father."

One by one God cleared the obstacles which stood like mountains in the road, blocking my path towards entrance to the Seminary, but one severe test lay before me.

It happened on New Year's Day, 1952.

I was out with Ada and Mrs. Amm trying to give them a few tennis tips. As I reached up to hit a ball, my left leg, which had remained weak and undeveloped, twisted and with a loud snap, buckled under me.

In terrible pain, with my knee locked in a half bent position, they rushed me to the Chamber of Mines Hospital in Johannesburg where I was readmitted. I was writhing in agony—the result of torn cartilage and tendons. The only recourse was surgery.

Once more, I was faced with a major decision. Dr. du Toit recommended the removal of my left kneecap. In the accident I had sustained numerous fractures, some of which had only become apparent with the passage of time. This was one.

I chose to keep my kneecap, but have the cartilage removed. Because of the wasted state of my leg, the surgery and recuperation were tiresome and prolonged.

Recovery from a menasectomy (removal of the cartilage) is usually straightforward. Five days in a leg cast, discharge from the hospital on about the seventh day and return to fairly normal activity in about two weeks. But for me, the process was long and agonizing. My wasted, weak leg took not weeks, but months to heal.

On February 16, my birthday, I had permission to spend the night away from the hospital. The Amm family planned a party for me that evening and the hospital agreed to take me to their home by ambulance. I was ready for my celebration by ten o'clock in the morning. My school blazer, resplendent with its crest and long list of athletic scrolls made a sharp contrast to my thin body and pallid complexion.

Armed with a pair of crutches, my leg stiff and specially bandaged to enable me to walk, I waited for the promised ride to Roodepoort where the Amm family lived. Talk about trials; the vehicle did not arrive until almost 3:00 p.m. I was already tired from the long vigil, but the ambulance driver, no doubt with other urgent calls to make, dropped me about half a mile from the Amm's house.

With a small overnight bag slung across my shoulder, almost spent from my ordeal of waiting, I was no match for the walk. I struggled down the road on my crutches with an awkward gait that made the bag thump me with a bang every time I lurched. The skin under my arms chafed with the rubbing of the crutches and my arms ached under the strain. I lost not only my joy, my eager anticipation and my physical well-being, but I lost my spiritual victory too. I began to curse and as my anger rose; tears of frustration stung my eyes.

But somehow I battled on. And the pain of defeat gave way to happiness in the loving concern and consolation of Ada's vivacious welcome when at last I stumbled up the front steps of their home.

Chapter Fourteen

t was March 1952. Feeling awed and apprehensive, I presented myself at the office of the Rev. A. J. Barnard, principal of the Baptist Theological College of Southern Africa. The red brick building at 20 Wellington Road, Parktown, appeared cold and forbidding. The term had begun nearly two months previously and I felt like an intruder. I arrived expecting to find a band of men who demonstrated the best of Christian virtues. Naively I imagined a seminary to be a haven of warm, loving fellowship, where men were prepared in heart as well as mind for the task of serving Christ.

I was rudely awakened. The atmosphere was cold, formal, correct. After a while, I, too, succumbed to the prevailing cynicism. My once sparkling, pristine faith soon bogged down in a mire of formalism.

The training was rigorous and demanding. In the realm of education and preparation for the mechanical function of the ministry, the college was superb. Rev. Barnard was a brilliant scholar and a masterful teacher. His lectures and practical classes in preaching were handled with skill and proficiency. The college trained men with precision for the mechanics of the ministry.

But among the students there was a hard, competitive spirit. Corporately we were guilty of allowing the environment to rob us of our warmly intimate relationship with Jesus Christ. My "first love" was overshadowed by long hours of study and constant academic pressure. Interchanges between the students were often acrimonious and there was a woeful absence of Christ-like love.

Theology and related subjects were taught in the austere buildings which housed the seminary, while the language courses, English and Greek, were taken at the University of the Witwatersrand, a couple of miles away. Each day the students had to walk up the long hill which stood between the two institutions and I was immediately in trouble because I found it impossible to make the arduous climb. My left leg, still weak from the surgery, simply would not carry me up the steep incline, nor take me down the hill back into the valley. Sitting on the curb side to rest my weary body, I decided that the only course open to me was to buy a car.

My choice, dictated by my purse, was a used mini-automobile, a Fiat 500; cost, about $200. The first weekend it was mine, Ada and I drove the little "bug" a distance of 50 miles to fulfill a preaching engagement. A few blocks from the church, the snub-nosed Fiat broke down. Everything seemed to fail; brakes, clutch, gears. Eventually, we parked it against the curb to prevent it from rolling away and walked the remaining distance to the church.

We made it in time for the service, but our minds were anxious. We were not sure how we would get home and we did not know the extent of the damage. After the service I was handed the customary preaching fee, the princely sum of $2.50! I knew that would not pay for repairs! But my spirits rose when one of the men said, "When you come to collect your car later in the week, drop by my store, I'd like to see you." I had optimistic visions of the church or this man helping to pay for the repairs to my forlorn little car.

Repairs were completed by Thursday and I made the long journey by bus and train to the town. I cleared my savings account of its remaining fifty pounds ($120) and went to reclaim my car. The bill was an even forty pounds! I stopped expectantly at the businessman's store and we chatted casually for a few minutes. He then dismissed me with a handshake and a cheery invitation, "Drop in and see me any time you are in town."

With only two front seats and a narrow shelf for luggage at the rear, the car was so light that pranksters would often carry it away and hide it! After attending a service in the Krugersdorp City Hall one Sunday, we came out of the meeting to find the car perched at the top of a steep flight of stairs on the landing at the front entrance!

During my first year at the College a remarkable man was used by God to anchor my faith, stir my vision, and quicken my spirit.

He came to Johannesburg a stranger; his name was Dawson Trotman, founder of the Navigators. "Daws" (as he was affectionately known) just "dropped in" on South Africa. With a few days in hand between training counselors for the Billy Graham crusades and establishing the work of the Navigators in Europe, he came unannounced to our country. His only contact was the Rev. Wilfred Edmunds, minister of the Troyeville Baptist Church in Johannesburg.

"Daws" attended the Sunday morning service and at the door introduced himself to the preacher, who immediately recognized in this stranger a mighty man of God. Rev. Edmunds, who was lecturer in evangelism at the college, invited the visitor to address the student body.

Dawson Trotman burst into my life like a whirlwind. Dynamic and forthright, with a unique combination of zeal and compassion, he made a tremendous impression on the students.

The effect of his visit on me was so strong that the next day I "played truant" from college and spent twelve hours with him. In that one day Dawson Trotman brought a breadth and depth to my Christian experience which remains a powerful influence to this day. He whetted my appetite for personal study of the Bible, for committing Scripture to memory, for witnessing and discipleship. He introduced me to the little book *Power Through Prayer* by E. M. Bounds. That book would become one of the most cherished works in my library. I would go on to study it, quote it often, and seek to apply it's truth to my life. One of the memorable statements from that mini-classic affirmed; "The Church is looking for better methods. God is looking for better men — men of prayer, men mighty in prayer The holy spirit does not anoint machinery, but men. Men are God's method." Dawson shared with me many of the principles which he had developed in training men to become disciplined soldiers of Christ. His anecdotes, stories and experiences fired my own desire to see God at work.

As we walked by the tree-lined banks of a small lake, he urged me to be a man of God, a man of the Word, a man of prayer and a faithful follower of Jesus Christ. The special emphasis which he pressed heavily upon me was that I should be a pace-setter. He quoted the example of St. Paul, who said, "Follow my example, as I follow the example of Christ."(1)

He challenged me to be a man who could say to others, "Follow me and I will lead you in the footsteps of Christ." That evening, he spoke at a meeting in the city. His skill in handling the Word of God and his phenomenal program of Scripture memorization inspired a longing in me to know the Word of God as he knew it.

Without boast, or appearing to be arrogant, Dawson Trotman could say to the audience of 200 people,

"If you quote to me any verse of Scripture which you know by heart, I will give you the reference in the Bible, chapter and verse."

"And if you give me the reference of any Scripture which you have learned by memory, I will quote it for you—word perfect."

He had memorized 3,000 Scriptures verses and could quote them, giving the exact place they were to be found in the Bible.

It was awesome.

Oral Roberts also visited Johannesburg. Christian friends urged me to attend the crusade meetings. Reports of healings and miracles caused a stir and an air of expectancy seldom experienced in our land.

Earlier I had attended a William Branham Crusade and had waited expectantly in hope of God performing a miracle of healing for me. The prayer lines had been so long that Branham could give only a few fleeting seconds of prayer for each of the multitudes who came for a miracle touch.

Now Oral Roberts was being hailed as God's man of miracles. I went to several meetings with an openness of faith which said, "God, if you want to do it, I ask you please to heal me." As the prayers for healing were offered there could have been no person in that audience of thousands who longed for a miracle touch more than I did.

I had heard of signs and wonders. Deep in my heart I said, "God, if you straighten my back and restore me to 100 percent fitness it will be a miracle obvious for all to see. It will make your name famous!" But, it did not happen. I came away from each healing meeting, forlorn, disappointed.

In February, 1953, at the commencement of the new academic year, I met Merold Stern. Newly graduated from Wheaton College in Illinois, Merold brought a broadening influence to my life which expanded my narrow vision. Because of my "pagan" past and my hospital confinement, my knowledge of Christianity was limited to my reading and the personal contacts I had made to that time.

With a sensitive attitude to my weakness and a Christ-like compassion, Merold became the closest friend I had ever known. With wit and candor he regaled me with anecdotes and incidents about life in America. His father, Dr. J. C. Stern, was minister of the Baptist Church in Cape Town. On his various visits to the Reef, the preaching of this godly man opened new vistas of Christian possibility to my wondering eyes.

I was still having trouble with horrifying dreams at night. In addition to his understanding friendship, Merold led me into the secret of victory and deliverance over these nocturnal nightmares. He encouraged me to claim the power and efficacy of the blood of Jesus. I had known from my earliest Christian experience that I had been "redeemed with the precious blood of Christ."(2) But now I came to grasp the truth of Rev. 12:11, "And they overcame him (the devil) by the blood of the Lamb, and by the word of their testimony." The horrible dreams would come to me at night, but I soon learned as I struggled into wakefulness that the first thing I should do was speak the words of authority and power and overcome these evil attacks by saying, "Satan, I withstand you in the name of Jesus. I claim the power of the blood of Christ. I overcome you by the blood of the Lamb. I claim the protection of the blood of Jesus Christ."

Gradually, the nightmares became less frequent and eventually I knew the joy of complete deliverance and victory.

I graduated from the Baptist Theological College in December, 1954, while it was caught in the wake of a violent controversy. The college council was demanding the resignation of the principal, charging that his views on the authority and inspiration of the Scriptures were suspect. Rev. Barnard had described himself as a "thoroughgoing Barthian" and the issue divided the Baptist Union sharply. A section of ministers in the Baptist Union rose to the principal's defense and the outcome of the confrontation was a temporary closing of the college in that October of my final year.

The toll of the grueling three years and the crisis in the college proved too much for me: I became ill with chronic physical exhaustion.

In addition to the rigors of the College, I had worked through every vacation to support myself and had pastored the infant Baptist church which I had helped to found in Randfontein. My body simply gave way under the strain, so Merold invited me to spend the month of November at his home in Cape Town. There, the sunshine, the fresh air and the relaxation brought swift renewal to my ailing body.

This was the first time I had returned to "the fairest Cape" since my mother had left it in defeat with her two fatherless boys twenty years before. With wonder and praise to God I retraced some of the paths of my first years of life. I began to see that God had "done great things" for me and I was truly grateful.

I began to grasp a deeper significance of what Jesus Christ had done for me in my salvation. The distant view was still misty in many respects but I was beginning to understand the words of John, "How great is the love the Father has lavished on us, that we should be called children of God."(3)

I returned to Johannesburg for the college graduation ceremony in December and Ada and I set our wedding for a day in April of the coming year.

Also, I went back to work in the aptitude testing center on the Randfontein Estates Gold Mine.

The year was to be crowned with a special event: God gave me the inestimable joy of leading both Hilda and Eddie to receive Jesus Christ as their personal Savior.

For several years a strengthening bond had drawn us closer together. Unfortunately, Sam resented this deepened love and understanding, seeing it as a force which might alienate his two children from him.

This cancer of jealousy and misunderstanding increased the tension and tragedy of our family life.

Chapter Fifteen

was now 23 years of age. The harsh environmental influences of my life had worked to produce in me a nature which longed for love, tenderness and acceptance, but had also created a strange inability to demonstrate affection. I could not recall anyone ever throwing arms of love about me in an uninhibited display of affection. I could not remember a time when someone spoke the tender words, "Peter, I love you." In turn I, too, found it difficult to express myself in human affection.

One person changed that: Ada. From the tentative first expressions of concern and companionship had grown a strong and compelling love. In my weakness and physical dependence she had demonstrated a steady strength. Into the often dark and gloomy aspect of my life she brought a glowing radiance. And into my awkward, often clumsy attempts at expressing human love and tenderness, she brought a simplicity and warmth which irresistibly drew me out of my sullen world of rejection.

We were married on April 16, 1955.

Our wedding day dawned gray and forbidding, with heavy rain clouds which threatened a typical highland storm. And rain it did. The heavens opened and poured water in torrents on guests and bridal party alike. But Ada and I were undaunted. It was the joyous climax to the five years of growing understanding, commitment and deepening love.

Merold Stern was the best man and the groomsmen were Maurice Kirk and Johnny Buchler. In escorting us from the church to the waiting car after the ceremony, our attendants held a large canvas canopy above the bride and groom. Ada made it safe and dry into the automobile, but as I bent to duck into the car, the weight of rain water in the canvas made a spout and the entire load came cascading down my neck and back. Fortunately, the euphoria, combined with a sense of humor, stood me in good stead!

We started our married life of service for Christ with few material possessions. Ada had shortly before graduated from teacher training college. Her salary as a school teacher was a lowly forty pounds ($80) a month!

My years in seminary had been austere and frugal. But happy in our love and with single devotion to Christ, we set out on our adventure of united service.

I had accepted a call to be pastor of the Baptist church in the delightful seaside resort of Fish Hoek, 20 miles from Cape Town, the place of my birth. It had been called "the Fairest Cape" by the early seafarers and became that to us.

The sparkling white church building was a landmark in the community. At our first Sunday evening service the sanctuary was crammed with people. These were the "regulars" as well as the curious who had come to look over the new pastor and his bride. As I reached the climax of my first sermon to the new congregation, a lady in the front row fainted. She slid from her seat with a clatter and slumped in a heap on the floor. The disturbance shattered the attention of the congregation.

What a chaotic start! But God gave me promises which spurred me on. "The desert shall rejoice, and blossom as the rose."(1) "As the rain and the snow come down from heaven...and water the earth, and makes it bring forth and bud, so shall My word be...."(2)

People came in large numbers to hear the Word of God proclaimed. I devoted many hours of each week to study and preparation of my sermons.

The church prospered; this in turn fired our hearts with greater zeal. I claimed Isaiah 55:10 and 11 as the promise of God for my ministry; "My word...shall not return unto me void (empty) but it shall accomplish that which I please, and it shall prosper in the thing whereto I sent it."

In my study I had a stuffed chair which I had salvaged from my parent's home. I knelt beside that relic and draped my body over it as in earnest prayer as I cried to God for His anointing and blessing on my preaching and teaching.

As the church grew so did I. I was coming to understand the vital principle in God's dealings with His people which Dawson Trotman had pointed out. It was: God uses the man! One person influences the life of another.

In his book, *Power Through Prayer*, E. M. Bounds lays great emphasis on the truth,

"Men are God's method. The church is looking for better methods; God is looking for better men...What the church needs today is not more machinery or better, not new organizations or more and novel methods, but men whom the Holy Ghost can use—men of prayer, men mighty in prayer. The Holy Ghost does not come on machinery, but on men. He does not anoint plans, but men—men of prayer...."

"The training of the Twelve was the great, difficult and enduring work of Christ. It is not great talents or great learning or great preachers that God needs, but men great in holiness, great in faith, great in love, great in fidelity, great for God—men always preaching by holy sermons in the pulpit, by holy lives out of it. These can mold a generation for God."

I could trace the truth of this running through my own personal pilgrimage.

Now, as I faced the challenges of a life in full-time Christian service, God reinforced these principles. I saw my service for Christ not in terms of programs and projects, but in terms of what God could do in and through people. In turn, God shaped and molded my own life through the influence of other godly men. I wanted to be a man whom God could use to mold my generation. I was twenty-three years of age, a young, eager preacher starting out to win my spurs on the battlefield: I was impressionable and wide open to the influence and direction which godly men brought into my life.

Mediocre men never impressed me, but men mighty in the Scriptures, powerful in prayer, men involved in dynamic Christian service, affected me deeply.

Wherever possible, I sought them out and tried to discover the secrets of their effectiveness. I read the biographies and journals of the heroes of faith; John Wesley, Hudson Taylor, George Mueller, David Brainerd, William Carey, Adoniram Judson and C. T. Studd. Other mighty men of faith played an important role as I sought God's best for my ministry. I longed to see a New Testament church in action.

God has a sense of humor. He even gave me two men with apostolic names to be my closest aides and friends; we were Peter, James and John. Peter the minister, James (Jim) Matthew the church secretary, and John (Jack) Pearce the treasurer.

Billy Graham also entered the arena of men who dramatically influenced my life and ministry.

Not in person, at that time, but through the release of the landmark Christian Films, *Mr. Texas* and *Oil Town, USA*. I had read in seminary about a distinguished English preacher who urged, "Gentlemen, always preach for a decision." This was patent in all Dr. Graham's preaching. I longed, with a deep yearning, to see men and women come to know Jesus Christ as Savior and I began to preach expecting the Holy Spirit to work. I expected a response to the proclamation of God's Word and worked hard to provide every sermon with a compelling motivation for people to "choose this day whom you will serve."(3)

I was disturbed by the lethargy and perfunctory performances which I saw in so many professed worship services. I prayed for God to show me how the dozing mass of people who called themselves "the Church," could be stirred from their apathy. I grieved over the mediocrity with which so many seemed content.

From Wales, Maynard James, evangelist, preacher and mighty man of God, came to stir my soul. I was spellbound by his accounts of the great revivals which had energized the church in generations past. I shall never forget his distinctive manner, his earnest prayers and his passionate preaching. Ours was not among the largest congregations, but when I invited him to preach in our church, he graciously consented. And preach he did!

He challenged us to pray for revival. After his stirring delivery, I announced from the pulpit that we would meet each Wednesday morning at seven o'clock to pray.

I arranged to pick him up and duly knocked on the door of his hotel room at 6:45 a.m. that first morning. I waited several minutes and was about to leave, thinking I had somehow missed him. He finally came to the door, his eyelids heavy with sleep and his great shock of grey hair looking like the mane of a lion. He had been following a grueling schedule and was weary with travel. I apologized profusely for disturbing him, backed away and drove on to the church.

We started the prayer meeting without his presence at 7:00 a.m. Within minutes the door burst open and there was Maynard James, his tousled grey hair standing wild on his head. He had run all the way from his hotel to that early morning rendezvous.

When he prayed, heaven seemed to come down and fill that church. I saw, by example, how revival comes: by prayer—fervent and believing prayer. I saw a man filled with the Holy Spirit.

To that point, my teaching had been strictly academic regarding the person and work of the Holy Spirit. In this man I saw a mighty power which I had seldom seen in any other. A longing was born in me to know the power of God as I saw it in Maynard James.

Also from England, God sent Dr. Martin Lloyd-Jones, a master in the exposition of the Word of God. He enthralled his listeners as he expounded the Scriptures and fed us with the Bread of Life.

At a minister's meeting in Cape Town he challenged the servants of God to pray and preach till revival came. He counseled the men of God to return to their churches and preach through the book of Acts.

I did! I earnestly desired to experience a true revival.

From America came Dr. Edwin Orr. His book, The Second Evangelical Awakening was fuel for the fire in my soul. Over a period of many years he visited South Africa periodically and was mightily used of God to motivate the Christians to pray and believe for revival.

The Rev. Duncan Campbell brought a unique perspective to our lives. He had written an eye-witness account of one of the most momentous events of Protestant church history. His book *I Saw the Welsh Revival* bridged the time span of an almost-forgotten era with the longings of my own spirit. His first person accounts of the Revival which stirred nations and demonstrated the awesome power of God in answer to prayer were enthralling, challenging, stimulating. They fueled the fire of my young heart.

Dr. Oswald Smith of the People's Church in Toronto was used by God to focus my attention on the missionary responsibility of the church. He directed my gaze to the whitened harvest fields of the world. He told how the vision for missions had changed his church and I determined to do the same. Consequently, the first Sunday of every month, we turned the evening service into a missionary meeting, inviting a missionary or a representative of a foreign mission to be our guest. Those services were memorable. We drew large crowds, sang the great missionary hymns of the church and encouraged our people to give generously. The offerings at these missionary services were given entirely to the mission represented and were by far the biggest single offerings in any month.

God blessed our church; it prospered and grew and, "the Lord added to our number those who were being saved."(4)

I invited Dr. J. C. Stern (Merold's father) to conduct a week of Bible teaching in the church and at the conclusion of the week I went forward at the end of a Sunday morning service with many of my people, knelt down before the pulpit and with all the faith I knew, asked the Holy Spirit to utterly possess me, fill me and empower me. Dr. Stern used Luke 11:13, "If ye then, being evil, know how to give good gifts unto your children, how much more shall your heavenly Father give the Holy Spirit to them that ask him?"

I asked, and in faith believed that God had filled me with the Holy Spirit. However, it was to be many years before that decision bore the full and ripened fruit of its desire.

Chapter Sixteen

n the early days of my ministry in Fish Hoek a singular event touched deep chords in my spirit and brought back vivid memories of a time long past. One weekend I opened the newspaper and gasped as I saw the picture of a young man, tattooed chest thrust out in defiance, swaggering insolently from the Johannesburg magistrates court.

It was my best friend of Mayfair days — Zoes!

The headline screamed, "Guilty of murder!"

When the shock wore off, I was able to grasp with wonder the magnitude of what God had done for me in His mercy. Not only had He directed the movements of my life and taken me from the sordid streets of Mayfair, but His redeeming power through Jesus Christ had transformed my life. With humble thanks I had cause to ponder the words of Jesus, "...to whom little is forgiven, the same loves little."(1) The converse was true in me: I had been forgiven so much, and, in turn, I owed my Savior so much; I owed Him my whole life, my total being, my all!

Our ministry drew students from the nearby Bible Institute to the fellowship of our church. Many of those young people consequently volunteered for missionary service in our church and today are serving on the far-flung mission fields of the world.

The most important single "program" which we promoted in our church was lay evangelism. We organized a weekly program of house visitation; I trained our lay people in personal witnessing and one night each week I led them as we went door-to-door and house-to-house, sharing our faith in Christ. The program did as much, if not more, for those who participated as it did for those upon whom we called.

In October of 1955, Ada and I had traveled back to Johannesburg for the annual Assembly of the Baptist Union where I was ordained; set apart for full-time ministry in the church. I saw it as a pinnacle in my life and the culmination of the call which I had received from God while in my wheelchair. I looked forward to that night with a spirit of awe and wonder. Ada was with me. But next to that I wanted, more than anything else in the world, for my family to share the sacred moment.

However, Dad was taciturn and declined our invitation to attend the ordination service. His harsh attitude grieved me, but even more difficult to bear was his refusal to let Hilda, Eddie and Mom attend.

On several occasions, when I was still living at home, Sam had tested my willingness to abide by the scriptural principle, "Honor thy father and thy mother," but this was his most defiant challenge to date.

Mom might have asserted her independence and attended, but she and the two young children were in a quandary. To emphasize his defiance, Dad entered Hilda and Ed in a swimming gala for that same night. For them to have attended my ordination would have meant open rebellion. It was heart-breaking for them because of the close bond of love which tied us together. The five of us — Ada,

Hilda, Ed, Theo and I—were now a team. Our combined prayers were offered constantly for our parents. We interceded for them with a deep longing because we could see the havoc which sin, rebellion and rejection of God was playing with Dad's life.

The marriage bond between Mom and Dad was dangerously frayed. They were on the verge of a calamity, yet Ada and I could not understand the turn events were taking. We had prayed, witnessed, pleaded; all to no avail.

And now Sam was turning in defiance, not only from the truth but to seeking answers in other religions. We discovered he had been attending spiritualist meetings as well as reading books on Hinduism and Buddhism.

He seemed to be saying, "I won't do it your way. I'll make it on my own."

In the process he was destroying himself and, with him, all those around him. Crestfallen, defeated and discouraged in our faith, we gave Mom and Dad each a beautiful, leather-bound Bible and made our way back to the church in Fish Hoek.

Shortly afterwards, in the bitterness of his resistance, Sam plunged the family into further chaos. He resigned his position with the Randfontein Mine, placed Hilda and Ed in boarding schools and with Mom left the country.

He headed for the Gold Coast, high on the tropical northwest bulge of Africa. He thought he had put a safe distance between himself, his conscience, and God.

He did not know that the Bible says, "Whither shall I go from Thy Spirit? or whither shall I flee from Thy presence? If I ascend up into heaven, Thou art there. If I make my bed in hell, behold, Thou art there. If I take the wings of the morning, and dwell in the uttermost parts of the sea; even there Thy hand shall lead me, and

Thy right hand shall hold me...Yea, the darkness hides not from Thee."(2)

Restless from the turmoil in his soul, Sam became even more difficult.

Mom left him.

Immediately following Hilda's graduation from High School, they made their way to England while Eddie was all but abandoned in South Africa.

The family was finally torn apart. Ed was the most deeply affected, for he was growing into a superbly athletic young man, but his spirit was tender and gentle. He visited with us during school vacations. We often ached inside as we saw the hurt in his sensitive eyes whenever he had to leave and go back to the bleak loneliness of the boarding school.

In July, 1956, Dawson Trotman drowned at a Bible conference in the State of New York. He died as he had lived, saving the life of another.

On November 15 of that same year our first child was born. I had said, "God, if this child is a son, I'll name him Dawson."

It was a boy and we named him Peter Dawson.

For Sam Church every endeavor turned to gall. He was defrauded in West Africa and lost his entire life's investment in a timber company. By his harshness and headstrong actions he had alienated all his loved ones.

Now, alone and bereft of friends and family, he made his solitary way back to South Africa. He came to our home in Fish Hoek in December 1957, like the prodigal son in the story which Jesus told in St. Luke's Gospel.

Ada and I welcomed him with open arms and the kiss of love. His greatest delight in those sobering days was to take his little grandson to the beautiful white beach which lined the bay where Fish Hoek nestled. How he loved the little lad!

Early in 1958, he sat one night in our church service and listened with rapt attention as I preached from God's Word. My mind went back to just such an occasion, seven years before, when he had stood behind my chair listening to Ivor Powell.

But tonight was different.

God's Holy Spirit had long been at work in Sam's life.

He was ready for a miracle.

After the service, he returned to his room. There, in a personal encounter with God, he gave up the struggle. Simply, and with child-like faith, he opened the door of his life, received Jesus Christ as his Savior and was born again. How the heavens rang that night with the sound of singing as the angels rejoiced over this sinner who had repented! (3)

Like Saul of Tarsus, Sam Church rose from the ground a new man. A miracle of conversion had taken place in his life. I witnessed the fruit of a truth I had clung to — "Never lose faith in the power of Jesus Christ to save!" From that instant, my Dad was "a new creature;" he was made new within by the presence of Christ coming to live in him. (4)

Now I really believed in miracles. I knew, without the shadow of a doubt, that God answers prayer! If the Good News of Jesus Christ could so profoundly touch such a rebellious, wayward sinner, I knew the power of Christ could change any person who was willing to acknowledge their human helplessness and believe on the name of Jesus to save. (5)

For years, Sam had seemed like a hopeless, helpless case. Yet here we saw him, radiant and transformed by Calvary love. I could never again doubt God's promises or His power to save.

I wrote to Mom in England. I appealed to her from my heart, pleading and urging that it was time she made her decision to receive Christ.

She did! Hilda was with her and led her into the joy of God's salvation. How we praised God. We added our "hallelujahs" to those of the angels in heaven.

Regeneration is the work of the Holy Spirit by which a person is transformed from the inside. Conversion is the outward evidence of that inner transformation.

Dad's conversion was evident everywhere. He sent to England for Mom; she returned to South Africa and they made a new beginning together.

Sam took the most menial job with a gold mine because it paid the most. He became a "shaft sinker" in a remote area of the gold fields in order to make money so that they could start married life anew.

But, he was plunged, immediately, into fierce spiritual warfare. It was not easy to overcome the habits of sin and the fruit of rebellion, but he fought and won great personal victories. I spent time with him. I passed on to him many of the principles inculcated into me by Dawson Trotman.

I taught Dad how to study the Bible, memorize Scripture, develop a regular devotional life and how to witness for Christ.

On one of my visits with him, we were in a hall crowded with gruff, foul-mouthed miners. One of the officials constantly took the name of the Lord in vain. I waited for an opportune moment, then asked the gentleman in question if I could see him in private. We stepped into a side room and I said to the blasphemer, "Sir, you have just offended my best friend."

He was startled and asked incredulously, "Who?"

I said, "Jesus Christ; He is my Savior, my Lord, and my Friend. You take the name of God in vain, you blaspheme, you swear and curse and you cause me deep offense, but more than that, you are offending almighty God. You are guilty of breaking His law."

I left him a very sober man. On the way home Sam asked me how I had handled the situation and I explained it to him, just as Dawson Trotman had explained to me, "A man is different when you get him alone." I told Sam, "Don't try to argue in public. Pray for a man, then look for an opportunity and, in private, speak to him about Jesus." Sam was a quick learner. It was thrilling to see his development.

Sam Church became a shining light among his peers. Often, in our early prayers and deep longings for this outstanding man, we had said, "If ever he would become a believer, he would be a dynamic Christian witness."

He did! A man of great personal presence, he was a born leader. He had been robbed of his potential through the tragedies of his own childhood and youth, had squandered his early manhood in rebellious self-will, but now he began to literally glow and sparkle as his life underwent miraculous changes.

One day, as he was being lowered into a new shaft on the flat, open-sided "platform" with which shaft sinkers descended into the open pit, the edge of the huge structure hooked on a railing and tipped the crew of black and white miners into the vertical shaft. They fell hundreds of feet to a grisly death at the bottom of the black hole.

Only Sam survived. Miraculously, he managed to cling to the edge of the platform.

When they finally rescued him, dangling over that waiting grave, his fingers were so tightly wrapped around the railing which he had grasped that the rescuers had to pry his grip open to get him to release his hold.

Through many agonizing struggles with his old life, Dad rapidly grew in grace and in the knowledge of the Lord Jesus. He attended church, studied his Bible and wrote out memorization verses on small cards which he attached to the dashboard of his car. It was a modern-day miracle to see him so full of love and compassion.

Ada was pregnant with our second child when we visited Mom and Dad in their humble apartment in the far-off Orange Free State gold fields. She slipped on the stairs and Sam rushed to her aid, embraced her and tenderly cared for her.

He even hurried us along to be ready in time for church on Sunday mornings. He was compassionately concerned for others and became a vibrant witness.

Lovingly concerned for his sister Ethel, who was passing through deep sorrow in her own life, he arranged for her to visit us in January 1959. Ours was the joy of introducing her to Jesus Christ as Savior and Friend. In her, too, we saw an instant wonder of transformation. God was miraculously at work in the family.

That month, our daughter Jenny was born. Six weeks later she suddenly became alarmingly ill.

Our family doctor admitted her to the Children's Hospital in Rondebosch, Cape Town, where the specialist diagnosed her as suffering from pyloric stenosis, a condition in which the valve at the bottom of the esophagus closes tightly, and the pressure build-up ejects the baby's milk back through the mouth. This prevents the milk from entering the stomach, quickly causes dehydration, with serious consequences and even the death of the infant.

By the time of diagnosis, our Jenny was almost dehydrated. The doctors urged surgery but we called our church and all our friends to prayer. We could not bear the thought of that precious bundle undergoing the trauma of an operation.

Just before the time appointed for surgery, she began to accept and hold her nourishment. God had granted us another evidence of His love and healing power.

Chapter Seventeen

ur years in Fish Hoek were the years of "first things."

Our first home.

Our first church.

Our first child.

And many other baptisms into new experiences. But the time came to move on.

In May, 1959, we transferred from Fish Hoek to take pastoral charge of the Fynnland Baptist Church in the city of Durban, on the eastern seaboard of South Africa.

The move catapulted us into an environment very different from the one we had just left. I was about to learn some hard, yet valuable lessons in the school of life. I was aware that my special gifts for the ministry were preaching and teaching, but here, in this different community, I discovered that what the people demanded and expected was intensive home visitation and continuous "stroking."

One Saturday morning soon after our arrival, an emergency telephone call sent me rushing to one of the homes. A young father had been electrocuted through a fault in an extension lamp which he was using to work on his automobile. The faulty lead had carried the lethal 220-volt shock through his body as he was standing on a patch of wet grass.

I reached the house within minutes, arriving before the emergency ambulance. Every attempt to revive him failed and mine was the agonizing task of telling his young wife, expecting their first baby, that he was dead.

I visited the family several times over the next two weeks, offering comfort, prayer and spiritual encouragement, but other duties and demands of that pastorate clamored for my attention. About a month later, word came to me that the young widows' mother was implacably angry and spreading criticism in the community against me because I had not called on her daughter in two weeks.

I began a serious quest to find answers to the questions of how the Founder (Jesus Himself) had intended the church to function. I was familiar with the King James Version of Ephesians 4:11,12. "He gave some, apostles; and some, prophets; and some, evangelists; and some, pastors and teachers; For the perfecting of the saints, for the work of the ministry, for the edifying of the body of Christ."

I began to discern why so many ministers were frustrated and acutely unhappy. They were faced with extravagant expectations, while not equipped for all the duties their congregations demanded of them.

The minister was expected to be pastor, preacher, teacher, counselor, visitor, evangelist, administrator and youth leader. He was expected to preach like St. Peter, pray like St. Paul, be nursemaid to the infant saints, physician to the emotionally ailing and ready to make instant house calls upon every demand. These frustrations were exemplified when, a few years later, several vacancies occurred in the government educational department: three positions needed to be filled and twenty-seven Baptist ministers applied for the posts!

One Monday night, we returned from our customary "day off," having traveled several miles down the coast where we had enjoyed a day on the beach. Despite the relaxation, I returned tired and eager for an early night. I fell asleep about 8:30 p.m.

When the telephone rang rudely in the night, I struggled with my wits, not certain for the moment whether it was day or night.

A woman's voice asked, "Are you the Rev. Church?"

I replied, "Yes."

She said, "You have to come and see me immediately."

I asked who was speaking, but she declined to give her name. Still a little dazed and confused by the sudden awakening from deep sleep, I asked if the call could wait until the morning.

She retorted angrily, "I thought when you phoned a minister he was supposed to come immediately!"

She refused to give me her name or address, but retorted, "I am going to commit suicide" and hung up.

By now I was thoroughly awake; I enlisted the aid of Doug, the church secretary, and finally, by a process of elimination, we deduced who the woman was. She had pulled the stunt with the previous pastor. I dressed hurriedly and together we went in search of the threatened suicide.

We arrived at the house where we believed she would be, and sure enough, she had attempted suicide. But not very seriously. She had taken a slight overdose of sleeping pills, more as an act of spite it seemed, than in a serious attempt to kill herself.

Deeper understanding, years of experience and clear exegesis (examination) later unlocked for me the true meaning of the Ephesian passage. It is not the intention of the Architect and Engineer that the pastor function in every role required to make the Church function according to design.

The gifts given to the Church are men whose task it is to train the people so that the body of believers should do the work of the ministry. Later versions of the New Testament would correct the age-old misinterpretation of the role of the pastor. They would show that the work of the pastor is to "equip the saints for the work of the ministry" so that every person should be part of the function of building up the body of Christ.

We inspired an enthusiastic group in the church to embark on a remodeling project to improve the appearance of the old, worn and tired-looking building. The transformation was stunning.

I solicited donations for the project, and motivated my parents as well as Ada's Mother and Father to contribute the funds to install a gorgeous new pulpit. The "new-look" sanctuary attracted new people and we embarked on a building fund project with the view to erecting a beautiful new facility.

In August, Lorne Sanny, Dawson Trotman's successor, made the long journey from Europe to South Africa. He brought with him the Navigator staff member from Nairobi, Ed Reis. Mom and Dad joined us for the weekend.

On Sunday, Lorne preached in our church and I had the joy of baptizing my parents.

The experience for me was indescribably sweet; one of the spiritual "highs" of my life.

Dad submitted to baptism by immersion, the act of obedience, with a humility which was so characteristic of his new life. He was a living demonstration of the deepest meanings of the death of the old self and the rising to newness of life in Christ.

My dear mother was already showing signs of the illness which was to claim her life. To avoid undue shock to her system, I baptized her as she knelt in the baptistry, by gently lowering her head forward into the waters. What a day!

Dad was also powerfully affected by Ed Reis' vivacious spirit of joy. It was good for Sam to see that a believer, so godly and sincere, was also a joyful, jubilant man. How badly Sam needed that example. Through the bitter years of his life there had been little joy. Again we witnessed the effects of God using one man to influence the life of another. They were never to meet again, but Ed Reis left a legacy that remained with Sam Church.

During Lorne's stay in South Africa, plans were made for us to undertake two years of training at the headquarters of the Navigators in Colorado Springs.

In 1960 a near fatal accident cast a shadow across our home.

Our little Jenny was an early walker; at nine months she had set out to explore the world on her own two feet. One Saturday afternoon, while still a cuddly eighteen-month-old, she was playing in the driveway of the parsonage. A young mechanic, who had come to the house to help me do some work on our car, pulled into the driveway and parked. After working for some time, he decided to move his car.

Just as he started the engine of the huge American sedan, the Holy Spirit prompted me to ask, "Where's Jenny?"

As the big brown car rolled forward, I screamed with a blood-curdling yell for the driver to stop.

People heard me scream and came running from all directions. I raced around the front of the car in time to see the massive front wheel rolling off Jenny's lower body. My desperate screams had caused the driver to stop and back up.

Our little blond doll lay crushed beneath that monstrous wheel.

I picked her up in my arms and rushed into the house; her little body hung like a limp rag doll over my arms.

Ada called the doctor.

We thought our hearts would break as she lay on the bed with questioning eyes , her right leg twisted and bleeding.

I blamed myself over and over and over again.

The horror of my own accident and paralysis leaped like a monster onto my back. I prayed to God for a miracle for my helpless little angel. I said, "O God! Don't let her be paralyzed. Please, God, forgive me for my folly. God, please heal her. Lord, don't let my carelessness cause her to be damaged or harmed in any way."

At the hospital, the X-rays showed two fractures of the pelvis and two fractures of the femur; one simple, one compound.

The compound fracture had snapped the thighbone just below the ball and socket joint. I was sick with remorse and guilt.

I blamed myself.

But I prayed over and over and over again, "Please God, don't let Jenny suffer any permanent injury."

Ada was my anchor. Jenny had been God's special gift to her, but as we shared the agony, wept and prayed together, Ada kept me from punishing myself needlessly.

In the hospital, Jenny was suspended from her tiny heels in a steel frame with only the nape of her neck resting on a pillow.

A new crisis followed. She would not eat.

In mute frustration, unable to talk and not knowing why she was suffering so, she struck out at anything offered her. The hospital staff were as distressed as we were. However, we had a Zulu maid in our employ—a genial, motherly woman called Jemima. Jemima had lovingly cared for Jenny for nearly a year, often carrying the little white baby on her back in true African style. We had often chuckled at the contrast—Jemima so dark, Jenny so fair.

Our baby had not eaten for several days and, once again, she was in danger of dehydration. How we prayed for a solution!

Ada arrived at the hospital one afternoon and noticed to her amazement that one of the Zulu women who worked at the hospital cleaning the wards was sitting beside Jenny, cooing softly and coaxing gently as she spooned baby food into our little girl's mouth.

Jenny was smiling sweetly at the woman whom she identified with Jemima. Our crisis was over.

After six weeks in suspension, our darling was released from the frame. She had to learn to walk all over again, but she was safe. God had heard our prayers. The bones knitted, she grew strong and very, very affectionate. She would cuddle up to us whenever we held her in our arms. We knew then that she was a special child.

By January, 1961, I was faced with a dilemma. I knew God was leading us to leave our church and to go to Glen Eyrie, the Navigators' headquarters in Colorado. But I had no financial resources whatever. Our salary was barely enough to keep groceries on the table. Many of the churches espoused the view that, in a minister, poverty was next to godliness and endorsed the prayer, "Lord you keep him humble, we'll keep him poor." I was drawing fifty pounds ($150) per month. We lived in a parsonage, and the church provided $15 a month to run the car and—that was it! We'd never see Colorado at that rate. I prayed, "God, you'll have to do another miracle if you want us to go."

It was a traumatic time for Ada. Unlike my shifting, restless childhood, hers had been settled, secure. She had lived all her life in the house where she was born and only left it to marry me.

Now I was asking her to leave home, friends and family and accompany me on an uncertain journey to a strange land. I knew God would have to grant a special work of grace in Ada's heart if she were fully to share this step of faith with me.

One day Ada stood in front of me and made an announcement which was to mark a milestone in our marriage.

"Peter, personally, I don't want to give up my home and my possessions," she said.

"I don't want to leave my family and friends, but I have come to a decision. As your wife, I will do whatever you want me to do. I will follow you, love you, take care of you, and go wherever you believe God is leading you."

Chapter Eighteen

I resigned as pastor of the Fynnland Baptist church on February 1, 1961 and booked passage by sea for the four of us to New York via England. I said, "Lord, your Word says, 'In his heart a man plans his course, but the Lord determines his steps.'(1) Father, I'll make my plans, but you will have to open or close the doors."

I shared my desire with several Christian friends but received little encouragement except, surprisingly, from one person—my Dad. He sent me the first donation with which to start a savings fund for our passage. He said, "I know it is God's will for you to go."

In his God-given wisdom, King Solomon had supernatural insight into the relationship between human desire and Divine will. He wrote, "The lot is cast into the lap, but its every decision is from the Lord."(2)

I determined to trust God.

The way I would know His will would be by the provision of the money we would need to cover our travel to the USA years before, when Ada had announced our engagement to the principal of the school where she was teaching at the time, the gentleman had remarked:

"You shouldn't marry a Baptist minister; they're so poor. You should marry a Rabbi or a Dominee (the Dutch Reformed Church word for minister). They are well paid!" What insight!

There is a natural balancing tension between faith and works. I had to find the median between just sitting back, doing nothing, waiting for God to rain "pennies from Heaven" and the other extreme of taking the bit and doing it all my own way.

Years before, my life had been impacted and powerfully influenced through reading the book, Hudson Taylor's Spiritual Secret. It told the story of a young man's utter reliance on God to provide for every need.

Now, there followed for me 3 months of intense prayer, faith and the kind of abandonment I had read in the story of Hudson Taylor. But I also realized that I would need to make a total commitment, which would call for uncommon sacrifices.

Ada and I agreed on a plan of action. We would do all we could, and trust God to do what we could not! We sold our car and anything else we could not take with us!

We knew it was God's will when, in May, 1961, we had all the money required for our fares to the United States.

We sailed from Cape Town to England in the luxury liner, Windsor Castle.

In planning our visit, we had written to the headquarters of the Navigators and asked what we should take with us from South Africa. "Bring only your clothes," they replied, "we will provide housing and everything else you may need." We flew from London and touched down in Chicago. America—at last!

Our introduction to life in the US was a Fourth of July barbecue in the backyard of a young American Missionary we had ministered to in our church in Fish Hoek.

We took a rental car from Chicago and struck out for Denver.

In early July we drove wide-eyed onto the magnificent estate where the headquarters of the Navigators nestles at the foothills of the Rocky Mountains. I walked up to the reception office at the gatehouse and, trying to suppress my excitement, asked where I could find the key to our house.

I had to keep reminding myself this was no dream. I was here; in America. I gazed with wondering eyes at Pike's Peak, its summit towering like a monarch above the plains. Awestruck, my gaze roved over the ragged, tree-covered crags and canyons. I could have been in paradise.

My reverie was broken when the young man at the window asked me to wait while he made a phone call. I went back to the car; it was hot. Ada, Dawson and Jenny were tired from the long journey and when Ada asked what the delay was, I said they were probably looking for the key.

About twenty minutes later, Roy Robertson, director of overseas personnel, arrived to greet us. He explained we would need to spend a few nights in one of the lodges on the estate. Suddenly, there was a lump like lead in the pit of my stomach. I tried to hide my disappointment.

Next day, the news was broken to us. There was not a single house for rent in all of Colorado Springs! The United States army had just reopened its local Fort Carson base and had, sight unseen, rented every available house in the city.

We spent two prayerful weeks in a single room at the lodge, but then a break came. An elderly gentleman called the office. He explained that he and his wife lived alone. They owned a house in the elite Broadmoor area, another up in the mountains and also a three-bedroom house in the valley, close to Glen Eyrie. They did not want to rent to the army and wondered if there was a Christian family who might need a home.

We jumped for joy! Ada and I tumbled into the car with our two children and went to look at the house. It was old, but in good shape. We now faced another obstacle. The rent was $126 a month.

The financial arrangement at the Glen at that time was that they would pay us the minimum monthly allowance of $300. This was based on the assumption that missionary families returning from overseas would retain a sizable portion of their support. The minimum allowance would offset the drop in income while they were home on furlough.

Our problem? We had no other income. I had resigned from my church and it was unheard of in South Africa for Christians to support anything except the local church. Members were strenuously forbidden by their ministers to give to individuals or non-denominational programs.

We were in a quandary, but we decided to take the plunge and agreed to rent the house. The old man and his wife offered us a few odd pieces of furniture: a bed, a sofa, a table and some other odds and ends.

We salvaged beds for our children and other household pieces from the barns on the Navigators' estate.

The arrangement lasted two weeks. One day the old gentleman arrived at the house in a state of agitation. He was profusely apologetic but said they would have to ask us to leave the house because his wife was physically sick at the thought of someone using her furniture and living in her house!

The Lord used the incident to illustrate to us the meaning of His words, "Do not store up for yourselves treasures on earth...for where your treasure is, there will your heart be also."(3)

The equation stunned me: one elderly couple, three houses, but a possessive spirit which was unable to rent out even one dwelling.

One evening, as we were driving through the delightful valley which runs past the fabled Garden of the Gods, close to Glen Eyrie, we spied a quaint house with a sign in the window; it read "For Rent." It was God's provision for us. We jumped at the opportunity and rented the tiny dwelling.

I was assigned to work with Jim Downing, treasurer and financial director. With the patience of a kindly father, he shared with me from the rich store of his experience.

I entered into the domain which Dawson Trotman had so tantalizingly pictured. Disciples making disciples. One-at-a-time.

I saw "faithful men" committing their lives and knowledge of Christ to other "faithful men."(4) I experienced the reality of Dawson Trotman's vision. In the same commitment to the Word and work of the Master, women, both the young and those mature in years, were engaged in personal ministry with other Christian women.

Two dreams were taking on more than phantom illusiveness; I was living in the "West" I had loved vicariously through authors like Zane Grey, and I was also realizing the dream of being at Glen Eyrie.

Small things happened along the way to add humor to the reality of living on meager financial resources.

Our Dawson was attending elementary school in the valley near Glen Eyrie and Ada could always tell when he was coming home, because his clear little voice could be heard as he came singing down the street each afternoon.

One day he arrived home with a note from a speech therapist who was visiting the school. It read, "Dawson needs speech correction."

We were flabbergasted. He had been a great and clear talker from his baby days. He had learned to talk before he could walk!

At 10 months, scuttling along the floor on his seat, he had picked up a scrap and proudly held it up with the word "paper." By the time he was two, he could carry on an intelligent adult conversation. On his second birthday we had recorded him reciting the Lord's prayer, singing dozens of children's songs, naming about twenty cars which he had seen on the road and exhibiting other unusual verbal skills. We were proud parents.

Now, at six, we were told he needed speech correction!

We wrote to the school asking for an explanation. The reply came back, "He must work on his pronunciation, because he pronounces his words like a Britisher!"

Shortly before Christmas Billy Graham came to Colorado Springs to address the cadets at the nearby Air Force Academy. Ada and I were invited to attend as part of a small group of civilians. We arrived early to take a tour of the breath-taking facilities and were sitting quietly in the chapel, waiting for the cadets to be ushered in, when one of the chaplains whispered to us that Dr. Graham wished to see us. We were surprised, but went willingly to a side room where Dr. Graham was waiting. This was to be our first meeting.

I sensed the anointing of God upon this gracious world-renowned evangelist as we talked with him and then prayed together. I was able to share with him the story of how, through his films, he had shaped my preaching emphasis as a young minister in 1955. I asked him to pray seriously about coming to South Africa for a crusade. I spoke urgently about the great spiritual need of our land. The country was still reeling from the effects of the 1961 riots and subsequent police action at Sharpeville. He looked at me with his piercing blue eyes and expressed the immense burden which he carried on his heart, "Peter," he said, "There is great spiritual need all over the world."

Back at the Glen I talked with Lorne Sanny and requested permission to work with the Billy Graham Team in a crusade.

He arranged for us to participate in the Greater Chicago Crusade in the summer of 1962. The four of us, Ada, Dawson, Jenny and I, made the 1,000 mile journey to Chicago in our old brown Pontiac and eagerly checked in at the missionary home where reservations had been made for us. It seemed natural to us to have Dawson and Jenny with us, but it did not appear at all "natural" to the caretaker at the home, however.

When they discovered we had two small children, they gave us one day's notice and asked us to leave. They didn't allow children in the suites, "Because," the caretaker explained, "they might mess up the carpets!"

I had a breakfast appointment that morning with Grady Wilson, Dr. Graham's associate, and I told him of our plight. Without batting an eyelid, Grady said, "You will move into the Hilton hotel with us, as guests of Dr. Graham." I floated on air back to the missionary home and we "went out with joy" as we moved to our new quarters overlooking the park and the shoreline of Lake Michigan. God was showing us that He hears the prayers of His children and, "is able to do immeasurably more than we can ask or imagine."(5)

In that summer of '62, I realized one of the cherished dreams of my younger years. In the days when I had frequented the aisles of the silent library halls in our gold mining towns in South Africa, I had lived in the brilliant scenes painted by the vivid images of Zane Grey. I had longed to roam the plains, climb the mesas and wander among the canyons of the world described in classic tales of the West.

That dream came true. In the grandeur of Colorado's Rocky Mountains, and then in the summer of '62.

At the conclusion of the Billy Graham Crusade we packed our big brown Pontiac and set out on an idyllic trip which carried us across the great plains and into the wild and breathtaking scenes of the Great Northwest. We feasted our eyes on the wonders of the New World. From Wyoming, through the Dakotas, across Idaho and into Washington, we thrilled at the sights, the sounds, the scenery.

In Seattle we "cheated" on our kids. We stood with them on the sidewalk and pointed out the Space Needle, the monorail, and other long-distance sights of the World's Fair.

We then sent them off with a sitter (one of the girls from the Navigators) and went by ourselves to enjoy the Fair. They could always say, "I saw the World's Fair."

As we approached the end of our agreed two-year stay at Glen Eyrie, I faced another major decision: should we remain in the USA or should we return to South Africa?

I knew that Baptist ministers who had previously dared to leave the shores of South Africa were often viewed with suspicion when they returned and sought pastoral appointments.

Fierce, independent nationalism runs like an invisible thread through every phase of South African life. It invades even the churches. I wrote to the secretary of the Baptist Union, but received a discouraging reply. His comment reflected the prevailing sentiment: "Since you have spent two years away, I don't think any church in South Africa will call you."

I wrestled in prayer and considered my options.

I felt I was in darkness. God gave me a word to cling to, "Who is among you that fears the Lord...that walks in darkness...let him trust in the Lord and rest upon his God."(6)

In seeking God's will I fasted and prayed, retreating for several days to the grandeur of the mountain slopes which rise so majestically all around Glen Eyrie. I hiked up to the mountainside grave where Dawson Trotman's body had been laid to rest. I sat on the rocks where Dawson had spent many hours in prayer. I yearned to know God's will for my life and I sought the counsel of Dr. Jack Mitchell of Multnomah School of the Bible in Portland, Oregon. He gave me gracious advice.

"Walk by faith, one step at a time." His comment was, "After all, that is good walking."

Oswald Sanders, General Director of the Overseas Missionary Fellowship, was ministering at a conference in progress at Glen Eyrie. He made a statement which gripped me:

"God leads me by suggesting reasons to my mind for doing things."

I could not find God's will until direction came from an unexpected quarter; a letter from my Dad.

It brought sad news! He was seriously ill. He told us he had gone to see his mine doctor with a minor complaint—listlessness and loss of appetite. That was so unlike Sam Church.

The doctor sent him to a special clinic in Pretoria and when the tests were returned the verdict was: cancer.

The prognosis, "Six months to live."

It was April 1963.

Making plans to return to South Africa presented a dilemma. Should we drop everything and rush home?

We talked by phone with Ada's Mom and Dad, and with my sister Hilda who herself had completed her nurses training in England and had sped to Dad's side.

The opinion they offered encouraged us to take a few weeks to work our way through a planned trip to California, and also make stops in Europe and Israel. We gratefully took the opportunity to enrich our lives, and have been ever thankful for the privilege of visiting Rome, Cairo, the pyramids, the Sphinx and then—The Holy Land.

In Israel, the Word of God came alive. I could sense the presence of the people who had lived and died in the Land of Covenant. My understanding of the Bible, its message and especially the Life of Christ were molded for all time.

We took the final flight of our odyssey from Cairo, arriving home in Johannesburg two years after our departure.

A small incident brought comic relief to the somber homecoming.

Mom and Dad were living in a frontier mining town on the edge of the vast Northern Cape wilderness. I could only reach them by rail so I called the South African Railways office. I dialed the number and said, "I am inquiring about a train to Kuruman. Can you tell me when the train leaves, whether there are seats available and how much it will cost?"

There was a slight pause, then the male operator said, with a heavy Afrikaans accent, "But, sir; you're now asking me for three different departments!" It reminded me of a South African adage, "There are two ways of doing a thing; the right way and the railway."

I finally reached the "three different departments" and took the first available train.

A dreadful shock awaited me at the hospital in Kuruman.

Sam Church was a wasted, gray skeleton of a man. I tried to be composed when I saw his emaciated body lying on the hospital bed, but when I buried my face in his pillow, I let the tears flow unchecked.

I said, "Dad, I'll bring Dawson and Jenny to see you. You will really enjoy them. They have grown into such lovely children."

He replied sadly, "It's too late! Too late!"

During our two-year absence, God had spoken to me one day about my attitude toward my Father. He had showed me that I had harbored resentment and anger toward him.

As a young man I had not appreciated all he had done for me. He had given me a home, a name and had sacrificed his own life and liberties that I might have the opportunity of growing up decently.

The Lord had said, "Write to him. Tell him you're sorry. Confess your faults. Tell him you love him and appreciate him." I had done it.

That letter from America had been written with joy and had brought Sam deep peace and great happiness.

It had also brought a wonderful healing in our relationship.

Now, here I was, sitting beside the man who had done so much for me. I embraced him, kissed him, told him of my love.

I borrowed a car, drove to Johannesburg and brought Ada, Dawson and Jenny back to Kuruman.

Mom was not well either, but she was brave. The years had taken their toll. Hilda had returned from England and taken a nursing position at the hospital in that lonely outpost.

She nursed Dad night and day and also cared for Mother.

Our young brother Ed, after his high school years, had graduated from the South African Air Force Academy and had worked his way across the Atlantic as a steward on an ocean liner. He had enrolled at Moody Bible Institute and set his sights on becoming a missionary pilot. We sent for him because the end was near.

It came on an October morning of 1963.

Samuel Montague Church folded up the tent of his earthly tabernacle and was transferred into the presence of the King. He had lived but five brief years as a Christian, yet had accomplished more in those fleeting years than many people do in fifty.

I reflected on that night in 1950, when he had said, "I could never live up to your standards; I could never live the Christian life. I couldn't keep it up."

In the eight months of his severe suffering, he proved he did not have to keep it up. Jesus did it for him. He was "kept by the power of God through faith unto salvation."(7) He found the Word of God true, "My grace is sufficient for thee."(8)

In his months of suffering he displayed a love and graciousness that led several employees at the hospital to a saving knowledge of Jesus Christ.

He had fought a good fight, he had finished his course and there was laid up for him "a crown of righteousness."(9)

We laid his wasted body to rest under the vast blue skies that arch above the wide open plains of the Northern Cape.

He died in Kuruman, the lonely frontier that had given birth to the missionary zeal of David Livingstone. Sam Church was at rest.

Soon, very soon, two more graves would dot the dry, rugged earth which surrounds that lonely outpost.

Chapter Nineteen

avid Livingstone.

Andrew Murray.

Robert Moffat.

The history of South Africa rings with the sound of the names of men and women who have given their lives in service.

Robert and Mary Moffat arrived at the mission station in Kuruman in 1820. Spellbinding accounts tell of their dedication, heroism and self-sacrifice among the Batswana people of the Northern Cape. For 50 years they worked relentlessly to bring "the knowledge of the glory of God"(1) into the lives of the native people.

It was there that David Livingstone began his daring, illustrious career.

It was in the garden, under a tree, at that Mission Station, that David Livingstone "gave his heart" to Mary, the daughter of Robert and Mary Moffat. From Kuruman, David Livingstone set out on his epic journeys which brought him the fame and gave him the recognition which, at his death, prompted Florence Nightingale to say, "We have lost one of the greatest men of our generation."

That same Mission Station has come to play a nostalgic role in the history of my own family.

Shortly after Dad's death, Hilda married Alan Butler, an Episcopal missionary priest in Robert Moffat's church. Together, they have served the Lord in the same district where the dauntless Moffat had held high the light of the gospel for 50 years.

Eddie returned to America. He married his sweetheart at Moody Bible Institute and pressed on with his aviation career to win his pilot's rating, his instrument rating and his instructor's rating. He qualified as an aircraft maintenance engineer as well. Together with his American bride, Sondra, he bought a flying school in Arizona.

Mom, still in South Africa, moved 100 miles south to be close to Theo, who had settled in the city of Kimberley—famous for its diamond mine.

Although the need to pursue our separate lives caused the family to drift apart after Sam's death, there was a change in all our relationships. A subtle tenderness now pervaded every family contact.

Ada and I were faced with a cross-roads decision. Should we re-enter the ranks of active service in the Baptist Union or should we seek a broader field in which to apply all we had learned in our two years in the United States?

Again, times were hard. We had sold all to pay our expenses to and from the USA. We owed more than $1,000 on our return passage money.

I went back to the first priority of my ministry; preaching and teaching as I traversed the "Golden Reef" speaking in churches, ministering in men's meetings and teaching at camps and conferences.

The years of travel, learning, and the experience of naked faith, having to trust God wholly, had given a new impetus to my preaching.

My heart was warmed as never before. The years of challenge had drawn me close to God and taught me lessons which could not have been learned in the security of a safe pastoral position.

But I had to earn money to support my family, so I took a position with an insurance company. It gave me flexibility of time, and weekends free to travel in ministry.

I became a "tent-maker."

Each night Dawson and Jenny prayed, "Dear Lord Jesus, please help us to get a home of our own and, God, please help us to get a car." Their prayers seemed like dreams of fantasy. But gradually, as we "found our feet," our Heavenly Father slowly answered each prayer.

Another nightmarish event came to plague my troubled body. In February, 1965, while walking along an uneven sidewalk in the city of Johannesburg, my right leg buckled under me. A few days later, as I walked in our yard, I twisted my knee and felt a ripping, crunching pain as I fell to the ground.

A visit to the Chamber of Mines Hospital confirmed my own darkest diagnosis. The cartilage in my right knee had torn. There was only one solution: surgery—again. Only now it was a bilateral meniscectomy. That meant removing the torn cartilage on both sides of the knee.

As before, the inherent weakness in my muscles made the surgery and recuperation an extended ordeal. In April my leg was still very thin and my knee was stiff. There were angry scars from the stitches on either side of my blue and swollen knee.

The surgeon at the hospital concluded there was only one solution; to put me under an anesthetic and break the knee joint.

I had seen the procedure done before: it was torture. The joint was broken under anesthetic, and the heel tied to the buttocks. The attendants would come a few times each day, release the thongs which held the leg tied back, stretch the offending member a few times and then tie it back again. This would be accompanied by a chorus of screams, moans and pleading from the patient. All to no avail. The torture was legal. That's the way it was done!

I decided that treatment was not for me. So, with Ada and the two children, we set out for a hot spring spa near the coast. I had two weeks in which to perform my own "miracle" of bending the locked knee joint.

Dawson did it for me!

One evening while I was wading disconsolately in the hot pool, my lively nine-year-old, tired of a daddy who could not run, jump and cavort like other dads, yelled, "Daddy, catch me."

Without waiting for my frantic, "No!" he jumped right on top of me. The impact drove me under the water. I nearly drowned, but the sudden weight snapped the lesions in the joint.

I cried out in agony, but after the rescue operation of pulling a sobbing, gasping, nearly drowned father from the wading pool and administering first aid, we were overjoyed to find I could bend my leg; painfully and not completely, but the main lesions has been snapped!

I received my discharge from the hospital in May, but I was now classified: "Sixty percent totally, permanently disabled."

Two months later I was invited to become the director of Youth for Christ in Johannesburg.

God brought a dedicated Christian couple into our lives, Heinz Dedekind and his wife, Vera, who offered to support us for one year while we established ourselves in the work. How we praised God for their generosity, their vision and commitment.

However, we faced a serious handicap: we did not have a car, nor were there funds available in the YFC coffers to purchase one. Without adequate transportation it was impossible to do our work.

So I prayed, telling the Lord I believed we needed a station wagon. I said, "Lord, you have promised, 'My God shall supply all your need.'(2) Father, this is not just a fancy or a whim. We desperately need a station wagon."

A couple of days later Timo Crous, a distinguished Christian businessman, phoned me. He said, "Peter, I have something special for you."

I queried, "Timo, what is it?"

He replied, "It's standing outside my window; you'd better come over and see." I hurried to his office and, sure enough, there it was: a beautiful, gleaming Volvo station wagon!

1966 witnessed the fulfillment of a vision which I had carried for ten years.

During my years as pastor of the Baptist Church in Fish Hoek, in the days when God was shaping my ministry, I had become intensely interested in the use of radio as a means of proclaiming the Gospel of Christ. With Ken Terhoven, a notable young South African evangelist, I had prayed that God would give us the opportunity to use radio to reach the South African masses.

In South Africa, all broadcasting was government owned and operated. Historically recognized denominations were allocated time on Sundays, when church services were broadcast. On weekdays specially approved ministers offered devotions, homilies, prologues and epilogues, but no one was permitted "to rock the religious boat." Everything was very proper. Radio time was almost condescendingly allotted to the very staid and proper religious figures.

On the eastern seaboard of Africa, north of South Africa, lay the Portuguese territory of Mozambique. From the city of Lourenco Marques, an independent radio station beamed popular music into South Africa.

LM Radio commanded the largest youth audience in South Africa, as eighty-four percent of those in the sixteen to twenty-four year age bracket tuned into its programs. The managing director was a Christian gentleman, Mr. Sidney Low. I had met him several years before, but in 1966 we discovered our common interest in using radio to reach South Africa's youth with a positive presentation of the Christian message.

At his invitation I prepared an audition program and presented it to the directors. The station managers accepted the pilot and, in September of that year, I commenced a regular Sunday morning broadcast, *Faith for Our Times*, which I produced and hosted for eight years.

The format for my program included popular songs (usually from the Top Ten chart) which expressed the deep longings of people's lives; commentary from myself; always a scripture reading or text, and a personal testimony from some noted or well known personality.

In February 1968, LM Radio, under Mr. Low's direction, sponsored me on an idyllic international trip to capture recorded interviews with outstanding Christian personalities. I combined this odyssey with attendance at the International Convention of Youth for Christ in Kingston, Jamaica.

My travels took me to the Caribbean Islands, the USA, Great Britain and Europe.

In New York city, I met Dr. Norman Vincent Peale, who gave me an autographed copy of his best-seller *The Power of Positive*

Thinking. Later, he would be a benefactor in ventures which would be a great inspiration to many in South Africa.

Another prominent New York pastor who received me cordially and gave me the privilege of an interview was Dr. Stephen Olford, minister of Calvary Baptist Church.

An experience which deeply affected me was my excursion into East Berlin. The Wall was an awesome sight.

Since my early years of learning had been shaped by hearing the harrowing stories of missionaries and ministers who had braved the horrors of Communism, I viewed the Berlin Wall with a wonder salted with anger and indignation.

I brooded at the places where people had been cut down in cold blood as they made their dash for freedom.

Passing through Check-point Charlie into East Berlin was tense. I carried a portable tape recorder and chronicled my journey into the darkness of oppression.

An eerie silence hung over the austere city. The streets were almost silent; very few cars were to be seen. And the people were strangely quiet. I saw no smiles, met no friends.

Coming out again was like leaving a dark, oppressive chamber of fear. At the check point, mirrors were rolled under our bus. Naively, I asked, "Why?"

I returned to South Africa armed with interviews with people as diverse as Miss America, the "Strongest Man in the World," a circus clown, an astronaut, and a baseball Hall-of-Famer. I loved my role as producer, radio emcee, and disc jockey.

One dark night, after my radio program had been on the air for a few years, I became lost while driving my car in a sparsely populated rural area far to the east of Johannesburg.

Weary after a trying day, and many miles from home, I came upon a lonely country house set in the solitude.

When I rapped on the door to ask directions, I was invited in. Inside was a small knot of young people. One of the young men eyed me quizzically. The youth stepped forward and asked,

"Aren't you Peter Church?"

I was surprised. He continued, "I am in the South African army. Every Sunday our entire barracks listens to your broadcast. I recognized your voice."

My voice became so well known across Southern Africa that on beaches, in restaurants and other public places across the nation, people would hear me talking, walk up to me and ask, "Are you Peter Church?"

I would always respond, "Why do you ask?"

The reply would invariably be, "I recognize your voice."

Thousands of letters came to us over the years. The question I was most often asked by listeners was, "Is Peter Church your real name, or is it assumed for stage and radio?"

In 1969, Dr. Paul Smith, pastor of the People's Church in Toronto, was a guest in our home. Cut of the same cloth as his illustrious father, he encouraged me in my zeal to proclaim the gospel message over the airways. He donated 1,000 copies of his book, *Daily Gospel,* which we mailed free of charge to listeners who wrote to us.

My weekly guests included such international notables as Dr. Stephen Olford, Dr. Norman Vincent Peale and Senator Mark Hatfield. I featured South African sports personalities and other celebrities who could bear a clear Christian witness.

Chapter Twenty

t was 1969, the year of conquest, adventure, heroism and triumph. In July, Neil Armstrong uttered the words from the surface of the moon which struck pride in the heart of America:

"One small step for man; one giant step for mankind."

For me, the euphoria of the conquest of space was soon to be wiped out as our family tasted the bitterness of a dramatic personal loss. We plunged from the high flying world of rockets and outer space to the depths of grief through the heart breaking tragedy of a plane crash.

Early in the year, a striking young man in a white "safari suit" walked into the YFC office in Johannesburg. He introduced himself and said he had just moved from Durban and was about to make his home in Johannesburg. Recently appointed as area manager of a large fabric wholesaler, he was a highly motivated, successful salesman. He expressed an enthusiastic interest in Christian service and asked, "Can you use me?"

I recalled a word which Dawson Trotman had spoken. In referring to the training of men for Christian discipleship, he applied the rule, "Use me or lose me." 'Daws' had stressed the fact that in order to keep a man in Christian service you must put him to work. I did!

The young man was Tony Louch. He immediately became the most valued layman with whom I had ever worked and was destined to become an important person in my life.

That same year Mom became seriously ill and my brother Ed decided to return to South Africa with his little American family. He brought Sondra and their two baby girls, Charlotte and Suzie, to visit their Grandma.

Once back in South Africa, Eddie thought he might stay for a few years and talked of working as a pilot with the South African Airways. He spoke of buying a large piece of land and building a Christian health center.

He was a picture of rugged young manhood, with a superb physique. Handsome and strong, he exuded the same dynamic characteristics as had his Dad. His strength, his faith and his radiant witness for Christ won him immediate respect and admiration wherever he went. With his magnificent build, he was a strong man among men. His presence was a joy and inspiration to the whole Church family.

He took a job with an aerial survey company operating out of Johannesburg. The assignments were grueling, calling for low-level flying at 500 feet across the wastes of the Eastern Transvaal. The task demanded flying as many as eight hours a day without landing. It was toilsome, hazardous work.

On Thursday afternoon, August 7, 1969, my Aunt Ethel phoned me.

I knew instantly that something was seriously wrong. She was crying bitterly, "Have you seen the newspaper?" she asked.

"No."

She blurted out, "Peter, Eddie has been killed in a plane crash!" The words stunned me.

Eddie—dead? It couldn't be! No, it couldn't be. There must be some mistake. It was that nightmare moment that every person somehow anticipates, but you hope it will never come; sudden, violent death.

I rushed out into the streets of Johannesburg to see the story and picture emblazoned across the front page of *The Star*. On Friday, the *Rand Daily Mail* featured the tragedy on its front page. The newspaper, together with chilling pictures declared; "Mountain Crash Kills Three."

I was dazed and bewildered.

Three men had perished in the flaming wreckage of the survey aircraft. Coming out of one of the low runs, the plane had been caught in a down-draft and crashed into the top of a mountain.

I raced home to break the news to Ada, Dawson and Jenny.

The first one I saw was Dawson who was walking slowly home from school. He dearly loved Ed and had just spent the month of July with him, Sondra and the girls. Now I had to share this terrible news. I could hardly speak. I sat there with Dawson in the car as the tears rolled down my face.

"Uncle Eddie is dead; he was killed in a plane crash."

I bundled Ada and the two children into the car and, in dazed disbelief, made the hurried journey to the city closest to the scene of the crash. Sondra was already there with her bewildered little girls. Charlotte and Suzie were too young to fully comprehend what we told them. It seemed impossible, unreal.

"Your daddy has gone to be with Jesus."

I felt as though a deep chasm had opened in front of me.

First Dad, now Ed.

I loved these two men more than any on earth, but they had been taken from me; again I pondered the mystery of death. Its finality engulfed me like a dark cloud.

I was at the foot of the mountain when they brought Ed's body down.

Ada, Sondra and Ethel had all urged me, "Don't look at the body."

"Remember, that's not Eddie. Ed is with Jesus. He now has a glorified body."

"Don't look at the charred, burnt remains."

"Remember him as you always knew him; tall, strong, manly and handsome."

I resisted the urge to go and look at the solemn, green canvas that bore his remains.

On Saturday afternoon we held a memorial service for him in the Rosebank Union Church, the sanctuary Ada and I had made our spiritual home since our return to South Africa.

Two conflicting emotions contended inside me. I knew that for the Christian, death is victory: entrance into the presence of the King, the gateway through which we pass from mortality to immortality.

My faith was firmly anchored in the encouragement of God's Holy Word and I knew that Paul had alleviated the anguish of the early Christians with his comforting declaration, "Absent from the body, present with the Lord."(1) But the heart pain, the deep soul anguish was unbearable. It hurt at the core of my being. I cried many tears.

I struggled desperately with the sense of personal loss. I looked at Sondra and her two little girls, aged three years and eighteen months, and I asked.

"Why? Why, God? Why us?"

The answer came, "To be with Christ is far better."(2)

God showed me that we should not grieve for those whom He has taken, because they are at rest and infinitely better off than we who remain. It seemed as though the Lord said, "Do you wish him back?"

To this I could honestly answer, "No." I knew he was in the presence of One whom he loved and served.

The following Monday, we laid his body next to his Father, Sam, under the same clear, open sky on that lonely plain outside Kuruman.

Alan, Hilda's husband, read from Psalm 121, "I will lift up mine eyes unto the hills; From whence cometh my help? My help cometh from the Lord, which made heaven and earth."

Far off in the distance, the blue-tinted mountain peaks stood in silent confirmation. They seemed to say, "Eddie is gone, but the Lord remains; steadfast and immovable. His faithfulness is as vast as the heavens, as strong as God's mountains."

Dave Barr, of the Billy Graham team, was in the city of Johannesburg visiting me at that time. We were discussing opening a Billy Graham film library in the city. Tenderly, lovingly, Dave shared words of comfort with our bereaved family. God knew we would need someone special in those moments and in His mercy He had sent Dave to be with us.

Mother would not move away from the area but chose to live in solitude.

How much we had all changed.

The unhappiness and strife of our early years were washed away and replaced with the love of God which had filled our hearts.

God's love now bound us together.

Whenever we could get to Kimberley, Ada, Dawson, Jenny and I visited Mom.

My dearest recollections of her are seeing her sitting in her tiny living room with her Bible in her lap, listening to my voice as I broadcast each Sunday across the nation on the network of LM Radio.

She was my most ardent fan.

Chapter Twenty-One

"Mission 70." 1970 was a landmark year for the Churches in the City of Johannesburg. Under the leadership of Michael Cassidy and the leaders of his Missionary organization, Africa Enterprise, the Christian leaders of the "City of Gold" had banded together for an all-out evangelistic crusade to touch the heart and nerve of the millions, of all races, who lived in the seething metropolis.

I had been invited to serve as the Director of the youth outreach for this bold milestone endeavor which had been designated "Mission 70."

Youth for Christ had released me from my commitment and Tony Louch had become my successor as the director.

One afternoon I was in my car, inching my way along in the congested traffic on the concrete-canyon streets of Johannesburg. As the engine idled at a traffic light, I casually dropped my right hand to the side of my right leg. For a brief second I did not comprehend the sensation, then with alarm I made the discovery: my leg was numb! I pinched my calf, my thigh, then the right side of my chest; they were all numb! Most of the right side of my body was dead to feeling.

Another alarm broke in upon me with a shock. My right foot was "asleep," yet it ached terribly.

My back also ached constantly.

The symptoms had crept up on me like a thief but now I was jolted awake. There had been a marked deterioration in my physical condition over the months; or was it years? I didn't know, but suddenly I realized that my entire lower body twanged like an exposed nerve.

I had lived, now, for twenty years with my disability. I had learned to cope with discomfort, pain and severe restrictions. But this was different.

The pain was relentless. I realized I was weary, tired and drawn.

Wild thoughts raced through my mind. The specter of my wheelchair days rose before me. I thought I might be losing the use of my legs again.

I kept my discovery a secret and at first told no one, not even Ada. I indulged in the fancy of thinking that the symptoms would vanish, but they didn't. The pain throbbed in my back, leg and foot like toothache. Day and night I lived in secret distress, till finally, I could conceal it no longer. Ada saw that something was wrong.

We made an appointment for me to return to the Chamber of Mines Hospital. Dr. du Toit was now retired; his place had been taken by one of his protegés, Dr. McGregor. After examination, he recommended I consult an independent neurosurgeon.

Following exhaustive questioning and numerous tests, the opinion was handed down: there were bone fragments in my spinal column pressing on the nerves. The prognosis; I would have to live with the pain because the condition was inoperable. The doctors prescribed a new drug, Brufen, which had recently come on to the market. They could offer nothing more. I was consigned to live with the pain and discomfort.

I went about my duties inwardly concerned, but outwardly cheerful.

The Mission 70 office staff, drawn from a wide segment of denominational persuasions, included a small group who believed in and practiced Divine healing.

One morning, following the devotional period observed by the staff, the small group gathered around me. They knew I was suffering and asked if I wanted to be healed. What a question! Naturally, I replied in the affirmative. They placed me on a chair, closed in on me, laid their hands on my head and began to pray.

The action signaled the commencement of a life in which countless people who knew of my condition became anxious to witness God "do a miracle for me." I became a prime candidate for prayers of healing.

Burdened with constant pain and numbness in my back and right leg (my left leg had continued, since the accident, to be thin and weak). I nevertheless plunged headlong into the responsibilities of coordinating and organizing the network of activities planned for the city's youth.

The high point of the outreach was a giant one night concert with the British pop star Cliff Richard. Added to his fame as Great Britain's most popular entertainer and recording artist, Cliff had fairly recently experienced a real and dramatic spiritual conversion, becoming a dynamic Christian witness.

Months of preparation culminated in an event that "rocked" the young people of the City. It was a powerful incentive for the youthful Followers of Christ to be able to identify with so charismatic, popular and dynamic a person.

He was a matchless role model.

His visit was a raving success.

It also plunged me into a personal conflict!

On the "big night," the night of the concert, thousands of young people converged on the auditorium. The only suitable place we had been able to secure was the conference auditorium of a leading Afrikaans denomination. We had young people of every race in attendance. The air was electric with excitement and music.

Suddenly, a middle aged white man accosted me. He fairly yelled at me. I could almost see the demon of anger in his eyes. He was furious.

"You have desecrated my temple by letting these black and colored people come into this place!"

Somehow, I seemed to be the lightning rod for insults and outbursts. More were to follow in the years to come.

With the conclusion of Mission Seventy I did not return to YFC because a new vision had come to birth in me.

Chapter Twenty-Two

n February 16, 1971, the day I turned 39, I opened the offices of the unique twentieth century missionary movement which was to be the focus of my Christian Service for many years to come.

Two men, soon joined by a third, were partners with me in that "dream-become-reality."

The first man was Tony.

We were the visionaries who brought the idea to life.

Our vision was to harness the power of modern media to proclaim the eternal gospel.

Tony was an Evangelist. His heart beat was to bring people to a saving knowledge of Christ.

He was also a gifted and eloquent communicator, and spearheaded the negotiations which would enable us to bring radio, the print media and later television into the arena of our commitment to "Tell the World."

In a moment of inspiration God gave me a name which would sum up our Mission. It came to me as I wrestled with the challenge, "Go-Tell Communications."

Based on Matthew 28:7, "Go, tell that He is risen," the name summed up our vision.

Shortly, we were joined by Keith Strugnell, a young man of rare ability and grace who brought his skill as a chartered accountant to our organization.

The third man was little more than a teenager. He appeared at that time to play such a small part in the overall scheme of things!

His name was Simon. But there is a strange and enthralling story behind that life.

My name is Peter, and I am white of skin. Simon was black; a native of the Venda tribe.

I had been born into a paradox. Though, as with all babies, I have no recollection of the religious rite of baptizing infants, I must surely have been "done," the term we used to indicate that the rite had been performed.

The Afrikaans word is doop. It is equivalent to the English "to dip," which is the literal translation of the Biblical word, "to baptize." My mother, as a girl, was a staunch member of the Dutch Reformed Church, the most powerful Denomination in the land, with fifty-two percent of the white population registered as members.

And that is the paradox. As the son and grandson of faithful adherents to this monolithic institution, I was most certainly christened. (Another term for the same rite of passage.) On the other side of the dichotomy, my mother never, to my knowledge ever attended the church.

The institution was, for a vast number of its initiated, purely a convenience if, as was facetiously said, you wanted to be "hatched, matched or dispatched." The church was viewed as a necessity because, without it you could not be christened, married or buried.

How naive!

Like the millions of other South African white children, I was raised without the understanding of how our entire philosophy of life was governed by the theology of the Dutch, German and French settlers, whose descendants later became known as "Afrikaners." Through nearly two centuries, these pioneers, joined over decades by other European settlers, attained a separate identity and a hybrid language, "Afrikaans."

The leaders of this new nation called themselves Nationalists and ultimately crafted the system of separation of the races which they called apartheid, which literally means "separateness."

As a white child, I simply grew up accepting this political point of view. It was espoused without question in my limited circle of acquaintances. But stirrings grew within me as I heard the adults talk, and witnessed their attitudes and actions.

My personal journey of questioning the political system which discriminated against the black people of South Africa began first with tentative questions, and then, later, with out-and-out arguments with a wide circle of family members.

One night while I was still living at home, during dinner, my mother voiced a commonly held prejudice.

She exclaimed, "The blacks are not like us; they don't even have a soul. They are just like animals."

I challenged her, "How do you know that?"

What ensued was a verbal war. The vicious exchange ended as my enraged father threatened to throw me out of the house, literally, physically—forever!

I was 14 years old.

Perhaps it was the slow progress of years. Possibly a slow grasp of the deep-seated religious conviction of the men who had crafted the Apartheid system which made many of us blind to the reality of what was happening all around us.

And that was another mystery. How could men, who professed very real and sincere religious beliefs, sit on the pinnacle of a system which brought such human misery and suffering to so many? Which allowed, even condoned, the acts of brutality perpetrated in the name of the law.

However, South African white people were not a racist island in a tranquil sea of international harmony. In growing measure I began, personally, to question all the evidence of "man's inhumanity to man."

In 1956, as the fresh young pastor of the Fish Hoek Baptist Church, I had received an unexpected visit from 3 well-dressed black men. They came to my study and introduced themselves as representatives of the African National Congress.

Perhaps I was not ready to hear. Perhaps their message was too veiled, but I declined their invitation.

They had come to ask me to join the ANC!

Only 4 years earlier, at a rally at the University of the Witwatersrand in Johannesburg, where I was studying my languages, Greek and English, Nelson Mandela had addressed the students on campus. One of the ANC radicals in the party declared, "When we have come to power, we will sweep the white man into the sea. Then, when we have established our government, we will consider applications for immigration."

A white student in the audience asked one of Mr. Mandela's attendants the question, "But what about your white friends?"

The zealot replied, "We have no white friends."

Such was the racial and political polarity!

In 1963, after our sojourn in America, we returned to a country which was beginning to rise, ever so slowly, from the mire into which the system of Apartheid had dragged it.

Yet, in the years from 1963, when we took up life again in our homeland, we saw opportunities to sow hope, dignity and progress in the lives of the African people who came into the circle of our influence.

There was almost a despair as were viewed the racial disharmony and inequality. There was a near fatalism which secretly said, "You can never change this system."

But we could help change individual lives and their circumstances.

One of those opportunities came in the person of that young, homeless, out-of-work migrant who had drifted down from his "homeland" to seek a future in the City of Gold, Johannesburg.

His name was Simon, the "third man" present at the opening of the Go-Tell office in 1971.

Simon came to our home, just a boy, looking for odd things to do. He was sleeping, sometimes out in the veld, sometimes in a sheltered place among abandoned farm buildings, and occasionally with an older African man who had a spot for an extra mat in his mud hut. He washed my car, did yard work, and occasionally worked in our kitchen.

Such was Simon's lot!

We could only use his services on a part-time basis, but gradually we found other households which needed yard work. Soon I was able to arrange a room where he could sleep.

I began the slow process of teaching him to speak English and bought him his first reader.

After speaking to him in the working language "Fanakalo," which I had learned in my gold mining days, and with a combination of pictures and English, I led him to express his personal decision to receive Jesus Christ as Savior.

A few years down the road in our journey with Simon, Ada had a brilliant idea.

I was (as most Christian missionaries have to) going through the humdrum, but important, role of getting out newsletters, mailings, flyers and other pieces of information. In those early days, we cranked out leaflets and letters on messy duplicating machines and spent long hours in menial office tasks.

Ada said, "Why don't you take Simon into your office and teach him to do that work."

I did! And the rest is history!

When we opened the Go-Tell Communications office in 1971, Simon was our first employee. His station was raised and we sent him to special classes to learn the skills of servicing, cleaning and preparing the films for rental.

He had learned to read and write. He even carried a briefcase to work! The savings account we helped him open began to grow.

Simon married a girl in his "homeland" and began to raise a family. We provided a living space for him in the basement of our home, and with the passage of years, Simon has prospered—in spirit, soul and body. Simon is now on the Board of Directors of Go-Tell Communications, an organization which continues to have a profound influence throughout the entire African continent.

Chapter Twenty-Three

O n a Saturday afternoon, late in 1971, I drove my car through the semi-deserted streets which run through the grey brick-and-mortar jungle which is named Johannesburg.

As if to rebuke the greed and pride of its beginnings, there is a twist of irony in the history of the building of Johannesburg, South Africa's City of Gold. Running from north to south, there is a kink in many of its narrow streets, like the proverbial "dog's hind leg." Rumor has it that, because the town sprung up like a mushroom in the wake of the gold rush of the nineties, two surveyors were called in to map out its streets. They started from opposite ends, working their way toward the center, but there was a miscalculation and, when the two met in the heart of the booming mining town it was too late to go back and correct an error 10 feet wide.

Today, tall new buildings seem to jostle each other for space on the narrow streets and the gleaming, modern edifices are gradually elbowing out the ornate structures of an earlier era. Built upon the vast wealth of its gold mines and industries, Johannesburg is the solar plexus of the country's financial network, the heartbeat of its economy.

The city dozes from noon on Saturday to early Monday morning as across the nation, business, commerce and industry all pause while the people take time to pray and to play.

There are no stores open during these leisure hours because the Sunday Observance Act forbids all non-essential trading on the Lord's Day and effectively prevents the opening of all houses of entertainment. Therefore, Saturday is unique. In a frenzy of pleasure-seeking, as though another day might never come, movie-goers throng the cinemas and theaters.

My destination on this Saturday was the stately old 20th Century Fox cinema in the heart of downtown Johannesburg. I was unprepared for what I saw. Crowds of people were milling about the still-closed doors; a line stretched, in double rows, the length of the block and disappeared out of sight around the corner. Pulled up on the sidewalk was an array of mean-looking motorbikes. The Hell's Angels were out in force.

Displayed on the marquee in front of the cinema was the title of the attraction, *The Cross and the Switchblade*, starring Pat Boone.

As in a sweet dream, my mind drifted back more than twenty years. In 1948 I had been one of the people in a crowd waiting to enter the 20th Century cinema. Those had been the "high days" of Youth for Christ. I was a new Christian then, and had dreamed of one day being able to accomplish something of great significance for the Lord.

This was the fulfillment of that dream!

We had sent Tony to the United States of America for three months, where he was to contract, on our behalf, to distribute Christian films throughout South Africa.

He phoned me from New York and proclaimed, "Peter, I have a contract for *The Cross and Switchblade*, if you can raise $10,000 we can have the film!"

I didn't know where to get even ten thousand cents, but in faith I said, "Yes! Sign the contract!" And I began the biggest financial undertaking of my life!

I started out with enthusiasm, thinking every Christian businessman would leap at the opportunity to invest in a project which would place a dynamic, no-holds-barred, true Christian story on the cinema screens of South Africa.

I was in for a rude awakening.

Apathy and disinterest and even opposition met me at every turn.

On the religious front I ran into an ingrained prejudice against anything "modern." In my own denomination, young people were fed a steady diet of warning against "worldliness." The cinema was labeled "the devil's church." Pastors were outraged at the thought of their young people being lured into a "bioscope." Ministers in the denominations which advocated Evangelism, and who should have been our allies, because of their opposition to the movies, actually became our adversaries. They actively supported, and engaged in evangelistic efforts, but would not conceive of showing a Christian film in a secular cinema.

Out of a seemingly endless round of personal calls, only two men responded positively and generously to my presentation; our friend Mr. Sid Low of LM Radio and the Reverend Doug Fischer, founder and pastor of the famous Norwood Church in Johannesburg.

However, we needed $15,000 to cover the contract price, print costs and publicity.

Finally time was running out and we were about to lose our deposit of $1,000 plus the contract.

Miraculously, at the eleventh hour, salvation arrived when all seemed lost. The Reverend Ross Main, a close friend and board member of Go-Tell, introduced us to the chairman of a large savings and loan association.

On the last day of the holding period for the contract, Mr. Canning, chairman of the Natal Building Society in Durban, called to say his society would advance the $15,000 to us as an interest-free loan! A unique new movement was born in South Africa. It would eventually take me to Europe, to England, Ireland, Scotland and Wales.

Chapter Twenty-Four

We were poised for one of the most unusual acts of evangelism ever to be launched in South Africa. We were going to throw the cat among the pigeons by putting a strong gospel film on the regular circuit of secular films in the public cinemas.

Grasping the significance of the coming release of the film, Tony concluded a transaction with one of the nation's largest book distributors, the Central News Agency. Through Go-Tell, the wholesaler bought 10,000 copies of the book, *The Cross and the Switchblade*.

As part of the sales contract, Tony asked for, and obtained, a commitment from the company to feature the book in major store front window displays across the country.

It was exciting to walk down Commissioner Street in the prime downtown section of Johannesburg and see a 20 foot long window display of the book, heralding the release of the film.

To further capitalize on the wave crest of publicity, Tony negotiated with the publishers of the nation's leading color magazine, Scope, for a ten-part serialization of the book. Our excitement ran high as we saw the story appear week by week with dramatic still pictures from the film.

When the movie opened, there were few people in the land who did not know an event of singular importance was to take place. Through press, radio, periodicals and general advertising, the country was readied for a "happening."

The Cross and the Switchblade, shown in the 20th Century Fox Cinema, was one of the most ambitious projects ever undertaken by a Christian organization in South Africa. The film was eventually seen by more than two million people and this led naturally to our next venture.

We invited Nicky Cruz to tour South Africa.

In a ten day crusade, which swept from Johannesburg to Cape Town and out to the eastern port of Durban, by night and day, young people streamed out in their thousands to see and hear the gang leader whose conversion was the basis of the story, *The Cross and the Switchblade.*

Just as we had saturated the media prior to the release of the film, we now capitalized on the uniqueness of the event to bring all available communication aids into the arena.

Our opening night was in the open-air Ellis Park tennis stadium. Like a sullen enemy, the weather was our major opponent; it rained sheets all through Saturday morning. Gordon Calmeyer of the Living Sound, who was our sound engineer, phoned me from the stadium at 3:00 p.m. and said,

"There must be 6 inches of water on the court; are you going to cancel the meeting?"

I replied, "Gordon, even if we have to get oars and paddle the loudspeakers onto the court, we must go on."

We did.

Young people arrived in droves, in spite of the driving rain. Threatened with an opening night disaster, we prayed earnestly. It was dramatic! As the rain was falling, Nicky stepped up to the microphone and, in his unique, picturesque, though broken, English, simply said, "Lord Jesus, I am asking you to stop this rain."

It stopped.

The young people listened; and responded to the invitation to receive Jesus Christ as Lord and Savior.

Next day the newspapers carried front page stories of the crusade meeting. One reporter said, "Game, set and match for Nicky Cruz."

For five consecutive days our crusade was on the front pages of the principal newspapers.

The historic event was captured in the production of our first film, *Jesus is the Answer*, a forty-five minute presentation featuring Nicky's dramatic story.

For many years, it will stand as a major achievement that we sold 20,000 copies of the Nicky Cruz story, *Run Baby, Run*. Of the 110,000 young people who attended the ten day crusade, 5,000 registered decisions to receive Christ as their Lord and Savior.

However, Go-Tell lost more than $10,000 on the Nicky Cruz Crusade; but we rode the loss by using revenues from the successful run of the film. Thus, the stage was set for our evangelistic assault on the country.

But the ranks of opposition were also being drawn into array. Our opponents would prove to be "those of our own household."(1)

Succeeding years saw us launch crusades with numerous visitors from America. The crusades with evangelists and the concerts with Christian artists were genuinely successful in impact and appeal.

We consistently saw 10,000 to 15,000 people each year make commitments to Christ.

Unfortunately, we were unable to make our ventures show the same success in the financial realm.

We had several strokes against us.

The first salvo fired against us came from Christians who resolutely and, often viciously, opposed the idea of charging an admission for any event; even a Christian concert with a performing artist.

One of our Board members observed, "You are 10 years ahead of your time."

Someone else commented, "You are pioneers."

The risk of pioneering is; forerunners are the first to be shot.

Our problem was simple: high expenses and low income.

At the end of every crusade we faced the same sobering fact. We covered airfares from America; there were local expenses; and there was always our commitment to a fair honorarium.

We constantly hoped that somehow our next venture would come out on top financially. We always hoped other Christian people would catch the vision, see the results of our labors and rally to our aid.

On another front, we espoused a system which also was custom-made to ensure a constant deficit. Through Tony's visit to the USA we had added hundreds of Christian films to our library.

We paid the same prices for prints that were charged to distributors in the USA, but in addition we had shipping and handling charges. There were also local promotional and advertising expenses, plus overhead and operating costs. To cap our predicament, because of the lower income level of the people in South Africa, we could charge only half the rental which American distributors received. We offered the South African churches a service unique in the world; a selection of the finest Christian films—all obtainable from a single source; the offices of Go-Tell Communications.

Ada and I had previously completed the building of a new home on the outskirts of Johannesburg and when we moved in, we declared, "This is our last move!"

Since our wedding in 1955, we had moved twenty-one times. We immediately opened our home as a place of witness for Christ in the community. We were members of the Rosebank Union Church, for which we had helped to establish several home Bible study groups. Applying the principles of Bible study and discipleship which we had learned from the Navigators, the group in our home flourished.

Part of our basic training for Christians who attended our fellowship group was a special outreach evening, to which each member invited a non-Christian friend. We witnessed a deep work of God's Spirit in many lives. Several years later, at an annual presentation of deacons in the Rosebank church, no less than three of the men testified that they had been led to Christ in these home meetings.

David Shimmin was one of these men.

God had given me a special concern for Dave. Following a career in the British navy, Dave had settled in South Africa. He was now a respected businessman in the city and a director of his own companies. One Sunday evening, when I was gravely ill following an attack of whooping cough, I invited Dave to visit me at my bedside. Everybody else in the house had gone to church, but as Dave sat at the foot of my bed (a safe distance away) I again shared the Good News of the Kingdom of God with him, and asked him if he would receive Christ as his personal Savior.

He nodded his head and said, "Yes."

He prayed the prayer of repentance and faith and received Jesus Christ into his life.

The effect on his life was dramatic.

Through our home Bible studies he rapidly grew in grace and the knowledge of Jesus Christ and, within a few years, was secretary of the church and serving as chairman of the YMCA in Johannesburg.

When Go-Tell Communications was formed, I retained my position with LM Radio as producer of *Faith for Our Times*.

On Easter Sunday, 1971, I broadcast a major two-hour program featuring the rock opera, *Jesus Christ Superstar*. Using the New Testament narrative, I wove the Biblical account into the lyrics and score of the musical.

The government-owned South African Broadcasting Corporation had banned the opera, but through the press and radio announcements the entire country was alerted and many eagerly awaited the moment when the opera would be broadcast in its entirety on LM Radio.

One of South Africa's noted radio personalities, Peter Lotis, was in Durban on the Sunday afternoon of the historic event. On his return to Johannesburg his comment was "On Sunday, the whole of Durban, with its beaches, parks and thousands of young people, was Peter Church and Superstar country."

The broadcast took the nation by storm. I received 2,000 letters from listeners. I had ended the relay with a challenge to read the New Testament and consider the claims of Jesus Christ. I urged listeners to search the Word of God for the real answer to the question, "Who are you, Jesus?"

I had previously written to Dr. Norman Vincent Peale, who donated 2,000 copies of his booklet, *Quotations from Jesus Christ* for my broadcast. I offered these to listeners.

We were swamped.

National newspapers and magazines carried the story.

Personality, the country's leading color magazine, carried a center-spread with a four-page story. They quoted from letters which I had received from young people. In a single bold action, we had broken into the secular media with our unique story.

But in the wake of this unprecedented witness for a living, contemporary Christ, another storm broke over my head: the wrath of numerous conservative evangelical ministers.

The ire of the pious was so deeply roused that I was banned from most of their pulpits forthwith. The critics had not listened to the broadcast nor heard my defense of Christ's deity, but I was effectively shut out of many churches; the consensus of opinion being that I would be a "bad influence on their young people."

On the other hand, public demand for the program was so insistent that we rebroadcast the presentation on Ascension Day. On that occasion I ended the two-hour program with the "Hallelujah Chorus"! The response was again overwhelming; a second flood of letters deluged my office. Hampered by lack of help and facilities, I was forced from that point on to refrain from inviting people to write in for special offers.

On May 13, 1971, weary from the struggles and battering of the storms of life, my precious mother quietly passed away. Her suffering was more than could be borne, yet peacefully her spirit departed from her toil-worn frame and went into the presence of her Lord.

I am sure Sam was there to welcome her, Eddie was there to greet her and, together, they now dwell in the courts of heaven, singing the songs of the redeemed.

On May 17, I presented a unique production of the Rock Opera *Jesus Christ Superstar* on the stage of the Empire Theatre in Johannesburg. It was a visual presentation of what I had produced for radio. Reading my own script and playing the sound track through a super audio system, I wove again the story of Jesus in a fashion which those young people of the 70's could understand. We ended the show with the final footage of the Billy Graham film *His Land* in which the powerful montáge of the people's of the world are woven into a striking rendering of the "Hallelujah Chorus." At the close of the concert, Tony Louch extended an invitation and we witnessed the miracle of dozens of young people responding to the question of "What do you think of Christ?"(2)

On May 19, 1971 I buried my mother in the same cemetery in Kuruman where we had laid my Father and Ed. Their earthly remains lie together, side by side, on that open, dust-blown plain in the Northern Cape wilderness, its loneliness so typical of their lives here on earth. But their spirits soar in God's vast, eternal heaven. I know they heard the voice of their Beloved saying, "Well done, good and faithful servants, enter into the joy of your Lord."(3)

Chapter Twenty-Five

n 1971 Dawson saw a special evidence of God's love and miracle-working provision for his own life.

An avid student, with highly developed verbal skills, he was uninterested in the usual pursuits of high school students. We earnestly desired an opportunity for him to attend a private school, but inquiry quickly convinced us that the financial demand of such a school was wholly outside the realm of possibility. We encouraged Dawson to pray, and, together, we asked our heavenly Father to open a way for him to attend the newly established Woodmead School which, we felt, would be ideal for him.

God answered in a surprising fashion.

Several weeks after we had begun to pray, a gracious couple from our church, Mr. and Mrs. Eric Freemantle, came to our home. A forthright businessman, Mr. Freemantle came directly to the point.

For several years he had financially sponsored under-privileged boys from broken homes, but had become discouraged because so many of them seemed not to appreciate the help. They often squandered their opportunities, were unmotivated, and seldom seemed to rise to the privilege Mr. Freemantle offered them.

He had come to see us, to ask if we would be interested in his sponsoring our son to attend a private school. His wife, Alice, had suggested that he shift his benevolence to a boy who would appreciate the gesture and benefit from the assistance.

It was Sunday afternoon. We rejoiced and praised God exuberantly and, on Monday, Dawson was enrolled in Woodmead.

Eric Freemantle kept his promise, but he became ill and passed on to his reward just before Dawson was to enter his graduating year. His wife, Alice, who had become a close and dear friend, assumed the responsibility and we saw Dawson graduate from high school with a heritage for which we were unspeakably grateful.

I became wholly engrossed in the administration of promoting speaking engagements for overseas visitors.

Over the years we acted as organizing hosts for notable personalities such as Nicky Cruz, James Irwin, Ron Susek, Dr. Norman Vincent Peale and Jimmy Swaggart. We promoted concert tours for artists and groups like Living Sound, Red Harper (Mr. Texas), Gordon Jensen, Larry Norman, New Hope, Richard Roberts and The Archers.

In the course of time we promoted concert tours with international stars Pat and Debby Boone, and British pop star Cliff Richard.

Each event presented its own set of peculiar challenges and obstacles, as well as the resulting benefits and blessings. Each stands out as a rich experience.

Among the most rewarding outreach activities of 1974 was a lecture tour by Dr. Norman Vincent Peale and his wife, Ruth. The preparations and practical aspects of a tour of that magnitude were staggering. The challenges and cliff hangers which attended my responsibilities were encapsulated in the drama of the first lecture of the series.

We opened in Johannesburg.

The most important responsibility is to find a suitable place to gather. No small task in the Golden City. I had secured the use of an exhibition hall at the famed Show Grounds, and diligently worked through my list of "must-do's" and "must-have's." One must have seals, a speakers platform and all the other essentials, but priority one is a good public address system.

The resident manager assured me that the "house system" was top-notch. As we say in South Africa, "A1!"

I should have known.

Murphy's law is more than jest.

On opening day, I was surrounded by a hurricane of activity at the auditorium. Then the moment arrived. I turned on the house public address system.

It produced a fuzzy, tinny blur of unintelligible sound. I had a crisis on my hands. We were anticipating a crowd of 5,000. People from every management, motivational and personnel organization in the city were attending.

Dr. Peale enjoyed a huge following of people who had been helped by his writing. Groups as varied as I have ever known were enthusiastic about the one-night wonder of having the famed speaker, author and motivator in our city. And I was about to be the fall guy for the biggest blunder in motivational history.

Murphy's law: it went wrong, at the worst possible time.

The crisis called for every resource I could muster. Prayer, push and an ability to just think the problem through and find an answer.

It was do or die!

After several desperate phone calls, I located a sound engineer who agreed to come out to the Show Grounds immediately and install a system. And yes, it would cost a lot of money!

But my life was worth it.

The angel in overalls worked like a whirlwind, but we had our backs to the wall. In addition to the voice quality sound for Dr. Peale, we had to provide a patch-in for a vibraphone to be used by the lady vocalist in his party.

As the doomsday hour approached, I was sweating great drops. With minutes to spare, I ducked into a dressing room, changed from my grubbies into a suit and tie, and reappeared for my role as master of ceremonies. The public meetings called for a person who could direct the proceedings in both languages, English and Afrikaans, and I had been invited by Dr. Peale to be "it."

The crowd had gathered, the platform dignitaries were seated, and everything else was on schedule and on target. The auditorium was buzzing, the decor was great, ushers, book tables, and attendants and every other detail from parking lot to stage was in place.

Only one thing remained. As Dr. Peale and his troupe were ushered onto the platform I asked the technician to turn on the sound system for a check

The lady handed me her electric vibraphone with the question, "Will it work?"

I gulped, mopped my brow, and with my most reassuring smile I said, "Certainly!"

We plugged the cord into the amplifier on the stage, and like the breathless moment when the switch is thrown to light the Christmas tree in Rockefeller Plaza, we waited for the magic moment.

I stepped to the microphone, the lady strummed her harp, and yes, it all worked; perfectly!

I believed in miracles.

The opening was a smash hit. So was the tour.

But I would never want to live that moment again.

In January 1974, amid this flurry of activities, the unseen but ever-present hand of God was quietly shifting the gears of my whirling lifestyle.

I received an invitation from Phil Butler, of Intercristo, to be a speaker at the International Congress on World Evangelization in Lausanne, Switzerland, which was being sponsored by Dr. Billy Graham.

I went as a speaker, but came away profoundly affected. The appalling gap between the compelling words of Jesus, "Go ye into all the world" and the unfinished task of evangelism was sobering. With the thousands of other delegates, I too, was humbled to be faced with the economic, social and physical needs of the world's multitudes.

My address, delivered to the delegates in the media division of the congress, dealt with the use of the film as a tool in evangelism. Statistics revealed at the congress showed that of the four billion people in the world, more than half had never heard the Gospel.

Two measures appeared imperative to me as I viewed the challenge before the Christian church.

One, the task of telling our generation about Jesus could only be accomplished by a supernatural visitation of God's Holy Spirit in revival. Christians would, by multitudes, have to be shaken from their lethargy and personal preoccupations, anointed with power by the Holy Spirit and thrust out into the fields. Little did I realize what God was going to do with me!

The other, and equally important factor which became apparent to me, was that in order to accomplish the task of proclaiming the gospel "to all the world," we would have to avail ourselves of all existing legitimate means of communication.

Jenny had traveled with us to Switzerland while Dawson remained in South Africa to complete his statutory military training of eighteen months.

In the months prior to the Lausanne Congress, working with British contacts, we had laid a strategy similar to our South African campaign.

At personal risk, we had purchased the distribution rights of the film *The Cross and the Switchblade* for Great Britain and had arranged releases of the film in both 35 and 16 mm.; for public screening in cinemas and for rental to churches.

Following the Congress, the three of us, Ada, Jenny and I, continued on to Great Britain where we had organized evangelistic crusades in which Nicky Cruz shared his testimony.

In England, Scotland and Wales, following the steps of great men such as John Wesley, George Whitefield and D. L. Moody, we saw great numbers of young people come to know Jesus Christ as Savior.

In key locations, such as the Royal Albert Hall in London, locations in Edinburgh and Glasgow in Scotland and Cardiff in Wales, local Christians said they had not seen such meetings in their generation. Some likened the meetings to the days of the great evangelistic services of a century before.

One Scottish gentleman said to me; "We have not seen such meetings since the days of D. L. Moody."

I was misty-eyed as I pondered his words.

From the heady days in England, Ada, Jenny and I set out on a proposed six month visit to the United States during which it was our intention to raise financial support for the work of Go-Tell Communications.

Chapter Twenty-Six

ugust 7, 1974. We arrived in New York at the apex of the Watergate political crisis.

On our first night in the United States we watched the compelling emotion-charged drama as Richard Nixon resigned as President of the United States. It was a drama which was to cast a long shadow over the USA and, in turn, over our own lives.

Misfortune seemed to dog our every footstep. Our initial destination was Tulsa, Oklahoma, where we were to stay with friends, Paul and Connie McClendon. They had been guests in our home in South Africa when Paul, a professor at Oral Roberts University, had been on a sabbatical and had devoted time to aid Christian organizations in realizing the maximum use of media for spreading the Gospel.

A matter of weeks before our arrival, a tornado struck Tulsa. In the wake of its fury hundreds of homes were damaged and many people injured. The storm had almost passed the McClendons by, but had lifted the roof from their family room and damaged the house. They could not give us the hospitality they had hoped to share.

One of my first engagements was to fly to Clearwater, Florida, where Abe Thiessen, president of International Christian Broadcasters, had set up meetings for me with John Bostrom, the founder and director of Total Impact Corporation.

I was elated to meet people who shared the vision I had presented at Lausanne. My visit was exhilarating, encouraging.

Just before leaving Clearwater, John asked if there was anything he could do to help me. He was a businessman who also pastored a church. I deeply appreciated his gesture of concern.

"Yes"—there was something he could do.

During my travels with Nicky Cruz in England he had promised to let me have his used car when we arrived in the States. Because I had no credit and was not a resident, I could not obtain financing to purchase the car and in addition, I was not sure I could afford the monthly payments. When John offered his assistance I explained my dilemma and, in a gesture of generosity which I had never before witnessed, he offered to advance the money for the car without interest or security. We would be able to use the car until we departed from the States, then sell it and repay John.

I arrived back in Tulsa on September 24, Ada's birthday, and a few days later we set off in Nicky's Lincoln Mark IV to cover the USA.

I had mapped out a trip which would take us to most of our Christian film producers but along the way we planned meetings and church services from which we anticipated receiving financial support.

Income from church gifts, unfortunately, came nowhere near meeting the accumulating costs of our journeying, let alone bringing support for Go-Tell Communications, and we "began to be in want;" serious want. To crown it all, we were now in New York City.

Ada was distraught. We thought of our colleagues back in South Africa and our plight seemed to mock us. Assured of a comfortable living, secure in their homes and enjoying the ministry of international visitors, they were looking to us to provide a financial breakthrough for the ministry; and we didn't have enough to live on. We were glad when we could afford a hamburger!

We felt baffled and alone. There seemed to be no way back and no way forward. Like the children of Israel, trapped at the Red Sea, we were hemmed in. I recalled a scripture which Jim Downing had described graphically years previously at Glen Eyrie. It was Psalm 139:5, "thou has beset me behind and before, and laid thine hand upon me." I knew that only the hand of God could extricate us from this dilemma now.

Our deliverance came a few days later when Morry and Carol Ruddick, a couple we had met in Tulsa, sent us a letter of encouragement and a check for $300! It was the tithe from the sale of a motor home.

Working our way down the Eastern Seaboard, including a stop at Richmond, Virginia, to meet Pat Robertson at the Christian Broadcasting Network, we arrived in Florida in November 1974.

We had heard of a missionary home which offered housing to Christian workers at a nominal rate. We made application for admission, but found the conditions painfully primitive and the staff grim-faced and cold. At one of the chapel services the atmosphere was so frigid, the faces so unrelentingly harsh, that I said to Ada, "I would hate to be tried by this group of people for any offense."

We seized the first opportunity to escape from the icy, atmosphere and took a plunge of faith by renting a condominium in Clearwater on a six-month lease. We moved in the day before Christmas, feeling forlorn and alone. When the end of January loomed I did not have money to pay the $300 rent.

During December I had met a businessman at a church in Clearwater who had said, "If you ever need help, just let me know."

I needed help; and I let him know.

But I made a serious error in judgment in taking him at his word.

We sat at breakfast one morning and I confided my problem to him. Strangely, he seemed to relish my predicament, yet promised to think it over for a few days.

The outcome was a definite "No!" He did not feel "led" to help.

I felt crushed, vulnerable, alone. The experience reinforced in me the vital principle of faith, "It is better to trust in the Lord than to put confidence in men."(1) It was the same principle God wanted Israel to grasp, "You will learn that the Lord does not depend on weapons to fulfill his plans; he works without regard to human means!"(2)

Panic lurked in the recesses of my mind.

But I had been invited to speak at the annual conference of the National Religious Broadcasters in Washington, DC and I felt I should go; it seemed pointless to wait around in Florida.

At the Tampa Airport we shared our cash resources; Ada had $1, and I could muster 50¢.

With a sinking sensation I boarded my flight for Washington where I found the convention a hubbub of activity. I asked around and was finally offered a bed in a dormitory-type rooming house. There were three other men in the room and they shared their coffee and tea with me. I had no money for food.

The next morning I almost jumped for joy when I saw a South African friend in the lobby of the hotel where the convention was being staged. I wanted to hug him, I was so thrilled to see a familiar face, but my elation was short lived. He was hurrying to a meeting where they were drawing final plans for the Presidential Prayer Breakfast next morning and he cut me short with only curt and distant recognition. He went on to his meeting, leaving me in the foyer with a sinking feeling.

With a hollow feeling in the pit of my stomach I addressed my meeting, but God was not about to abandon me. At one of the display booths I met Jim Gilbert, an outstanding young musician and vocalist, who had previously toured South Africa with the Living Sound; a group which our organization had sponsored. Jim and his fiancée Dolly invited me to lunch.

That evening I stood at the doorway of the banqueting hall as the delegates sat down to the $15-a-plate dinner to listen to Billy Graham. I was asking, "God, what on earth am I doing here? Back in South Africa my friends have bread enough to spare, while I perish with hunger."

Next day our good friend, Ken Curtis, of Gateway films, offered me a welcome ride to Valley Forge in Pennsylvania where he put me up for the night at a motel. Before leaving I was forced to ask him to cash a check which I could not immediately cover, but I was believing God to do something special for me. I had several services booked, so I boarded a bus and headed west.

I made a stop in Ohio and called on an influential businessman and author. He had just returned from South Africa where Tony and Keith had arranged services and evangelistic meetings in which numbers of businessmen had come to know Christ through his witness. I never spoke of my need, but graciously he gave me a check sufficient to pay our rent for several months.

It was God's precious provision.

America was gloomy over the prospect of a recession and none of the avenues along which we hoped financial assistance would flow brought results, so, by July 1975 it was apparent Ada and I should return to South Africa.

We had, by then, finalized plans with evangelist Jimmy Swaggart for a visit to our country.

Tony and Keith had made all the arrangements for major crusades and on August 1, we flew from New York with Jimmy, his wife Francis and their team.

We left Jenny in America in the care of a Christian couple in Clearwater, Florida. Bob and Gay Duncan had offered to care for her while she completed high school.

Our parting from Jenny was tearful and deeply emotional, but we knew it to be for the best.

The bitterness of the separation was sweetened by one happy event. Just before our parting I baptized Jenny at Calvary Temple in Fort Wayne, Indiana. Pastor Paul Paino had been one of the few who had helped and supported our endeavors in a year of great trial.

Chapter Twenty-Seven

immy Swaggart was enormously popular long before he ever set foot on South African soil. Go-Tell Communications had released and sold thousands of his Gospel recordings.

A tumultuous welcome awaited the Swaggart team at the Johannesburg airport.

Under the organizing auspices of Go-Tell Communications, the major Pentecostal denominations had joined forces for the Crusade. In an unprecedented display of cooperation, Christians from varied persuasions united to believe and work for a mighty moving of God's Spirit.

The meetings were charged with excitement and anticipation, but the South African winter was bitter.

As the temperatures dipped below zero every night in Johannesburg, we witnessed a touch of humor. Each evening, at about 8:30, the icy fingers of cold night air seemed to envelope the audience in the huge, barn-like tabernacle. The members of Jimmy's band huddled behind him on the platform, snuggling under blankets which they had smuggled out of their hotel rooms!

In spite of the blasts of the winter wind, we saw the Wind of God, the Holy Spirit, move in heart-warming and life-changing power. We saw crowds of up to 15,000 come nightly; the largest audiences ever to attend indoor religious gatherings in South Africa.

A poignant incident occurred, which served again to remind me personally of the love, mercy and miracle of redemption in my own life.

During my closing years in high school, one of my most bitter antagonists was an aggressive, belligerent fellow named Ken. He was always spoiling for a fight and, as a thorn in my side, had goaded and angered me continuously. After high school he passed from my life until the wet, wintry, last night of the crusade meetings in Durban.

My crusade responsibilities demanded that I remain at the stadium long after the audience had drifted away.

That night, a bedraggled, forlorn tramp sought me out.

He wanted to see Jimmy personally. His request was insistent, pleading, urgent. I told him that Jimmy had long since left the stadium and would already be in bed.

The man began to sob. He said he knew he could be delivered from alcoholism if only Jimmy would lay hands on him and pray for him. He told how for years he had listened to the singer-evangelist's records and had long felt that this man could bring him healing. I heeded his pathetic pleas.

From a call-box I phoned Jimmy, who was already in bed at the hotel, but he graciously consented to get dressed and come down and see the man.

On the ride to the city I was nauseated by the derelict's stench. He was unwashed and reeking from booze and had vomited over his clothes. I wanted to retch, but mercifully we arrived at the hotel before I was overcome.

Under the bright light of the marquee of the hotel entrance I was jolted to recognition. The evil-smelling man next to me was my former high school antagonist—Ken!

Once back in my room, a wave of emotion swept over me: compassion for the wasted life of my old rival; joy and gratitude for what a gracious God, a heavenly Father, had done for me!

At the beginning of 1976 South Africa was heading for disaster; economically and politically. The recession, which had crippled the American economy through 1974 and 1975, had spread to our country.

Go-Tell Communications fared badly. We suffered severe setbacks on three fronts.

First, we reeled under the financial losses caused by sponsoring musical groups from America.

Then the bottom fell out of the entertainment market with the long-awaited advent of television. With TV sets selling for $1,000 each, there was little left to spend on Christian records and tapes. Restaurants were abandoned and many businesses failed. The number of bankruptcies in 1976 was surpassed only by that of the Great Depression in the years from 1930 to 1934.

Thirdly, film rentals plunged. With TV commanding the attention of the public, there were fewer calls for Christian films.

At the same time, I was personally fighting growing discouragement and weariness from the chronic pain in my back, right leg and foot.

My physical handicap was etched in bold relief against the backdrop of the South African conflict. Ada and I were traveling by car one stormy night when rain and mist delayed us for hours, causing us to arrive at our scheduled overnight stop in the rural town of Ermelo at about 1:00 a.m.

In the foyer of the hotel was a bawdy group of young Afrikaans men. They were obviously intoxicated; their raucous laughter and coarse speech jarred the night air. When Ada walked past, they made obscene remarks and leered at her. I reacted with a muted, "Watch your words."

It was like a battle cry. Instantly the gang of about six young ruffians closed in and threatened to fight me. I was backed against the elevator door with the leader raising his fist in my face and threatening to beat me up. His brave cohorts egged him on. Only the prompt action of the desk clerk saved us. He jumped into the circle, shoved the belligerent thugs aside and got us into the elevator while his assistant called the police.

Once in the room I realized, with humbling clarity, what it meant to be physically weak and disabled.

But the show had to go on!

Each Sunday afternoon we rented the massive, 2,000-seat Colosseum Cinema in Johannesburg. We advertised extensively and showed major motion pictures with a religious theme. At the close of each film we brought a short gospel message followed by an invitation offering viewers an opportunity to receive Christ as Savior.

One Sunday, as I stood on the huge stage, with the spotlight shining on me, I asked the audience to be still, bow their heads and participate with me in a prayer of repentance and faith.

There was a stillness, but just as I began to pray, a shot from an air gun broke the silence. I felt the lead hit me on the right side of my chest.

I said, "Someone in the audience has just shot me with an air gun."

A gasp went up. I continued, "I don't know who you are, the spotlight is blinding me, so I cannot see. But I want to tell you, whoever you are, Jesus loves you. If you will let Him, He will forgive you and save you."

The gathering broke up with more than the usual excitement. A large group of seekers streamed to the front of the auditorium to be counseled and prayed for.

As I was gathering the inquirers, two young men half dragged a sobbing boy into the circle of light. He was visibly shaking, crying and saying repeatedly,

"I didn't do it; I didn't do it!"

The terrified youngster had been nabbed running down the broad curved stairway which swept up from the foyer to the balcony. Stuffed in his trouser leg the pursuers had found a large, powerful air pistol.

The police had been summoned, and close on their heels, a press photographer arrived.

Next morning, the daily newspaper flashed the headline "Preacher Shot, Prays On!"

I declined to press charges, remembering my own youthful days. Instead, I visited the boy and his father to find out the mother had abandoned the family. The boy's father was in distress, and could not control his son. I had the joy of introducing the teenager to the same Savior who had changed my life.

Miraculously, mysteriously the boy and his father were living —in Mayfair. The very place where I had lived through so many escapades when I was the same age.

The mercy, the goodness of God, the power of the Gospel were demonstrated to me again!

In spite of mounting physical weakness and fatigue, I allowed myself to be drawn into another taxing situation.

Morris Cerullo had been invited to South Africa in the afterglow of the Jimmy Swaggart Crusade, but the organizers of the Cerullo crusade could not meet Cerullo's exacting demands. There were serious problems, one of which was a woefully inadequate public address system. To go to a secular company would have cost thousands, so the South African sponsors appealed to us. The first approach was made to Tony.

He called me on Friday and said, "Peter, the organizers are desperate; they have asked if we will set up our public address system for their two stadium meetings tomorrow and Sunday."

The decision lay with me, because I was the only one who had the experience and expertise to set up and operate the highly complex, costly system. For Tony's sake, and for the witness of the Gospel, I agreed.

From the outset, I was confronted by major obstacles and found myself on the receiving end of a long list of negatives.

The sound system had to be loaded on the truck that same afternoon, but, without adequate warning, it was difficult to get help. I had to carry and unload the innumerable parts of the massive equipment with only our faithful office helper, Simon, to assist me. It was hard labor!

And the weather! It seemed we always had to contend with rain when we had outdoor stadium crusades.

Saturday morning dawned wet and bleak. I encountered problems from the moment I drove the truck into the stadium early in the morning. It rained continuously hour after hour.

For the next two days I worked like a lackey over cables, controls and consoles. Huddled inside the sound truck, cramped and tired, I bore the brunt of irate and unreasonable demands from every quarter and I asked myself a thousand times, "How did you let yourself in for this thankless task?"

The pace of life in Go-Tell Communications was furious. I had helped to open a trap in which I was myself now caught. It became necessary to travel with musical groups, often doing the menial work of hauling gigantic sound systems, setting them up for concerts, driving the truck and still being prepared to preach at some of the meetings. Frustrated, tired and aching, I found my days had become a weary round of joyless, frenzied activity.

Chapter Twenty-Eight

une 16, 1976 will live in my memory.

Like a volcano that had for years been silently brooding, violence erupted in South Africa. Tens of thousands of young blacks spewed out the pent-up hatred and bitterness of generations.

With a fury never before unleashed, students looted, killed and destroyed in unrestrained abandon. They burned schools, hospitals, community buildings, homes, motor vehicles—any unprotected symbol of authority. It was a vicious outburst that rocked the nation and propelled the problems of South Africa onto the front pages of newspapers around the world. By the time the riots had been quelled, the anarchy had left hundreds dead and the nation reeling under the impact. Stunned by the vicious outburst, people were left groping for answers.

Circumstances were also building to a crisis in my own life.

We were expecting Dr. Herb Bowdoin, of Methodist Hour International, to arrive in August with a team of American lay witnesses.

Tony and I decided that I should take the full responsibility for preparing the thirteen churches participating in this program because during our stay in the USA in 1974–75, Ada and I had laid plans for this crusade with Dr. Bowdoin. I gladly assumed the task now of preparing the South African churches. It required commuting back and forth on numerous occasions between Johannesburg and Durban, the two cities chosen for the mission, a distance of 400 miles.

I decided also that Ada and I should leave our beautiful home in Johannesburg and move permanently to Durban. The Johannesburg office was facing serious financial crises and Tony and I often went for months without drawing a salary.

The net was closing. It was our intention to expand our operations and I would trust God to bring my support in through our work in Durban. We made our move in June, 1976.

That same month, the riots in Soweto rocked the nation.

The country reeled under the blows as violence and bloodshed broke out in other concentrations of black peoples across the country. The scare intimidated would-be visitors and the number of lay witnesses which Herb Bowdoin was bringing from America dropped from an expected two hundred to a mere fifty-three.

But we proceeded with our plans.

The venture succeeded beyond expectation. Filled with love, devoted to Jesus Christ and showing their compassion by paying their own way to come to South Africa, the Americans won their way into the affections of the South African people. In home meetings, in personal contact and in church services, their ebullient witness reflected a vibrant experience with Christ which affected the lives of all who met them.

At the conclusion of the missions in both Johannesburg and Durban, Go-Tell Communications staged two mass rallies at which Dr. Bowdoin preached the Gospel. When the two week mission was ended, we saw grown South African men weep as they told of what God had done in their lives.

The movement of God's Spirit known as Lay Witness Missions was born on South African Soil.

Ada and I firmly believed the move to Durban and the resounding success of the lay witness mission would turn our financial crisis around. It didn't. Over the four months in which I worked preparing for the mission, I traveled thousands of miles, ministered in the churches which participated in the mission and met with their leaders. We handled the distribution of the materials and organized the public meetings.

We waited for a breakthrough. We waited in vain—it never came.

At the end of September, Dawson phoned from Johannesburg where he was preparing to write his end-of-year examinations at the University of the Witwatersrand. He said, "Dad, I can't write my exams because you haven't paid my fees! We still owe $300!"

That was it! I said, "Lord, I'm through! I quit!"

In the depth of despondency I cried out, "God, if I had worked for anybody else as hard as I have worked for you these twenty-two years, I wouldn't be in this predicament!"

It was a Thursday night. I spoke to Ada with a mixture of frustration, weariness, indignation and anxiety. I said, "Honey, it's all over. Tomorrow I am going to close the Durban office. I am going to give it all up. I am going back to secular employment."

She was hurt also. She had believed God for a miracle; and now this! We agreed that there was no point in continuing. The only way out seemed to be the abandonment of the path which we had pursued since that day in April 1955, when we had taken our vows together.

Friday morning I phoned Tony in Johannesburg. My voice was weary with fatigue and disappointment, but my tone was final. I called my secretary, Juliet Middleton, and told her the news. The hardest part of all was when I had to phone my Indian co-laborer, Gabrielle, with the news that all the staff was dismissed.

It was midnight in our souls.

Jenny had graduated from high school in Clearwater, Florida and was now home with us. She was pursuing a career as a beautician in Durban and when I picked her up that Friday afternoon I found her inconsolable. She was deeply distressed by the turn of events and wept brokenly.

Saturday found us at rock bottom. It seemed as though the end of our world had come.

My mind turned towards the gold mines. I determined I would go back and appeal for the position I had abandoned in 1955.

Ada spoke a solemn word of warning. Though just as distraught by the turn of events as I was, she nevertheless declared, "If you leave the ministry and abandon your calling, God will remove His hand of protection from you. And you don't know what will become of you."

Chapter Twenty-Nine

e were renting a house on the Natal north coast which looked out over the beaches and took in the rolling hills, the snowy white houses and the sparkling Indian Ocean. Days were sunny and warm. It was an idyllic spot.

However, on that Sunday morning in October 1976, following our black Friday, a pall of gloom hung over our home. I was defeated, miserable, out of touch with God. As usual, Ada and I reclined on our beds to observe our daily time of Bible reading and prayer together. A practice we had faithfully followed from the first day of our marriage. We had observed the opening and closing of each day as a time of mutual encouragement as we read God's Word and prayed. It was one of the cornerstones of our married life.

Jenny joined us in our room and the three of us read from the Bible. Gerald Griffiths, who had been our pastor at the Rosebank Union Church, had often admonished us with the words, "The Bible is God's manual for living. It is the Manufacturer's Handbook." As I took the manual to read that morning, my reading was purely perfunctory. There was no feeling, no inspiration. The future was a blank.

A dozen times those past hours we had asked, "Why?" We could not understand how a loving heavenly Father could bring us to this predicament. We felt friendless, forsaken, and there was no one to whom we could go for counsel, help or prayer.

I felt I was heading into a period of darkness more dreadful than any I had known before. It all seemed such a mockery. I questioned the whole basis of divine guidance and, finally, God's will.

I said again, "I am going to find a job, a job outside of Christian work and just do my own thing." Inwardly I echoed the lament of hopelessness uttered by King Solomon, "Vanity of vanities; all is vanity."(1)

I lay back on the bed, feeling dull and listless. It seemed that every event had led to broken cisterns; that the waters mocked me as they drained away.

Then, like a flash of sunlight, the Word of God broke through to me and, as He did with Saul of Tarsus, the Lord confronted me.

It was as though I heard an audible voice,

"Have you forgotten my words to you? `I the Lord have called you in righteousness, and will hold your hand; I will keep you, and give you for a covenant of the people, for a light to the Gentiles; to open the blind eyes, to bring out the prisoners from the prison, and them that sit in darkness out of the prison house!"(2)

From the inner reaches of my heart God brought into the sunlight the words He had spoken to me before,

"You are my witness, says the Lord, and my servant whom I have chosen: That you may know me, and believe me, and understand that I am He. I, even I, am the Lord; and beside me there is no Savior...."(3)

"Have you not known? Have you not heard? The everlasting God, the Lord, the Creator of the ends of the earth, fainteth not, neither is weary? There is no searching of His understanding.

He gives power to the faint; and to them that have no might He increases strength...they that wait upon the Lord shall renew their strength; they shall mount up with wings as eagles; they shall run, and not be weary; and they shall walk, and not faint."(4)

God spoke to me with the clear voice of authority, "I saved you when you were lost. I spared your life when you were dying. I raised you up from a wheelchair and called you to be my witness. I told you then 'fear not, for I am with you: do not be dismayed; for I am your God: I will strengthen you, I will help you, I will uphold you with my right hand...for I the Lord your God will hold your right hand, saying, Fear not; I will help you. Behold, I will make you a new sharp threshing instrument having teeth.'"(5)

It happened in a flash. I saw, in a moment of time, that I could not forsake the ministry to which God had called me. He had saved me and had called me to be His servant, to preach His Word. I suddenly realized I had no alternative, I must go on.

I jumped off the bed and said to Ada and Jenny, "God has spoken to me; I know what He wants me to do. I must return to my calling. God wants me to preach His Word."

Ada said, "Where will you go?" I instinctively knew I could not hope for sustenance as an itinerant preacher in South Africa.

I replied, "God wants me to go to America!" It was a revelation from God; a light piercing the darkness.

It took a few seconds for this to register with Ada, then she said, "I know that's right. I will not stand in your way: you must go."

The transformation was electrifying. One moment I had been in darkest despair; the next instant I was radiant with the light of God's presence. Psalm 34 declares, "I cried to the Lord and He answered me! He freed me from all my fears. Others too were radiant at what He did for them. Theirs was no downcast look of rejection! This poor man cried to the Lord, and the Lord heard him and saved him out of his troubles."

It was happening to me.

I went to my study and I knew the Holy Spirit was with me. He was flowing over me, through me and filling me with love, light, joy and power.

Years before in the church in Fish Hoek, in 1957, I had asked the Holy Spirit by faith to fill me. For years I had walked in that faith, believing I had been filled because I had asked on the basis and the promise of the Lord Jesus. I knew that, "We walk by faith, and not by sight."(6)

But oh, the joy of that moment when faith became sight and hope became experience.

I felt it in my heart and I knew that the Spirit of God was doing a fresh work of grace in my life. For years I had known that many great men of God, such as D. L. Moody and Charles G. Finney had experienced mighty subsequent anointings of the Holy Spirit and here I was, nearly thirty years after my conversion, after many years of walking by faith, experiencing a surge of joy, release and fullness, such as I had never known before. I began to sing.

I put a record on the stereo. The song was Annie Johnson Flint's hymn:

He giveth more grace when the burdens grow greater,
He sendeth more strength when the labors increase;
To added affliction, He addeth His mercy,
To multiplied trials, His multiplied peace,

His Love has no limit; His grace has no measure;
His power has no boundary known unto men;
For out of His infinite riches in Jesus,
He giveth and giveth and giveth again!

And I began to praise God.

I exulted, "Lord, thank You for making Your face to shine upon me. Thank You for speaking to me. Thank You for removing my burden. Thank You for the joy and the liberty and the peace which now is mine in the Holy Spirit. I know, I know, today, that You have filled me with your Holy Spirit and with Your Power."

My spirit glowed with happiness and I asked the Lord for two special gifts.

I said, "Lord, I want to know You. I want to understand the deep things of God. I want You to reveal to me the hidden secrets of Your Word. Lord, I want the gift of wisdom. Then, Lord, I want power to proclaim those secrets which You reveal to me. From this day forward, Lord, I want to know the unfailing anointing of Your Holy Spirit every time I stand to speak in Your name."

I said, "Like the apostles of the New Testament, when they were all filled with the Holy Spirit, I want to speak the Word of God with boldness…and with great power."(7)

I was asking God for something different from anything I had ever known before.

From a worldly point of view, I had accomplished many things. I had been to seminary, I had studied Greek, Hebrew and theology. I had preached hundreds of sermons, conducted seminars and Bible studies. I had memorized Scriptures and written papers. I had been an evangelist, a teacher, a pastor and a lecturer. I had won people to Christ and served the Lord in full-time ministry for more than twenty years, but, this day, God was doing "a new thing."(8)

The past years had been invaluable in gaining experience. I had discovered how to promote, organize and manage major evangelistic crusades. The scale of past operations had been enormous, with thousands won to Christ through the Gospel preached on radio, in print, in cinemas, theaters, stadiums and auditoriums across the country. But now, God said to me, *"Enough!"* "Be still and know that I am God."(9)

In the hustle and bustle of life and Christian activity, I had drifted so far away from God's best for my life that He had to use drastic measures to bring me back to the pristine clearness of my early call.

In an act of total commitment, I said, "Lord, I am willing to give you my life anew; I surrender to you, now, all that I am, all that I have. I will live for you; if need be, I will die for you. But God, I'll never again do anything other than preach your Word."

For many years I had carried around in my preaching notebook a poem by Oswald J. Smith. But that Sunday morning, it became the living experience of my heart:

Lord, anoint me with Thy Spirit!
Fill me with Thy power divine,
Take away the love of sinning,
Make, oh, make me wholly Thine!

Lord, anoint me with Thy Spirit,
As I wait and watch and pray;
Grant a pentecost from Heaven,
Send, oh, send Him Lord today.

I am hungry for thy fullness,
I am thirsting Lord for Thee;
Fill, oh, fill me with Thy Spirit —
Wholly Thine I want to be.

I am praying, waiting, trusting,
For the power of pentecost;
Lord, anoint me with Thy Spirit —
Send Him now at any cost.

Savior, cleanse and make me holy,
Burn out every base desire;
Fill, oh, fill me with Thy Spirit—
Lord, anoint and send the fire.

Lo, He comes, the Holy Spirit,
Now with joy my soul is thrilled;
Glory! Glory! Hallelujah!
All my heart with love is filled!

Worldly things no longer lure me,
I am Thine and Thine alone;
All I have is on the altar,
And my heart is now Thy throne.

Chapter Thirty

The hours passed by rapidly. Before I left my study I spoke again to the Lord.

I said, "Father, You have said in Your Word concerning spiritual gifts, that, 'One and the same Spirit works all these things, distributing to each one individually...but earnestly desire the best gifts.' Lord, I am open to any gift and work which You want to do, in sovereign grace, in my life."(1)

But I vowed I would not be seduced by anything which was not truly of God.

I had encountered great problems and, subsequently, had serious reservations about many of the things which I saw perpetrated in the name of the Holy Spirit and His fullness. I had often looked at the inconsistencies and living hypocrisy of many who claimed the baptism of the Holy Spirit and I had said, "If that's what it is, I don't want it." These excesses and inconsistencies had caused me to be more than cautious; almost cynical.

A couple of years previously we had encountered a problem in Johannesburg.

A group of people, who described themselves as Spirit-baptized Jesus people, had held a street meeting in one of the public malls in Hillbrow, the densely populated, cosmopolitan section of Johannesburg.

The police had arrested a bunch of them for trespassing and the situation had threatened to become ugly, because, following the incident, the weekend newspapers had carried headlines heralding the trespassers as "martyrs."

It seemed as though a great crowd would gather the next Saturday night to share the dubious honor of being "imprisoned for Christ." They were clearly in the wrong because they had violated the city bylaws and intruded on the privacy of citizens by being rowdy and unruly in the courtyard of a public shopping mall.

Who cared? They were being hailed as "heroes."

The mayor of Johannesburg, Dr. A. D. Bensusan, had called me to his home and we discussed the situation with the chief of police. They knew me and felt that, as a Christian leader in the community, I could bring reason to the situation.

I agreed to do what I could. I put out an appeal on radio and through the city newspapers, asking the Christians not to congregate on public property, to respect the privacy of shoppers and residents and to refrain from the threatened show of strength.

The police agreed to stay away.

The next Friday night I was there, a lone figure, as I cautiously walked around the mall.

It was eerie. The atmosphere in the mall was like the movie set of *High Noon*. People lurked in doorways and stared out from shop windows. The media attention had set the scene for an expected "shoot-out."

The onlookers were not disappointed.

The leaders of these zealous Jesus people stayed away for about an hour, praying themselves into readiness, then suddenly appeared.

The situation was tense as they quickly assembled in a group and, in defiance of city ordinances, police appeals and my mediation, began to sing, raucously accompanied by music which blared from a hastily erected portable sound system. The noise was ear-shattering, causing people in their apartments to throw open the windows and glare down on the martyrs-in-the-making.

Suddenly, one of the more vociferous and antagonistic young men stood out from the crowd and began to shout threats of judgment, hell-fire and doom on the passers-by.

I stepped forward to talk with him, when, without warning, the pastor's wife attacked me. They had concluded, rightly, that I would not fight back against a woman.

She began to shove, hit and verbally abuse me. She clobbered me with her long-handled purse, calling me, "Satan's tool" and "the devil's instrument."

When this diversion subsided, the crowd drifted away and the zealots disbanded. The crisis was over, but I was forever affected.

I knew I did not want to emulate their behavior.

But, now on this pivotal Sunday I felt the warm glow of the Spirit's love in me. I knew He had endued me with new power: that warmth, love and power I did not want to resist!

On Monday morning I phoned Tony in Johannesburg and said to him, "God has told me to go to America and preach the gospel."

He asked, "When will you leave?"

"In four weeks time—at the end of October."

I began immediate preparation for my departure. Many of the lay witnesses who had recently visited South Africa had extended invitations to me to visit in their homes and preach in their churches. I could see clearly, now, the hand of God moving me in this direction.

However, there was the usual obstacle.

Tony voiced it. He phoned me Tuesday morning and asked, "How are you going to pay for your trip? You haven't been paid a salary for four or five months and there is no money in Go-Tell Communications."

I came back with an answer which expressed my new-found joy, power and freedom. I said, "Tony, I am just going to believe God to send me the money."

His encouragement heartened me. He said, "Peter, if that's what you believe God wants you to do, do it."

At ten o'clock that same morning I had a telephone call from the Rev. Arnold Walker, author and editor of the devotional, *Faith for Daily Living*. I had been working with him on his upcoming visit to the United States, planning a tour which would take him to see some of his American readers, as well as a few of the American scenic wonders.

He was due to leave in four days' time. He invited me to call at his office at 11:00 a.m.

At the appointed hour, I sat across the desk from Arnold Walker, my emotions alternating between disbelief, joy, tears and laughter, as he said, "Peter, I have talked with my executive committee and we want to pay your airfare for a round trip to America."

It was like a thunderbolt.

The crises of the past days evaporated.

Like old grave clothes, the stifling unbelief of the past months fell away. Now I knew the Holy Spirit had done a new work in my life. When I had previously traveled to America, I had labored for years afterwards to pay the bills. Now God was saying, "Trust me and you will see signs and wonders following."

The days passed swiftly as I wrote letters and made contact with people in the USA. My plans called for my being away from South Africa for about four months.

Ada was willing to let me go because she knew it was God's will. The provision of my airfare was confirmation to her and we were moving in a new dimension of faith and obedience.

But two weeks before my departure date the full realization of what was happening dawned upon her. She was being asked to move from the house we were renting and would have to return to her parents for three months while I was gone.

The exact pattern of our future was uncertain. Depression overtook her; in fourteen more days she would be adrift upon a sea of insecurity, alone.

Distressed and dejected, she prayed, "God you have done a great thing for Peter, but what about me? Lord, I have given my life to be his wife, his partner and his helper. I have loved him, cared for him, nursed him. In good times and in bad, I have stuck with him; we have done everything together. And now, must I be left to fend for myself?"

She cried in her desolation, "Lord, speak to me from heaven, send me an angel or give me a vision."

She went down to the beach, one of her favorite places to meditate and talk with the Lord. That day the sky was heavy with moisture and the wind whipped the fine misty rain into her eyes. She went back home, her heart as heavy as the skies.

Sitting on the sofa, she wept in an agony of spirit and said, "God, you must speak to me." In reply, He said, "I speak to you through my Word. Go to your bedroom and read your Bible."

She had read through the Bible once already that year and was reading it through again.

Taking up where she had left off that morning she now read, "Since the Lord is directing your steps, why try to understand everything that happens along the way?" She accepted the word of admonition from the Lord and read on.

She then came to the words, "Don't envy evil men but continue to reverence the Lord at all times, for surely you have a wonderful future ahead of you. There is hope for you yet."(2)

The effect on her was electrifying.

She was transformed.

When I came home, she was radiant, bursting with confidence and faith. She knew God had prepared a wonderful future for her.

Indeed He had! Six days before I was to leave we visited our beloved friend, Michael Cassidy, in his Africa Enterprise office in Pietermaritzburg. Mike listened as we recalled the events of the past weeks and at the conclusion he said, "Peter, I don't believe it is God's will for you to leave Ada for four months."

He turned to Ada and said, "What would keep you from going with Peter?"

She replied, "Nothing, except the money."

Mike said, "Ada, you go out and buy a ticket to go with Peter. Send me the bill. We will write to some of your friends and ask them to help. Together we will trust God to send the money for your passage."

My mother—a picture taken about 1942.

A wartime picture—1943 or 1944. My brother Theo and me with our dad Sam Church.

In 1949 I was appointed Senior Drum Major of the Witwatersrand Command cadet bands. This photograph appeared in the Star on Sept. 28, 1949 — I am closest to the camera.

Very few photographs are taken of me in my youth but, Maurice Kirk was on band to take this picture at the Band Competition in 1949.

Winning the mile at a school track meeting.

In 1949 I also captained the school rifle team which won the West Rand Bisley Competition. I am in the back row on the left next to the teacher.

Our high school track team in 1949. I am seated fourth from the left on the row of chairs. Six months after this picture was taken I was a broken invalid in the Chamber of Mines Hospital.

A casual snap-shot taken by one of the students in 1949 shows me heaving the weight in the shot-put competition.

Refined gold bars at the Rand Refinery. One day's production.

Drilling deep below the surface on a South African gold mine. The gold-bearing ore is blasted free and hauled to the surface for treatment. I was in a similar working area when the roof caved in.

Ice cream at the Zoo Lake. My first
outing from the hospital. This casual
picture, taken by Maurice Kirk is the
only photo ever taken which shows the
leg irons, boots and crutches with which I
battled my way back from helplessness.
I am also wearing a special brace to
support my back.

A snapshot taken about 9 months after
the mine accident. Notice the leg iron and
the swollen condition of my left knee.

Ada and I were married on April 16, 1955.

Left to right: Johnny Buchler, Maurice Kirk, myself and Merold Stern.

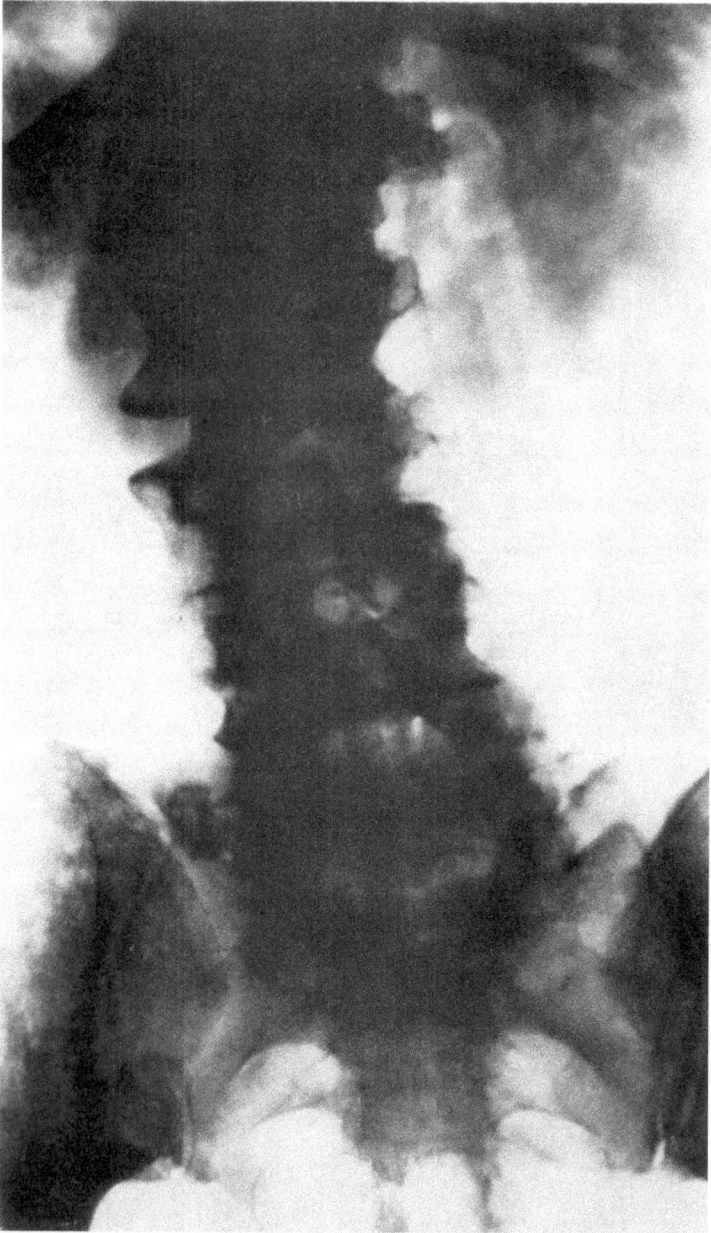

Not a flattering picture! The scoliosis (twisting of the spine) which resulted from the rockfall. This picture gives the reader some idea of the disability which has so dramatically changed my life.

My sister Hilda in London — 1958.

My brother Ed as an airforce cadet in 1959.

My brother Ed as a lifeguard on Cannon Beach in 1962.

Ed and Sondra — he met her at Moody Bible Institute, and they were married in California where they studied at Biola College.

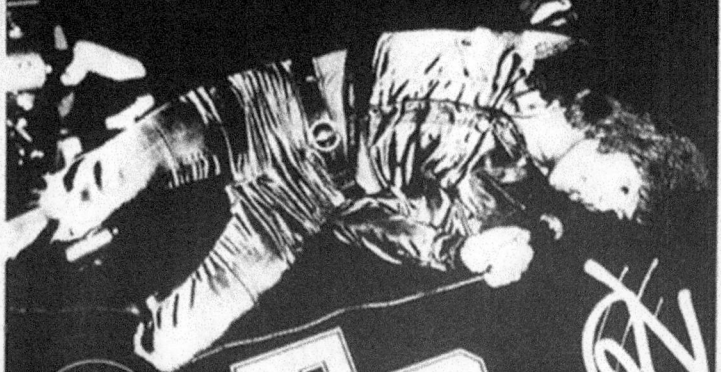

A poster advertising Cliff Richard & Band.

Ada and I.

Our daughter Jenny.

Our son Dawson.

With Angela, Lionel and Dawson in 2011.

Part II

Prelude

n Wednesday, July 16, 1997, I nosed the car through the city of Johannesburg, South Africa, which had once been as familiar to me as the back of my hand. It had been the playground of my youth. Now I felt as though I had landed on a different planet. I was a stranger where once I had been at home. An eerie sense of unreality engulfed me. Unfamiliarity hovered about the streets and buildings, once noble edifices that had been powerful symbols of stability and permanence to a boy seeking exactly that.

Today, Johannesburg in the tense grip of the social tensions and upheavals of the "New South Africa" seemed a shadowy, almost a ghostlike parody of what it had been. Apart from the natural change that overtakes all earthly things, the "City of Gold" was tarnished now and clearly suffering decay. A once familiar world had changed for me and worse than that, a foreboding disquiet and uneasiness was growing in me as it dawned on me that I was lost! Someone, somewhere I had missed an old landmark; or had it been moved? Or had it, one wondered sadly, disintegrated, succumbing to the relentless effects of the passage of time?

I wanted to stop and ask for directions as I maneuvered the borrowed car through the throngs of people that crowded the intersections. But friends welcoming me to the world's new high-crime capital had sternly cautioned: "Don't roll your windows down; Don't stop to talk to anyone; Always keep the car in gear; Keep your doors locked." There I was—imprisoned in a borrowed car, lost, and with no one to turn to for help.

I turned the radio on. It crackled as I pushed a button, and suddenly a familiar voice was giving the signature monologue to a talk show, plunging me into overwhelming nostalgia as the speaker reminisced about days gone by—days I myself had shared with him.

The voice belonged to my friend and erstwhile colleague, John Burks, with whom I had enjoyed the richest of companionships as together we had launched our broadcast careers with the wildly popular youth station LM Radio in the early sixties. It just so happened that on that particular day, July 16th, John was celebrating the anniversary of his debut in 1964. He invited anyone who remembered those good old days to call in and reminisce with him about the fads and fashions of that bygone year. I looked around anxiously for some haven from which a call could be made.

Ah! There it was! The fortified campus of the Rand Mutual Hospital. I swung the car into the parking lot and rushed to a pay phone. The call went through, and suddenly the years seemed to melt away as John and I talked about that halcyon era when the broadcast I had produced and geared for youth each Sunday morning on the landmark station of LM Radio had been the joy of my heart. But the euphoria of that renewed touch with John did not end there. There was a spin-off from that on-air encounter that was to bless me with even greater joy. A tapestry woven in living color by the hand of the God who is able to do seemingly impossible things began to unfold. It would bring fresh encouragement and motivation to continue faithful in one's quest to know and do the will of God. It would demonstrate the awesome ability of the Almighty to orchestrate the circumstances of life for His glory.

Just eleven days before, I had received a phone call from my sister-in-law, Pal in Pretoria, South Africa to say that her husband, Pastor Ed Roebert, had collapsed from a heart attack and had died almost immediately. This had happened at 8 o'clock in the morning just as 5,000 participants in an International Conference on World Evangelism were massing for a march from the Union Buildings to the City Square in Pretoria.

The news of Ed Roebert's death jolted the nation. Newspapers across the country carried front-page headlines and National TV News reports made people across the land aware that a great leader in the Christian community had suddenly been taken from them.

Twenty four hours later, and accompanied by my daughter Jenny, I flew from the USA to Africa. We would represent our family at the funeral and be available to the Roebert family to serve them in any way we could.

Which is how I came to be now driving through the streets of a city I had once known but had left so many years before. Listening in to the impromptu exchange between John and me on the air that anniversary day was a lady who had worked as a controller and producer for our programs on LM Radio thirty-four years earlier. Hearing John welcome me back to South Africa had her on her feet jumping for joy. Why the glee?

When Noeleen Tocker had worked as the controller for my program, *Faith for Our Times*, she had not been a believer. In fact, she was being consumed by her determined pursuit of happiness through self-indulgence, living solely for her own pleasure. It was the Sixties, the days of the Now generation, the "Me first" people; the era of Elvis, the Beatles, the mini skirt.

I was staying with Pal in Pretoria when, a few days after the on-air trip down Memory Lane with John, Pal called me from my room, and said, "There is someone to see you."

I walked into the living room. For a moment I was non-plussed, but when she gave her name it all came flooding back. "I'm Noeleen Tocker. Do you remember me? I used to control for you and John Burks at LM Radio." Then, her whole story bubbled out like the refreshing dance of a flowing stream. Years after my departure Noeleen had come into a personal experience of life-giving faith in Jesus Christ.

Now she was pouring encouragement into my spirit as she related that in the days when I came and went in the studio she had had no idea of the physical traumas I had undergone and what challenges had dogged my footsteps. But evidently my witness in conduct and words had dramatically affected her and prepared her for the day when she would hear the Savior at the door of her heart and, hearing His knock, invite Him into her life.(1)

Then, she read this book. She had been deeply touched, hoping that one day she would have the chance to see me again and so be able to thank me in person. In a remarkable engineering of circumstances, that day had been granted by the unseen, but Almighty hand of God.

It is Noeleen's story, and the many others like hers, that have prompted the conviction and given me the courage to write the second half of this book. It is my prayer that God's goodness to me will be an inspiration to you.

As we each pursue our own pilgrimage, none of us knows where the seed we sow will take root and spring up, how it will be watered, or when and by whom it will be harvested. Sometimes God permits us to catch a glimpse of His mysterious ways, but in the great scheme of living, He calls us simply to be diligent, to be faithful in the use of our talents and then to leave the yielding of the increase to His all-wise and loving care.(2) How true the words of St. Paul: "It is required in stewards that a man be found faithful."(3)

I pray that the account of God's love, faithfulness and all-wise providences as recorded in these pages will help some other fellow pilgrim, some tempest-tossed traveler to be steadied, encouraged, built up and made strong. In the end, when the shadows have fled and full light of understanding dawns, we will all be able to say, "He knows the way that I take, when He has tried me, I shall come forth as gold."(4)

Chapter Thirty-One

"You are going to die." It was September 21st, 1993, three days before Ada's birthday.

It was September 21st, 1993, three days before Ada's birthday. We were in the consulting rooms of Dr. Brent Norman in Santa Ana in Orange County, California. His crisp, dignified business card announced him as a specialist in Diseases of the Retina and Vitreous. The tension in the air was almost tangible; a cloud of apprehension enshrouded us like the foreboding atmosphere before a heavy storm.

Hospitals and doctor's rooms have a profound emotional effect on one's mental state. They spawn anxiety, nervousness, sweating palms and bring a knot to the stomach. Even strong men faint at the sight of a doctor's needle. Who has not felt the icy finger of fear when facing the uncertainty of a critical medical investigation?

We were waiting for the doctor to give us an answer to a question which lurked deep in the recesses of our hearts. Ada had asked the physician to call me into his office because she wanted me to be there when he announced the findings of the exhaustive four hour examination she had just endured. We sat very still, and tensed, as we waited for the doctor to speak.

"Mrs. Church, my examination leads me to confirm the diagnosis of my colleagues. You have a malignant tumor in your left eye. I am certain you have choroidal melanoma. This type of cancer spreads rapidly to the liver and the lungs and will cause your demise."

Silence.

What is there to say when you have just been delivered your death sentence?

A hint of the crisis had been given in July as a flash of light in Ada's left eye. She was kneeling at Morning Prayer in St. Michael's Church in San Clemente, California, when a brilliant silver wave rolled across her vision. We were attending a series of meetings with Malcolm Smith who was to be ordained that Friday, July 2, as a priest in the newly formed Charismatic Episcopal Church. Ada gave the incident scant thought.

Later that month we found ourselves on Interstate 95 in El Paso in the company of our good friend Steve Ingraham who had been prompted to visit us. He had come to El Paso on an impulse. Sitting at his desk in Houston that morning, the Lord spoke to him. The still small voice of God was directing him to phone me. By 3:00 p.m. he was on a plane to El Paso. He arrived at 5 o'clock. Steve had directed us to choose the restaurant of our pleasure, and as we sat in the stately dining room of a landmark old hotel, we sensed a new scenario was being unfolded by the hand of the Almighty.

That same evening the rolling light flashed across Ada's eye again. As we were parting, Ada asked Steve to pray for her. Steve had been a strong support for us in our ministry, but we little knew then that this was the beginning of a life and death drama that would mysteriously draw our destinies together.

By August, the occurrences of rolling light in Ada's left eye had become more frequent. At a fellowship meeting with long-time friends in the mountain resort town of Ruidoso in New Mexico,

Ada asked the group specially to pray for her. In addition to Steve's prayer, these were the first among our circle of friends and supporters to know about the symptoms and to pray for Ada. They gathered around her: Dennis and Becky Johnston, Dr. Earl Leslie and his wife Cheryl, and Rusty Steele. They prayed with passion and power. Earl prayed with both professional and practical insight, "Lord help Ada to find out what is causing these flashes of light to appear in her eye."

In those early months of 1993 we were commuting from El Paso, Texas to San Clemente, California where I was serving as a special assistant to the Archbishop of the newly formed Charismatic Episcopal Church. In February I had been ordained a priest in the denomination which was heralded as a church of "ancient altars and pentecostal fires." The movement, then just eight months old, would soon surprise the Christian community as the fastest growing denomination in the world. Embracing the three major historical streams of Christian history, the CEC blended the Sacramental and Evangelical past of the Church with the fresh spiritual life of the Charismatic Renewal.

The events leading up to my association with the CEC reflected a deepening understanding of what the apostle Paul spoke of as the mystery which one was hidden, but has now been made known. He was writing to the Ephesians about the church, his point being that it was God's eternal intention to reveal His glory, His bright radiance, through His many-faceted body of believing people.

My ministry, beginning with my memorable association with the Navigators, had taken me into churches whose forms of worship and liturgical structures varied from ordered, quiet and sublime, to free-form, loud and wild. Growing out of a search and a longing for the blending of the Spirit's renewing power and a dignity which honored the concept of reverence for God, I had written a booklet which I titled, *The Perfect Church*.

The announcement of my manuscript drew humorous jibes from friends. One said, "That will be a very short book." Another quipped, "Is it fact or fiction?" Another added, "Is it a book of jokes?" I defended my treatise by affirming that there no such thing as a perfect church. There is no perfect church because there are no perfect pastors. And of course, there are no perfect people, either.

In spite of the impossible dream which I carried in my heart, I was gradually drawn to an ethos of Christianity and an understanding of the church which found its expression in the dignity of the liturgical forms of the ancient church. But mere liturgical forms are rigid, icy, and even dead. I had also experienced the renewing and refreshing breath of the power and presence of the Spirit of God in worship where one knew and felt that God was alive and well.

I found the melding of spiritual energy and the dignity of liturgical order held in the closest balance in my association with The Reverend "Terry" Fullam at St. Paul's Episcopal Church in Darien, Connecticut.

In 1982, our ministry was headquartered in Tampa, Florida where I had launched a city-center outreach called "The Heart of Tampa Ministries." In association with out Tampa friends, Stan and Carol Skipper, and Larry and Margilee Carr, we presented a lunch-hour fellowship for business people. We also decided to hold a series of mid-day services to reach professional people in the heart of the city. Through the recommendation of Brenda Franciose, we chose as our guest speaker, the Rev. Terry Fullam, the rector of St. Paul's Episcopal Church in Darien, Connecticut.

On New Year's day, 1993, we attended an unforgettable service at St. Paul's in Darien, and when asked to introduce ourselves from the floor of the huge auditorium where the services were conducted, I publicly extended an invitation to Terry to come to Tampa, By his own admission, it was the most unusual invitation he had ever received. He accepted; and a defining relationship began. The Tampa Crusade was a resounding success.

I was invited to conduct a preaching mission at St. Paul's in the fall of 1984 and in 1985 was invited to assume a position as a pastoral assistant to Terry at the church that was featured in the best-selling book, *Miracle in Darien*. My ministry with Terry at St. Paul's was possible because of his unique views of ministry, the church, and Christian servanthood.

Among the many powerful and rewarding experiences of our years in Darien was the opportunity to work with people who had been deeply and significantly touched by the ministry of Dr. Fullam. I had the privilege of coordinating and leading the pastors' conference for the hundreds who came to investigate the secret and bask in the blessing of "The Miracle in Darien." People came from far and near to be refreshed and find healing in the grace and love at St. Paul's.

Another involvement of far-reaching significance was participating in the birth of a ministry which has since dramatically influenced the city of Greenwich and its surrounding neighborhoods.

A member of St. Paul's, Debbie Reynolds, had long nurtured the idea of starting a women's Bible study in Greenwich, the town where she and her husband Russ lived. Together, we planned the project, and with the help of Debbie's friends, with myself as the teacher, we launched the Greenwich Bible Study. It was an instant success. We held the morning meetings in the stately Episcopal Church, and the impact was so powerful that the vestry of the Church purchased Bibles to be placed in the pews! That ministry, under Debbie's leadership continues to prosper and flourish. From that singular beginning, there are now more than a dozen Bible studies which have proliferated in the area.

In the shifting times of life and ministry, both Terry and I felt that our season of service at St. Paul's was drawing to a close. At the end of 1989, we both resigned, each to pursue a different assignment, but committed to a continuing relationship as friends and fellow laborers. Ada and I returned to El Paso, Texas to resume our ministry of preaching and teaching. I stated the mission of my ministry to be:

To Encourage the Believers,
Establish the Church, and
Equip the Saints
To Evangelize the Lost.

With characteristic spiritual eagerness, Ada became actively involved in a ladies' Bible Study at St. Clement's Episcopal Church in the city. The experience proved to be of mutual benefit, and produced enduring friendships. In the ebb and flow of Christian communion, Ada enriched the group and they, in turn, provided an atmosphere of genuine love in which significant relationships flourish.

So it was, that on an early summer morning in 1993, as she picked fruit in the yard of one of the ladies, Dorothy Caldwell, Ada casually mentioned the recurring flashes of rolling light waves in her eye.

Dorothy asked, "Have you seen a doctor?" Strangely, the thought had not occurred to us, partly because we almost never were ill, and also because we had no medical insurance. We rarely consulted a physician.

I phoned our long-time friend, Dr. Gerry Miller, a physician in El Paso, who referred me to an eye specialist in the city. However, we were unable to obtain an appointment before our next scheduled trip to San Clemente.

In California we made an appointment to have Ada examined by the man whom we thought of as our family physician, Doctor Bernard Huss. He and his wife Lyn operated a family clinic in San Juan Capistrano, and had, for several years, provided us with loving professional care as the occasion arose. Dr. Huss examined Ada and recommended she consult an Ophthalmologist as soon as possible.

The appointment was set for September 10th. At 8:30 a.m. that day Ada was examined by Dr. Diana Kersten. When she had concluded her examination an urgency crept into her doctor's tone.

"I want you to see an ocular specialist," she said. My response was, "We have an important conference starting next week, can we see the specialist in two weeks time?" The reply took me by surprise, "No, I want you to see him today!" Her office made the appointment for us to see a Dr. John Lean immediately. The arrangement would cut into our lunch plans, but she was insistent. Like two innocents we drove to the rooms of Dr. Lean in Laguna Niguel.

There the hammer blow fell. Dr. Lean was a dignified, beautifully spoken English gentleman. But neither his gracious manner nor his soft English tones could dull the blow which fell on us. He called me from the waiting room where I had spent the last 2 hours, and solemnly gave us the somber findings of his examination.

"I am ninety-nine percent sure that Mrs. Church has choroidal melanoma, a malignant tumor in the left eye. I must also tell you that this type of cancer spreads rapidly to the lungs and liver, and will cause her death."

He recommended that we immediately consult his colleague, another specialist, who had at his disposal the most up-to-date, state-of-the art investigative resources. He wanted to make an appointment for that same day for us to see Dr. Brent Norman in

Santa Ana. However, the logistics were impossible. The examination would require preparation, would take four hours and would cost $1,000! We set the appointment with Dr. Norman for the following Tuesday, September 14, and soberly made our way back to the clinic where Dr. Huss and Lyn were waiting for us.

I was in a quandary. I was to participate in a House of Bishops retreat for the Charismatic Episcopal Church due to start on Monday, September 13th. Should we go to the conference in Tucson, Arizona, or should we keep our appointment with Dr. Norman?

I discussed the dilemma with Dr. Huss. His words were sobering: "When I examined Ada, I suspected a malignancy. Dr. Kersten called and confided her opinion to me, and now, Dr. Lean has confirmed our mutual diagnosis." He continued, "You could wait two weeks before seeing Dr. Norman, but I don't think you can wait two months."

The gravity of the situation was dawning on us. We had previously arranged a lunch meeting for that day with Bishop Adler, his wife Betty, Dr. Huss and Lyn. It promised now to be a rather somber occasion, with not much hope of good cheer.

God has perfect timing. Preparing to leave the clinic and head for the restaurant, we were standing in the hallway, when our South African associate and dear friend, Rev. Tony Louch, as if by some pre-arranged cue, walked through the door. Tony had immigrated to the USA and was pastoring a church, of all places, right there in San Juan Capistrano!

We shared the newly received diagnosis with Tony. I have known very few men who have the anointing and power that Tony has received from God. He laid his hands on Ada and prayed with a confidence and assurance that was both comforting and faith-building.

The doctor had solemnly pronounced Ada's death sentence, and his words still hung like a threatening cloud over us: "You have two options, enucleation (removal of the eye) or radiation. The cancer you have is very rare. Only about 1,500 people are diagnosed with this melanoma each year, and we do not know yet which form of treatment offers the hope of longest survival."

In striking contrast, Tony's prayer breathed hope and faith into the dark uncertainty which had so suddenly engulfed us. We went to lunch, meeting Bishop and Mrs. Adler in the entrance of the restaurant. While Ada visited the rest room I broke the news to them. They were stunned. Ada returned to a very serious group of people, some of us close to tears. But rather than commiserate with us, she instantly brought a spirit of cheer and sunshine to the group.

For seventeen years, since that magical moment in the airplane when we winged our way across the Atlantic from South Africa, Ada had continued to read the Bible through each and every year. Her life and faith were grounded in a knowledge of God and an unshakable confidence in the promises of His word. He had promised her, "Don't try to understand everything that happens along the way; Do not envy evil men, but continue to reverence the Lord at all times, for surely, *you have a wonderful future ahead of you*. There is hope for you yet."(1)

She had believed it for 17 years; she believed it now.

It was not bravado. It was not denial. Rather, it was the inner Spirit-given confidence to which the writer to the Hebrews referred when he wrote, "Let us then fearlessly, and confidently and boldly draw near to the throne of God's grace, that we may receive mercy (for our failures) and find grace to help in every need (appropriate and well-timed help just when we need it)....For He, God Himself has said, I will not in any way fail you nor give you up nor leave you without support. I will not, I will not, I will not in any degree leave you helpless nor forsake, nor let you down (relax my hold of you)! Assuredly not!"(2)

That confidence would be put to the test in the most grueling fashion in the months to come.

Chapter Thirty-Two

It was now September 11th, the morning after our appointment with the specialist, Dr. Lean. We were in Solana Beach, guests in the condominium of our dear El Paso friends, Wally and Betty Taber. The quaint seaside town of Del Mar is between Solana Beach and La Jolla in Southern California, and each Saturday a parking lot in the downtown area is transformed into an open-air market which offers casual browsers as well as serious shoppers the atmosphere of a busy bazaar exuding all the charm of a side walk café.

We wandered among the tables and stalls at the Del Mar market. The fragrance of flowers mingles with the aroma of the baked goods. We stop by the fish stand. Even the smell of the seafood seems to be more memorable. The sun is shining. People come and go, some smiling, some grim. There are the young couples who hold hands; the older ones who seem more occupied with shopping than with sentiment.

But on this Saturday morning, our lives seem eerily different. Everything is as if it was yesterday and yet strangely changed. The previous night we had talked by long distance telephone with our children, Dawson and Jenny, who were both now living in the USA. Dawson and his wife Brenda were quietly, deeply concerned.

When I broke the dark news to them, Dawson's first comment was, "Dad, do not do anything in haste. Do not consider radiation or surgery till you have explored all the other options available to you." He is profoundly knowledgeable, having researched and written books on the subject of health, healing and alternative medicines; his first anthology, *The Heart of the Healer*, brought together many of the leading medical luminaries of our time.

Jenny is a woman of unique spiritual wisdom, insight and power with an almost unequaled gift and anointing as a worship leader. She walks in a fellowship with Christ which is awesome. My call to her was one of the most emotional moments of my life. Four of our grandchildren were old enough to have grasped the gravity of the doctor's words.

Jessica was nine, Second Peter (to distinguish him from me!) was six and Bethany Joy four. When Jenny gathered them on Friday night and told them the news, collectively they burst into tears.

Their sobs were punctuated with prayers, "Please, Jesus, don't let our Granny die." Baby Ruth, only ten months old, was uncomprehending. They were 3,000 miles away in Jacksonville, Florida. If we chose to attend the House of Bishop's gathering in Tucson we could be with Dale and Jenny next week. If we elected to keep our appointment with Dr. Brent Norman on Tuesday September 14th, we would miss them.

Dawson and Brenda made immediate plans to drive from Northern California, their home, to visit us. Brenda was expecting their second baby in December. Lionel, nearly five, loved his Granny and was deeply concerned for her. I spent hours on the telephone, calling friends in the USA and family in South Africa. The calls evoked a uniform reaction: Total shock. There was silence at the end of each line as I explained the diagnosis.

So this was a special day. A Saturday to remember. Our lives could never be the same again. We would be forever affected. We held hands, meandering among the fruit stands and flower pots. Ada loved fresh cut flowers. The fragrance of the blooms seemed sweeter that day. We bought a big bunch to take home with us.

We did not talk about the cancer, but it was there, invisible and inescapable. One knew that from now on, it was a factor that would always be a presence just below the surface of one's consciousness. Like an air bubble, it was there, ready to escape to the surface of the water at the slightest provocation.

That week-end, time seemed to stand still even though we were busy with details of our ministry, making telephone calls, writing letters. Betty Taber had been a special angel of the Lord. She had invited us to stay in the condominium as long as we needed to. Every time I made a phone call, Ada quietly slipped to the seclusion of the beautifully furnished and appointed bedroom. She could not bear to hear the same death sentence, the same diagnosis, the same prognosis over and over again. It became my role to be the bearer of the bad tidings.

Finally, on Sunday, we made an important decision; we *would* attend the conference of the CEC in Tucson. Once made, we wondered why we had vacillated. Early on Monday morning we set out by car for Arizona with a cheerful confidence. We reasoned that to wait a week to see Dr. Norman would make absolutely no difference to the ability of God to "keep that which we had committed to Him."(1) The burden fell from our shoulders.

Knowing that on our return to California, Ada was to undergo the daunting experience of a four-hour examination at the consulting rooms of Doctor Norman, I carried a weighty sense of my responsibility as husband, care-giver and provider to the woman I loved. I shared every pang of anguish, every sorrow and every shadow of uncertainty that touched Ada.

Our time at the conference was like a soothing balm as we were bathed in prayer and experienced the personal love of our dear ones, Dale and Jenny. It was also the first time to meet our beloved "Ruthie," Jenny's fourth baby.

A monumental challenge lay ahead of me. We had to find $850 for the consultation—in one week!

With a sweet confidence, Ada wrote to the couple who, for so many years, had been to us the kind of friends who, in the words of Solomon, were "closer than a brother"(2): J. O. and Marlene Stewart. They had been among the first we had phoned, and at my first emotional outpouring, J. O. had said, "If we can help in any way, let us know."

In response to Ada's letter, J. O. and Marlene, true to their assurance, sent us the money to pay for the battery of tests which were to be performed. We kept our appointment with Dr. Norman in Santa Ana on Tuesday, September 21, 1993.

Leading to that consultation, Ada had been subjected to the usual examinations requiring dilation of the pupils and in which the doctor peers into the eye with an opthalmascope. This four-hour investigation involved, in addition, exhaustive and complex procedures causing severe irritation to Ada's eye, taxing her physical endurance to the limit. Sonogram readings recorded the size of the tumor. By means of intricate color photography through the pupil, the technicians obtained pictures of the tumor, and by means of an intravenous injection of dye into the blood stream, could monitor the flow of blood through the veins of the eye and observe as the dye passed through the tumor.

Following the four-hour ordeal, when all the data had been accumulated and analyzed, we were summoned to Dr. Norman's private room. There he solemnly pronounced the words which amounted to a death sentence, "You have uveal, or choroidal melanoma, a malignant tumor dangerously close to the optic nerve."

In the silence of the after shock, we were numb. Dr. Norman recommended immediate surgery. He offered us the same options Dr. Lean had presented. "Remove the eye, and you remove the tumor, giving you a greater chance of survival." He reiterated the reference to Ada's "demise!"

The second option was irradiation. A radioactive gold plaque is fashioned, charged with I 125 radioactive ions and attached to the back of the eye to exactly cover the tumor. The prognosis? "In either case, you will lose the sight of your eye. We just do not know which treatment will help you live the longest."

By this time the ominous message, "you are going to die," had gathered to itself the muffled beat of a distant funeral drum. No one else could hear it but it reverberated in our souls with a heavy beat.

Back at the condo in Solana Beach, I again made the round of phone calls. One call elicited a strikingly different response. It was my call to our friends Dr. Jim Gills and his wife Heather at the St. Luke's Eye Clinic in Tarpon Springs, Florida. I spoke first to Heather who put the doctor on the line. His questions were pointed, precise. "How big is the tumor?"

I told him, "It is 9 x 6.5 millimeters at the base; 3 millimeters in elevation."

His response was stunning: "Praise the Lord. It is small and can be treated."

His words birthed a quiet hope in my heart. Ada's reaction to the predictions of the physicians had been a firm, "I am not afraid of dying." Yet there was now the subtle specter of an unknown and uncertain future which hovered over us like a thin but dark veil. Ada's concern was not about dying, it was about what lay between this moment of diagnosis and the event the doctor had called her "demise."

In these moments of real life words memorized in days past came back by legions to strengthen our souls. How many years before had I learned the hymn, "Rock of Ages"? The words returned to me now and mounted a guard in my heart as the comfort of them saturated my mind.

Rock of Ages, cleft for me,
Let me hide myself in Thee;
Let the water and the blood,
From Thy wounded side which flowed,
Be of sin the double cure,
Save from wrath and make me pure.

While I draw this fleeting breath,
When my eyes shall close in death,
When I rise to worlds unknown,
And behold Thee on Thy throne,
Rock of Ages, Cleft for me,
Let me hide myself in Thee.

Returning from reveries, stirred by those lines to the stark reality of the doctor's room, I asked him two questions. "What do you recommend we do?" His response was, "I advise Mrs. Church to have the radio active plaque therapy and that we perform the procedure next week." He added, "You do not have the luxury of time. This melanoma spreads rapidly; time is critical."

The second question? "What do you estimate the cost of the procedure will be?" We sat in silence as he made some notations. "Twenty thousand dollars." When I heard this impossible number, the room swayed around me.

Chapter Thirty-Three

We returned to our haven; the Taber condominium in Solana Beach. Scholars, philosophers and theologians have wrestled from earliest times with the mystery of suffering. In my own wanderings in these valleys, I had absorbed some truths which would now be the anchor of our minds and emotions. I understood in the tension of these days the importance of the injunction of St. Paul, "Pray without ceasing."(1)

Much of the great wisdom passed on by the inspired authors in the Bible had been forged in the crucible of their own experience. King David had often faced the specter of death. Emerging from encounters in which he came face to face with fear and death, he wrote monumental epics such as Psalm 23. And so with us, it is in "the valley of the shadow of death"(2) that we are able to enter into a fuller and deeper understanding of the promise, "The Lord your God is with you."(3)

Those words live because they have their source in the life-giving breath of the Holy Spirit. They are not mere rhetoric, they are Truth and they stand the test on the battlefields of life. In our valley of shadows, we knew, not academically, but personally, that God was with us. His presence was real, almost tangible. We experienced what it meant to live in an atmosphere of conscious, constant and continual prayer. We prayed for guidance, knowing how much depended upon crucial decisions we had to make, and we began each morning and each evening by anointing Ada's eye with oil and praying the prayer of faith.(4)

Our lives were being subtly, yet distinctly changed from anything we had ever experienced before. We were dealing with a disease feared by millions, a killer which claims 1,600 lives a day in America and 21,000 worldwide.

Cancer.

For years we had treasured two of the richest blessings one can have; our family and our friends. Through days of praying and waiting, the endearing and enduring value of these enriched our lives. The love and the prayers of countless people touched us.

Among the first with whom we had shared the grave news were our friends, Francis and Judith MacNutt. Over years of acquaintance, they had prayed many times for me. Now, the focus of our faith was changed. Though I was no less needy, I realized that we were to give our full attention to seeking God and His perfect will for Ada.

To our delight, we discovered that Francis and Judith were to be in San Diego for a healing mission within a few days, so we arranged to meet them. In their hotel room, Ada recounted all the details of the events leading up to the diagnosis; she held back nothing. She revealed her heart to their attentive and loving concern. Her disappointments, discouragements and even the darkest hours of her soul, were all chronicled for them.

The past few years had witnessed fierce personal struggles. There had been disillusionments and broken dreams. As Ada bared her soul, Judith expressed her compassionate concern, "I am more concerned about your heart than your eye!" she said.

Judith was discerning the hurts, and measuring the depths of anguish in Ada's soul, burned by broken promises, failed relationships and the fickleness of people who had once pledged loyalty. Ada had, over the years of pilgrimage and ministry experienced disappointment and grief through the betrayal of people in whom she had invested confidence and trust. These pent up emotions poured out of Ada's broken heart as from a breached dam. Ada finally confessed, "I don't want anybody to say 'I love you.'" She had heard similar words often, followed only by betrayal.

Worst of all, Ada voiced the haunting fear: "I think I have brought this cancer on myself. I have harbored anger and resentment and have even wished in some dark nights of my soul that I would die and not wake up in the morning."

We knew, did we not, that good thoughts attract good consequences, and that bad thoughts take their toll in sickness, ill-health, poverty, unhappiness and all the host of evil things that lurk around negative, hateful, bitter and unforgiving people? The paradox was that Ada was by nature a bright and vivacious person. Her spontaneous laughter rang like a melody through every conversation. When she was a little girl, her grandfather called her Bright Eyes. Now her vision was threatened, her life was in jeopardy. What had gone wrong?

As we wrestled with unanswered questions and sought to understand the new emotions brought on by this malady, we were often steadied, quieted and strengthened by long distance conversations with priceless friends.

We felt bathed in the loving concern of two specially close friends, Jay and Pat Sindahl. Ada was counseled and upheld by the wisdom of Pat's words and her instant understanding of the trial through which Ada was passing. Whenever we talked with Jay, his mellow manner and the compassion of his huge heart always served to remind us of the Father Heart of God.

And we talked whenever we could with Terry and Ruth Fullam. Every time we talked with them we were encouraged by the love and concern expressed in their prayers. We drew strength and courage from all the prayers and words of assurance from many precious friends with whom the Lord had blessed us. We were sustained by the people who helped us in the spirit of Galatians 6:2: "Carry one another's burdens, and so fulfill the law of Christ."

Chapter Thirty-Four

As I wrestled with the tragedy of Ada's condition, I reflected on the long journey that had brought us to this point. It began eighteen years earlier, when our plane from South Africa landed in the USA on Friday, October 30. Our first speaking engagement had been at the Lockhart United Methodist Church, near Orlando, on Sunday November 1st.

The evening service was designated a "missionary meeting" and there was an air of solemn, compassionate concern among the congregation as we told of the troubled country we had left behind us just 72 hours before. Ada was in tears through most of the service, as she spoke of the co-workers we had left in the turmoil which was roiling in South Africa.

She told the story of one of our African team members, who had been brutally attacked a few weeks before. A band of marauding young African men had pounced on him, ripped the watch from his wrist and stolen his wallet. In the struggle one of the attackers had drawn a long-bladed knife and slashed our friend, who suffered severe wounds from the assault.

Ada had described the awful sight of his almost severed thumb and the gaping wound across the palm of his hand, weeping as she tried to describe her anguish. That night, Ada woke at the midnight hour with a burning word from God in her heart. She roused me at 1:00AM. It was now November 2nd.

She said, "Peter, God has spoken to me; I believe the Lord wants us to give away all our earthly possessions and begin to live by faith, trusting Him completely for everything we need." We talked till the sky began to lighten with the dawn of a new day. The first day of a whole new life. The Lord Jesus had said, "Except a corn of wheat fall into the ground and die, it remains alone. But if it falls into the ground and dies, it brings forth much fruit."(1)

It was to be a death, but also a resurrection. By daybreak, from memory, we had made a list of all the possessions we had left back in South Africa. We had, only weeks earlier, put all our furniture, household possessions and personal belongings into storage. Now we wrote a detailed list of all those things. The list included details of kitchen utensils and appliances. It included even my golf clubs. We wrote a letter to Ada's father and mother, and attached the list. Our directive was clear: Give everything away!

We named people to whom certain items should be given. Some were to go to members of our family, others to people in need, some to our friends. The gifts were not based upon the recipients giving us anything in return. Finally, as day broke, we experienced a sense of relief. It was as though a burden had been lifted from our shoulders. We were free.

The family back in South Africa was shocked. They were also alarmed. Had we lost our minds? Ada's mother wrote expressing her distress. She was especially upset that we had left our beautiful 17 year old Jenny in the YWCA in Durban. Mrs. Amm, though a woman of great spiritual stature, could not comprehend our commitment to the will of God.

On January 19th 1977, Jenny turned 18. We decided to call her. It was midnight in Dallas; morning in Durban, South Africa.

Jenny was in training as a beautician at a celebrated salon in the city and took the call in the busy beauty shop. Ada was anxious. What would she find?

It had been almost impossible to keep in close touch with our children because we were moving around the USA and had no fixed mailing address, but Ada kept her watch on South African time so that she could always picture where her children would be. It was her way of keeping a prayer-watch over them.

There was the usual tense pause in making an overseas connection. Then Jenny's scintillating voice broke the awkward moment. Bubbling with enthusiasm she said, "Mom, don't you worry about me, I am doing just fantastically!"

A miracle had taken place. As part of our preparations for making the journey to America, we had agreed to place Jenny in the YWCA in Durban and allow her to continue her apprenticeship and studies as a beautician and hair stylist. At that point in our planning, we were anticipating a four-month tour of ministry and visitation with the members of the Lay Witness Team that had so recently impacted South Africa.

The move from Johannesburg to Durban in the middle of 1976 had been a time of major upheaval and had left us in the all-too-familiar position of seeking a Christian fellowship in which we could be at home spiritually and in which we could serve our Lord. In the four months since the transplant, we had not found that special place, though we had attended many churches.

In consequence, Jenny was not regularly attending a particular church. However, Juliette Middleton, the young lady who had served as my secretary in Johannesburg had moved with us to Durban, and was attending a vibrant youth congregation which had a dynamic outreach and appeal to young people. It was called "The Invisible Church."

Soon after our departure, Juliette invited Jenny to attend the services, and there the miracle happened. The music was loud and the worship decidedly boisterous but the huge congregation was turned on to Jesus. It was a church alive with the power of the Holy Spirit; a charismatic church.

For Jenny, who had grown up under the strong influence of a conservative congregation, it was, to say the least, a very unusual and different experience. A few years before, her Grandmother, Mrs. Amm, had undergone a dramatic spiritual experience that had dismayed her traditional church friends and family. While in prayer one morning, Mrs. Amm had been supernaturally moved by the Holy Spirit. As a result of that visitation, she had begun to pray and praise God in what the Bible calls "tongues." She had not sought any such experience, and had often, before the manifestation, denounced the practice! Because of the opposition and misunderstanding which she knew would follow, she was hesitant at first to tell of her encounter. I had been one of the first people Mrs. Amm had told about her being "baptized with the Holy Spirit."(2)

One evening, in a home fellowship meeting in Durban, Jenny too was touched by that same Spirit of power and grace. She sat on the sofa in the home of one of the elders, John Watson, and at the close of the gathering, an appeal was extended, inviting anyone who wanted to receive the anointing of the Holy Spirit, and power to serve Christ, to come forward for prayer.

Jenny remained seated, just where she was, on the sofa. She did *not* want to go forward. Yet, in the strange and sovereign working of God, as John prayed for those who had come forward, the Holy Spirit came to Jenny in a gentle and almost imperceptible way. She was endued with unquestionable power. She lingered at the conclusion of the meeting, reluctant to leave. This was uncharacteristic, but there was now a compelling desire to be in the place where the Presence of God was real. The next day, she knew a dramatic transformation had taken place in her life. She began to read her Bible with relish, she had a new-born zeal for God, and as she says, "I fell totally in love with Jesus." It was as though the Holy Spirit had taken over her life. She was radically changed. So, when we called her on her birthday, the news she shared with us was electrifying.

Every day since leaving Dawson and Jenny, we had prayed earnestly, fervently for our two children. Jenny told us that Dawson, too, was well. She was reassuring, positive, bright. As an evidence of her having undergone the same experience which marked the beginning of the ministry of the Lord Jesus, Jenny had been "anointed with Holy Spirit and with power."(3) In the YWCA, she and another girl were initially the only two professing Christians. When we talked with her on this her eighteenth birthday, she had become, what the prophet Daniel describes as "a shining star." She had won a dozen girls in the YMCA to Christ and "turned them to righteousness."(4)

On the streets and on the beaches, with charm and with a new-found power, she had become, almost overnight, just like the 120 disciples on the day of Pentecost, a zealous witness for the Savior. It was the beginning of a life of devotion to Christ which would blossom in the years to come and prepare her for the incredible ministry to which God would call her.

Ada's experiences in South Africa moved her to pen this moving plea for a violent continent to the peace that only the Savior can bring.

Heart Cry for South Africa

Oh! Africa—South Africa,
Land of my youth and my birth;
Land of great beauty and sadness,
Rare gem on the face of the earth;
Amidst the specter of progress,

We see your anguish, your pains.
From the mountains majestic with splendor,
Your search for identity reigns.
We play on the beaches together,
But hate remains in our heart,
We *could* live together in harmony
And a new life for all we could start.
Who will rule this new nation,
Where the blood of many was spilt?
For the scourges of war and of anger -
We all bear the burden of guilt.
The cry of our hearts is for freedom,
To love, to live and to play
At one with our brothers and sisters;
Will we *ever* see that bright day?
Oh! Africa — South Africa,
Where the tribes of divergence have met,
When will you pause to acknowledge
The God who has plans for you yet?
We *can* live together in freedom,
With respect for everyone's creed.
There's room for us all without limit;
If we conquer the giant of greed.
Hatred and strife will destroy us;
What a price to pay to be right.
Won't you turn to the One who has made you;
Come into His circle of light?
 The white and the brown and the yellow,
With the black can all live in peace,
For the blood that flows in our veins,
Is the same 'til our life here shall cease.
We pray for this beautiful country,

Chapter Thirty-Four

One of the richest on earth,
Enjoy the great things God has given,
Oh! Land—great land of our birth.

Chapter Thirty-Five

n our circuit around the United States, we were visiting the pioneers who had spearheaded the historic Lay Witness Mission in South Africa in 1976.

In addition to our itinerant ministry in Methodist churches, we had been invited to speak at the Missionary Convention of a Pentecostal Church in Salisbury, Maryland. My heart was burning with a passion ignited by my own encounter with the Holy Spirit five months before. Whenever we had ministered in those intervening months, God had honored the contract I made with Him that October Sunday morning. Now, I was having the opportunity to preach to a congregation which throbbed with Divine life and to people whose hearts burned with missionary zeal.

We arrived in one of the most humbling automobiles I had ever driven. It was a relic, or more accurately, a wreck! A well-intentioned gentleman had offered to lend us his car and we had accepted because our destination was far from any major airport. When we saw the proffered chariot, our hearts sank; but we were obliged to go through with it. The old thing wheezed and rattled as we bumped into the heartland of Maryland. Finally it breathed a hot sigh of expiry as we pulled into the parking lot of the church. As I climbed out of the drivers seat, the exhausted car slumped at one corner; we had a flat tire to crown it all. The corpse looked utterly pitiful as it was towed away.

The church however, was already buzzing with activity in preparation for the opening meeting. Ada and I were delighted when we were offered a choice: "Would you prefer to stay in a motel or a private home?"

It was winter and we had just come through a harrowing experience. Throughout our tour, we had enjoyed the hospitality of our Lay Witness hosts and hostesses, but the accommodations often tested our physical endurance. At a recent stop we had arrived just hours ahead of a snowstorm. Our hosts were farmers and housed us in a room on the second floor of their old farmhouse where there was no heat.

To help drive the bitter cold out of the un-heated room, they had kindly provided a tiny electric heater. However, because there was no electric outlet in the room, it had to be plugged into a socket on a wall in the hallway.

The effect of the miserly little heater was minimal. Cold crept in through cracks between the window frames and the walls and under the door. As the storm raged outside ice and snow collected on the windowpanes. It was so cold we could see our breath vaporize as we exhaled. Although we put on every warm piece of clothing we could find in our bags and tried to sleep, we shivered between the icy sheets longing to be in some warm place.

I fared better than Ada. When I awoke early in the morning, she was gone. From the room, that is. During the night, for fear of a fire hazard, our dear old friends had unplugged the heater. There was ice and snow piled on the window outside, but now, our presence in the room had caused ice to form on the *inside* of the windowpanes.

When I finally coaxed my aching body down the stairs, I saw Ada asleep on the sofa in front of the dying embers of the fire in the living room. She had caught a really bad cold and was ill for weeks. So, here in Maryland, given the choice, we elected to enjoy the luxury of a motel room. It was the beginning of a memorable weekend. One of the speakers was a man whose biographical sketch listed in the bulletin made him sound like a bundle of contradictions and paradoxes; it was intriguing. He was a French Canadian, Charismatic, Roman Catholic, Lay Evangelist! His name was Ray Brooks.

Ada had been invited to sit on the platform, but chose rather to be anonymous in the congregation. Feeling both weary and wary, she eyed the proceedings from what she thought was a safe distance. Until Ray Brooks spoke.

He told of a recent ministry trip to South Africa, and in the telling of his story, Ada found a unique and sympathetic affinity with this man who spoke with a delightful French-Canadian accent, but whose words were both winsome and powerful. Though she was a complete stranger to him, he singled her out from the audience and gave her a word of encouragement and confirmation in a prophetic utterance which was so personal and appropriate that it was evidently a message from God.

Naturally, over the weekend we spent time in discussion with Ray and found an affinity of heart, mind and spirit. On Sunday night at the closing service of the convention, Ada was sitting with a family that had been extremely warm and hospitable towards us. They had a 20-year-old daughter who longed to be a missionary. But she was epileptic. This girl had attached herself to Ada and was holding tightly to Ada's hand.

While preaching on the power of the Holy Spirit for Christian service, Ray Brooks told of an experience in which he had witnessed the miraculous healing of someone with epilepsy. When he extended an invitation to seekers to come to the front of the church, Ada, moved with a deep compassion for this girl, reasoned that if she went forward, the young lady would follow. In Ada's heart, she felt the girl might receive a miracle of healing and have her desire for missionary service fulfilled.

Ada moved out of her seat and walked to the open space in front of the pulpit. When she reached the platform area, she looked around; the girl had not followed. But, having made the move, Ada felt she had nothing to lose, and remained as Ray Brooks was laying his hands on the heads of those who had come, praying for each one to receive the gift of the Holy Spirit's power.

Initially, Ada felt no emotion or any other physical or spiritual response. Ray passed her, and continued to pray for the many people who had responded to his invitation. He then returned to where she was standing, and laid his hand on her head.

I was, by then, standing to one side of the platform. I watched with concern and amazement as I saw Ada slowly slide to the floor and lie motionless on her back among others who had fallen to the floor under the power of the Holy Spirit. Some had fallen backwards like felled trees. Others had slid down like the folding of a sheet as though wafted by the wind. She lay there, as though deep in sleep for a considerable time. Finally, she sat up, and to her utter surprise and joy, the young epileptic was lying by her side.

We went from Salisbury directly to New York City and checked in at our favorite place to stay in Manhattan, Hephzibah House, the gorgeous Brownstone house which had been donated to a missionary society by the lady whose home it had been many years before. There, lying on a bed, on a Wednesday in March 1977, Ada was visited again by the Holy Spirit.

While praying, as she often did in her times of quietness, she began suddenly to pray in a tongue or a language that was completely foreign to her. She had, unsought, received what the Apostle Paul refers to as "the gift of speaking in tongues."(1)

D. L. Moody, the famed evangelist tells of a life-changing encounter he too experienced in the city of New York. Describing it as being "Baptized with the Holy Spirit," he would later say, "It does not matter what you call it, so long as you have it." In that personal, specific, dramatic, and Biblical experience Ada was "baptized with the Holy Spirit."(2) It signaled a definitive change, touching, not only the lives of both of us, but affecting our entire service for Christ. From that moment, Ada was transformed from a shy, reticent witness and reluctant speaker, into one whose joy, power and boldness knew no bounds. She spoke to every person she met about her faith in Jesus Christ.

On our return to Washington DC, I contacted Senator Mark Hatfield whom I had not seen in several years. As always, he was gracious, interested and asked about my ministry in the USA. I told him of the dramatic decision we had made in November. He listened intently. I added, "Senator Hatfield, my wife and I also believe that God wants us to make our home here in America." His reply took me by surprise. "Is there anything I can do," he said, "to help you?"

Putting action to his words, Senator Hatfield, personally initiated the process of our application for permanent residence in the United States. Later, while speaking at a conference in Florida, we were made aware of the gracious action of the Senator when a very prominent overseas preacher confided that he had made several vain attempts to gain legal resident status in the USA.

We immediately began the process of application for our two children, Dawson and Jenny, to join us. There was an element of excitement in our lives which was both exhilarating and at the same time daunting. We needed the proverbial miracle a day. One of those miracles came as we were making plans for Dawson and Jenny to be admitted to schools in America.

Back in South Africa, a dynamic lady from the US had helped me as an occasional secretary in the office. She told me that at one time she had worked for a Dr. Reynolds, a professor at Baylor University in Texas. She really meant it when she said, "If ever you are near Waco, Texas, please contact Dr. Reynolds. I will write to him and let him know that you might visit him." She was as good as her word.

Early in 1977, while in Dallas, I made plans to take a bus down to Waco to meet the man my friend had recommended with such high praise. My trip to Waco was one of the adventures that seem so improbable, even impossible, unless one has experienced the chilling feeling of despair which overtakes one in a time when there seems to be no way out of a tight situation.

I made an appointment to see Dr. Reynolds and the lady who was our hostess in Dallas dropped me off at the bus station. I had ten dollars in my pocket. It was all the money I had to my name. Naively, I figured the bus ride would be about two or three dollars each way, and I would have a couple of dollars for coffee and a roll into the bargain.

I stepped up to the window at the bus station, and innocently asked for a ticket to Waco. Without batting an eyelid, the cashier said, "Ten dollars!" Talk about culture shock!

I froze. I was between a rock and a hard place. Should I just give up my appointment? But would I have another chance? Thoughts raced through my brain like cars on the Indianapolis 500 Race Track. I had to make a snap decision. "One way," I responded. I boarded the bus with a strange feeling of abandonment. I was headed south, and I had no visible means of getting back!

Dr. Reynolds was graciousness personified. After the customary greetings he said, "Why have you come to see me?" I had to say, "I really don't know, but your former secretary told me about Baylor and spoke so highly of you."

Chapter Thirty-Five

His next question was, "Is there anything I can do to help you?"

At that moment, and not until that split second had the thought crossed my mind, but I told him about Dawson. The outcome was a staggering offer. Dr. Reynolds offered a full scholarship for Dawson to attend Baylor University!

That was one huge miracle, but I needed another. I had no way of getting back to Ada in Dallas. My parents had drummed some strict rules of etiquette into my brain. "You never ask strangers for money." But even without my parent's savvy and social wisdom, I would never have dared asked Dr. Reynolds for a hand-out.

Only one avenue of action seemed open to me. On leaving Dr. Reynolds, I asked his secretary if there was any way they might cash a small check for me. I figured I could get some money in my account in a few days and cover the promise. The secretary was immediately helpful and invited me to write out my check. I did.

Then came the embarrassment, she said, "I need to have Dr. Reynolds approve the check." My heart sank like an elevator that had snapped loose from its cable. I could almost feel it hit the soles of my shoes. A few seconds later she re-appeared and said, "Dr. Reynolds would like to see you in his office again."

I knew the feeling. I had lived through it many times in my school days. "The principal wants to see you." It could make a boy feel like he was having a heart attack.

The Dr., however, was kindly. He asked me why I needed a check cashed at the school. I was trapped. I was found out. He knew now that I was a pretty poor provider. Not much of a money-maker on the preaching circuit. I felt embarrassed.

But I gave him the truth. Told him just what had happened. I explained my miscalculation, my meager resources, and the alternatives I had faced. His response was unforgettable. He instructed his secretary to return my check and asked her to give me my bus fare home out of their petty cash.

God is truly good. And He does have some really wonderful people in His family. King David called them, "the glorious ones in whom is all my delight."(3)

Three urgent necessities still pressed us. If Dawson and Jenny were to join us we would have to pay all the expenses related to their relocation. We did not have a car, and, perhaps the most basic of life's necessities, we did not have a house—a place we could call home. We did not even have a fixed address!

We were to see God demonstrate that He is our provider, the meeter of every need, but that He works the wonder of His providing love through people who hear His prompting and obey His directing voice. Ada and I were in Vero Beach, Florida, where we had conducted a series of meetings in the United Methodist Church. Our hosts were Duane and Pat Safer, a Spirit-filled couple whose commitment to hear the voice of the Shepherd was total; to the point of genuine sacrifice. As we sat at their dinner table one day, they spontaneously asked, "How much will it cost to bring your children to America?"

I had already tabulated the expenses, and gave them the figure. They stole a sly glance at each other and said, "We prayed about this and agreed that if you gave us a certain figure, we would know that God wanted us to sponsor your children. The figure you have given us is exactly the amount we agreed upon." Jenny arrived in New York on July 7, 1977, and Dawson followed two weeks later.

We also needed a physical location, a real place to record as our domicile in order to qualify for our application as permanent residents. We were simply believing God for this, our most urgent and most basic need. Our prayer was "God, where you provide a house, we will make our home."

The answer came as one of those incredible tapestries which only the Hand of an all-caring God can weave. As part of our planned itinerary, we had made a scheduled stop in northern Louisiana to visit one of the couples who had been on the memorable Lay Witness Team. Hale Shadow and his wife Margaret were our hosts in the quaint little town of Ruston, Louisiana.

We ministered in the beautiful United Methodist Church, and at the conclusion of the service I invited people to respond to the call of God and to the renewing work of the Holy Spirit. There was the same response we had been witnessing in every place we visited. In fulfillment of His promise, the Lord was mysteriously, powerfully touching peoples hearts as I preached and Ada shared her living examples of God's grace and goodness. They came to the altar rails to experience the dynamic of a new beginning in Christ. People responded to the offer of power to live an effective Christian life. They came for healing, for rededication, and renewal. We witnessed God answering prayers and fulfilling His promises to bless His people with "goodness and mercy, for power to live an effective, dynamic Christian life, for healing and for rededication.(4)

On Sunday, among the many who came to the altar rail, were two very different people. One was a tall, handsome, athletic young man. He had a pair of large, powerful hands that made even mine seem small. I prayed, and God gave me a special word of encouragement for him. Unknown to me, this outstanding young man was the quarterback for one of the National Football League teams. Also, unknown to me was that he was facing a critical choice that was to decide his future. I was seeing the gifts of the Holy Spirit at work, giving wisdom, knowledge and discernment.

The other person whose heart God touched was so different. He was just a lad kneeling at the rail with shoulders drooped and his head resting on his hands. A love welled up in my heart as I knelt beside the boy, put my arm around his shoulders and prayed with him. My prayer for him was for comfort, encouragement and for the Lord's guidance in his life.

As we walked to the waiting car in the parking lot, Mr. and Mrs. Shadow told of the tragedy which had touched the boys' life. A few months previously, he had been in the woods on a hunting trip with his father and his uncle. The boy, mistaking a form among the trees for a deer, had accidentally shot and killed his uncle! He had been inconsolable since the tragedy. He came to the altar for healing of his brokenness.

The miracle of God's provision was to follow that service. The daughter of the Shadows, Loretta, had inherited a portion of a farm from an uncle who had died, and, hearing of our need, approached me with an offer. She said, "There is an old house on the farm. It has not been lived in for a number of years and it needs a lot of work, but if you want it, it is yours to live in as long as you need it."

We had a home, we had a fixed address, and we could apply for our permanent resident status. To this new home we brought Dawson and Jenny in the August of 1977.

Chapter Thirty-Six

hat same month, August 1977, Elvis Presley died in Memphis, Tennessee. I was in Memphis a few days before his death, and carried in my heart a real concern for the man who was, even then, a legend in his time. I did not meet the man they called The King, but felt a deep stirring in my heart and obeyed a prompting in my spirit to pray for him.

I was there to consult with a well-known orthopedic surgeon, Dr. Marcus Stewart. We had met his daughter Betty a few weeks before while teaching at Reach Out Ranch, the ministry headquarters and conference center of the prominent Bible teacher Kay Arthur. We had met her husband Jack years before when he had ministered in our church in Cape Town. They now received us with grace and generosity. Betty told Ada that her father, a former president of the American Society of Orthopedic Surgeons, had been a guest lecturer for the Chamber of Mines Hospital in South Africa! She arranged for me to consult her father in the hope that his skill could alleviate the chronic pain and spreading numbness in my back, legs and feet.

Following the initial consultation and after several further visits, Dr. Stewart scheduled a major surgical procedure to be performed on my spine for February, 1978. However, several major obstacles had to be overcome before that could take place. The mountains to be moved included such practical things as a suitable place for the recovery period, estimated at 6 months; nursing care, transportation from the hospital following the surgery and the ever-present financial liabilities.

One by one we witnessed the awesome ability of God to do the impossible. The community of believers in the seaside town of Vero Beach in Florida were the angels of God's mercy and provision. We had experienced an unusually significant and successful teaching mission in their midst in the fall of 1977, and now, at the dawning of 1978, they became our family.

Ken and Margaret Atha had taken us into their hearts as a father and mother and had both graciously and generously supported us financially. They had also introduced us to their close friends, Jerre and Betty Haffield who financed the renting of a small house where I would be able to recuperate following the surgery. Pat Patteson was a pilot with Pan American. He coordinated and then co-piloted a small aircraft to air lift me from Memphis back to Vero Beach following the surgery. I would be in a body cast from my chest to my left knee, unable to sit upright for 6 months. Other members of that unforgettable family responded as the true body of Christ for us.

Dick Long, with his wife Julie, headed up the support team who arranged for the ambulance to meet the plane at the Vero Beach airport. A young lady named Jean volunteered to come each day to help with the chores which attend the full-time care of a patient. When the rental time on the house expired, Bill and Ann Howard offered us the sanctuary of their rental condominium close to the beach. It was a dramatic and moving demonstration of how a group of loving, caring people can make evident the principles which Jesus decreed should demonstrate His character to the world. We experienced love, caring, sharing and the upholding prayers of a group of people, many unnamed, who rose to the challenge of the Master, who had said, "By this shall all men know you are my disciples, that you *love* one another."(1) We experienced the truth that God's love, demonstrated by His people, is not just emotion, it is action.

A heavy blow came just weeks before the surgery. Dawson was at Baylor University, while Jenny was at Oral Roberts University where God had also graciously provided for her continued study. On January 18 it was Ada's mother's birthday. Dawson arranged a conference call with Mrs. Amm in South Africa. Though she had been in hospital a few weeks earlier, she was in much worse condition than we realized. The interaction of the three generations on the phone was warm, caring and loving. Five days later, she died. Her last words were, "I'm going to the Glory Land. I'm going to the Glory Land."

Ada was devastated. There had always been the thought, "If anything were to go wrong, I could always go home." She enjoyed the quality of relationship with her mother and father that assured her of a loving, open door of welcome. She knew she had a home of last resort if all else failed. Now, it seemed that her last bastion of earthly security was gone. She felt alone, stripped of security. Death is so final. She would never on earth hear her mother's sweet voice again or see that cheerful smile.

As all the preparations and plans for my admission to the hospital were being put in place, a strange and powerful opposition began to raise itself against the approaching surgery. It came from an unexpected source: the people who spoke of themselves and their theology as "the faith movement."

We were living, as closely as we knew how, by the principles of faith. We really did believe God for the supplying of our every need. We were not novices in the Christian Way. Yet we were suddenly assailed by numbers of people, many relative newcomers to The

Faith, whose claim to a revelation of a particular dimension of faith revealed a woeful lack of balance and sound doctrine.

Statements such as: "If the Apostle Paul had understood the principle of faith he would never have been in jail" and "God has revealed to one of our teachers that we will soon see miracles like the growing out again of severed limbs" and "Women who have been robbed by Satan in having a hysterectomy will begin to see their wombs grow back again" were dished out. Their ultimate delusion was to declare that, "We will soon make the Apostles look like Sunday School children!"

These zealots maintained that if I assented to the surgery, I lacked faith. In their eyes, I would be a "second class" Christian, one who lacked faith. I would be rejected as a teacher. There were churches in that theological mold that banished people if they committed the sin of consulting a doctor. If an offender repented he could be re-admitted, but only to sit on the back row.

One Pastor who "in faith" claimed that he had been healed from a serious allergy later died as a result of an ant bite he sustained while collecting his early morning newspaper. His last directive to his flock was, "If I die, don't bury me because God will raise me from the dead as a testimony to this city." He died. His followers said that, like Christ, their pastor would be raised on the third day. That didn't happen of course, and eventually the health authorities were forced to seize the decaying corpse and bury it.

Considering the implications of these preposterous declarations, and setting the doctrine of faith in what I believed to be Biblical balance, I decided that God had opened the doors and that it was His plan for me to have the surgery. On February 14, 1978, I was admitted to the Baptist Hospital in Memphis Tennessee.

The day before my 46th birthday I underwent the extensive procedure of fusing the lower five vertebrae of my spine. The surgery immobilized my entire lumbar region and, securely bound with steel wire, I would never again have flexibility in my lower back.

In the early hours of my birthday, February 16th, a radiance filled my room. Even though I was still in deep trauma, Ada came into the hospital with a glow that shone like a brilliant light. She was radiant with a promise God had given her in the trying hours of waiting. She burst into my semi-conscious state, beaming as she said. "God has given me the promise; 'The Sun of righteousness has risen with healing in His wings.' I know the surgery will be a success."(2)

During the months of recovery, first Jenny, and then Dawson, each spent 3 months at Ada's side. Dealing with my disability drew us closer together than any crises we had previously experienced.

A short while before the surgery, the Lord had touched the heart of a business man in the quaint Swedish settlement of Lindsborg, in Kansas, and Rodt Sveven and his wife had felt moved by God to provide us with a car for our ministry. It was an oldish Chrysler, huge from bumper to bumper with a voracious appetite for gas. But 8 miles to the gallon was not too bad in the days when gasoline was about 60 cents a gallon. Unknowing what lay ahead, but definitely directed by the Holy Spirit, Rodt had located this 1972 Chrysler Le Baron, and presented it to us for our ministry with great joy and enthusiasm.

Like some other classics, this car had the suicide doors; so named because the two rear doors swung outward, hinged, one at the back, and the other at the front end of the body. If the rear doors ever opened while the car was moving the wind would have ripped them from their hinges causing great damage. Because of this design feature, the doors opened without a central post giving a wide open space for access to the front seat. It was perfect for a patient in a body cast who could not sit erect. Who knew? As Jenny might say, "God is awesome."

Our daily routine, apart from the tedious tasks which accompany the care of a spine patient, included a full scale production of dressing me in the outsized clothes which Ada had purchased to fit over the huge body cast. We often chuckled, sometimes howled with laughter, at my appearance. Getting me off the bed and standing me in an upright position was a feat of ingenuity. I was like a lamppost lying on the bed, held rigid by the ghastly body cast. Ada, by a stroke of genius, came up with the solution. She and either Jenny, then later Dawson, would roll up a bed sheet, slip it under the body cast and under each arm, swing my feet off the bed and then literally lift me into a standing position with the sheet. Stuffing me into the reclining front seat of the Chrysler was another call for ingenuity. Someone always had to guard my head or I would bump it against the edge of the roof.

Ada insisted I get out of the house on some interesting excursion every day. On one of these outings, she and Jenny took me to the Boardwalk at Vero Beach, and against my muffled protest, pried me out of the car. They assured me the sea air would do me good. I stood next to the car wobbling unsteadily, all the while protesting, "I don't feel like walking along the Boardwalk." All I could accomplish in the body cast was an uneven shuffle, not really a walk.

We saw a group of people running along the beach yelling some sort of warning. They came abreast of us trailing a cloud of "no-seeums." For the uninitiated, which was us, "no-seeums" are jokingly (which is not really funny) described as "two wings and a big mouth." Tinier than mosquitos, these minute flying pests are invisible individually. Only when they swarm in their countless numbers can you see a moving haze. By then it is too late; the scouts of the swarm have already begun the attack. The bites are worse than those of mosquitoes.

The fringe of the tormenting cloud descended on me even as Ada caught the cry "no-seeums." If there was any comedy to the scene it was provided by my two blond attendants (Ada and Jenny) trying to stuff my almost rigid frame back into the car. Alas, too late! The insects had attacked my head and my neck, and found their way *inside* my body cast.

Ever irrepressible, Ada saw the comedy of our hasty retreat and laughed us through the episode. Two weeks of sheer torture followed as I searched for anything I could find to reach down into the body cast and scratch the angry, itching welts I carried on my body. Ever since then, I have had a particular appreciation for fly swatters! The wire handle was about the only implement I could safely push between my burning, itching skin and the hot, sweaty plaster cast.

Then it was time for a changing of the guard. Jenny had been with us for 3 months, but she needed to return to Tulsa. Dawson came by bus from Baylor University in Waco to stand guard with Ada. He moved into my room, and kept the night watches.

As we lived together through those testing days, there grew in us an awareness of that peculiar tie that separates humanity from all other creatures. It is the utter dependence of the new-born child, which, when nurtured in the cradle of God-directed principles, will blossom into a love which later is returned by children who have been cherished in their impressionable years.

Through the years of their childhood, adolescence and young adulthood we had, I assume, like all parents, made our share of mistakes in the learning curve of raising our children. Yet somehow, by the Grace of God, we had forged a family life that then, as now, caused us to be unspeakably grateful for the principles upon which we built our home life. The guidance of God's Word, family life conferences, the reading of appropriate books and the daily desire to raise our children with love had collectively shaped the development of the lives of all of us.

The trauma of my own marred childhood worked as a force to keep me from repeating a cycle of dysfunction. Our family relationships were a miracle of God's making. The pursuit of my calling and the demands of the endeavors to "fulfill the ministry which I had received of the Lord"(3) had necessitated sacrifices and separations over the years. Our children were assured of two things, however; that our love for them was unconditional, and that home is wherever Mom and Dad are. This, by their own confession they knew. This time of trial saw the flourishing of a reciprocal love for us, and the genesis of succeeding years in which they demonstrated a unique loving care for their parents.

Chapter Thirty-Seven

t was July, 1978, and Jenny was back in Tulsa, living with Dr. Bob and Nancy Staab. The family had taken her under their care, giving her a home and security. She was also working as a beautician, which meant she often had to keep late hours. She had no means of personal transport and was dependant on someone meeting her each night after the salon closed. One evening, due to a breakdown in communications, she was left waiting anxiously for a ride home that never came.

Alone on the curb, in a deserted strip mall, she became alarmed. She could not get back into the beauty shop because all the staff had left, and she was afraid to walk alone in search of a telephone. Eventually the family missed her and dispatched someone to fetch her. They found her in tears in front of the salon. She called us to tell us of the frightening ordeal. Ada's immediate response was, "We *must* buy Jenny a car."

Providentially, Ada's mother, before she died, and of her own volition, had sold Ada's piano and had sent her a thousand dollars to buy another, knowing how dearly she loved her music. Life could never be quite complete for Ada without being able to spend time lost in the rapture of worship at the piano.

The money was earmarked. It was precious. It was also the only money we possessed in the whole, wide world. Characteristic of her spontaneous generosity, but linked with her anxious concern for Jenny, Ada said, "Let's take the piano money and buy Jenny a car." She added, "Dawson can drive it west to Tulsa, deliver it to Jenny, and then take a bus down to Baylor University in Waco for the start of his new semester in September."

The very next day Dawson and I set out in the Chrysler and cruised the used car lots. I was barely able to see above the door-line because of my reclining position on the fold-down passenger seat. I had an innate love for cars. They had been my hobby in my Technical College and motor racing days.

Perhaps that is why I spotted it. I just knew the small white two-door Mazda RX3 was "it." Dawson swung the lumbering Chrysler into the lot and helped me to a rigid standing position next to the cute object of interest. He went in search of Honest Bob, the used car dealer. The salesman didn't have to do any selling. I wasn't able even to kick the tires, let alone drive, but Dawson started the motor (how silently, how silently the rotary engine runs!), and took the car for what the English call a "spin." He came back with a very positive report.

I asked the salesman, "How much?"

The reply, "One thousand two hundred dollars."

I told the salesman I had only one thousand, and offered him cash with the request that they put 4 new tires on the car. He disappeared to discuss the offer with the sales manager and came back with a "Yes." The deal was done. New tires included!

Before setting out for Tulsa, Dawson drove south, to Miami. We thought it would be a good test run for Jenny's new car, but misfortune was his companion. He called from Miami with the news that the gas pump had broken. It would cost about two hundred dollars to repair. What were we to do?

I phoned the manager at the used car lot and explained our predicament.

As we always did, we depended upon God's provision. Everything we attempted or sought to accomplish was attended with prayer. Not just a perfunctory "God help me!" Rather, we recognized that God was the source of our very life and breath. Everything came to us from His good hand. Equally, we recognized that God worked the miracles of His provision through loving, concerned and obedient Christian people. So we prayed.

The manager responded with the answer, "Have the car fixed and we will pay for the repair." We were elated; we also were grateful to the Lord for leading us to a dealer who was the antithesis of the characters about whom we had been warned. Dawson set out for Tulsa. Jenny was ecstatic. This was her *first ever* car! She waited with bated breath for the promised gift. It never came!

In Tennessee, approaching the city of Jackson, a few hundred miles before Memphis, the rotary engine of the Mazda RX3 seized up and burned out. Dawson was to have spent the night in Memphis with Jim and Rose Marie Pace, the dear people who had hosted us prior to the surgery in February, and who had so lovingly cared for Ada and Jenny during the ordeal of my operation. Dawson phoned Jim late that night, and he graciously drove to where the Mazda stood forlorn beside the Interstate. He helped Dawson secure the services of a towing company, and Dawson watched disconsolately as the little car was parked in the lot of a garage in Jackson. It was passed midnight, and there was nothing to do but go on to Memphis and, after a rest, take a bus to Waco. All seemed lost.

Yet in those small but mysterious situations, God was in control! Dr. Stewarts' daughter (the one who had introduced us to her father) had recently married, and, was living in Jackson, the very town where the car was abandoned. The telephone lines between Vero Beach and Jackson began buzzing. Jim Rhodes, her husband, drove to the garage where our Mazda was parked. You guessed it; it was a Mazda dealership.

Jim gave me a first hand report by telephone. The news was not good. I then began a series of telephone conversations with the service manager at the garage. The interchanges went something like this:

"How much will it cost to fix the car?"

"It cannot be fixed, you need a complete new motor."

"What will that cost?"

"Anywhere from eight hundred to one thousand dollars, depending on how many parts we can use from the old engine."

"I have just paid one thousand dollars to buy the car and I honestly do not have a dollar more to spend on it."

Silence.

My next question, "How much will you give me for the car?"

"Two hundred dollars."

"But," I protested, "the four new tires are worth two hundred dollars."

The bottom line was, there was absolutely nothing they could do for me. Through all this, we were reporting every move, every question and answer to a tearful Jenny. Dawson, too, was deeply grieved. The final blow seemed to fall when, in despair, with stinging tears, Jenny said to me one night on the phone, "Daddy, why is God so mean to you?"

I was, in every human sense, helpless. My plaster cast had recently been replaced by a rigid back brace to which was attached a steel rod which ran down my left leg. It was anchored at my thigh and knee with leather straps. I could not bend at the waist. I could do nothing to help my distraught family. Yet we continued to pray.

We spent much of our time in reading, study, prayer and contemplation. I was also writing Part One of this book. A couple, George and Sylvia Brown, who for that time in our lives were a great encouragement and a blessing, provided me with a tape recorder into which I dictated the first draft. I could not sit up to write, but lay on my bed recording event after event.

When Jenny asked, "Daddy, why is God so mean to you?" I gently explained the principle that is the heart and soul of this book.

I said, "Jenny, God is not mean. God loves us, and all these trials come to us as part of living. It is how we react to the test that counts. The trials of life are opportunities for us to trust God. We have two options when trials and testings come. We can become bitter, even angry, blame God and go down in defeat. The other alternative is to believe God and the words of God." I quoted the title which God had given me for my story. "He knows the way that I take, and when He has tried me, *I shall come forth as gold.*"(1)

I personally was cast wholly on the truths of Dawson's favorite hymn, "How Firm a Foundation":

How firm a foundation, ye saints of the Lord,
Is laid for your faith in His excellent Word!
What more can He say than to you He hath said;
To you who for refuge to Jesus have fled?

Fear not, I am with thee, O be not dismayed,
For I am thy God, I will still give thee aid;
I'll strengthen thee, help thee, and cause thee to stand,
Upheld by my gracious omnipotent hand.

When through the deep waters I cause thee to go,
The rivers of sorrow shall not over flow;
For I will be with thee thy troubles to bless,
And sanctify to thee thy deepest distress.

When through fiery trials thy pathway shall lie,
My grace, all sufficient, shall be thy supply;
The flame shall not hurt thee, I only design,
Thy dross to consume and thy gold to refine.

The soul that on Jesus hath leaned for repose,
I will not, I will not, desert to its foes;
That soul though all hell should endeavor to shake,
I'll never, no never, no never forsake!

Two weeks after my last conversation with the service manager at the garage where the Mazda had been abandoned, and my sobering talk with Jenny, the phone next to my bed rang. The service manager was again on the line.

He said, "Rev. Church, the Mazda Field Representative has just been to our dealership. He has looked at your car, and *the Mazda Corporation has offered to put a new motor in the vehicle for you.*" We wept tears of joy and we poured out our praise to God with unbridled thanksgiving. Our happiness was complete. A week later, Jenny and a friend took the bus to Memphis. Jim and Rose Marie Pace drove them to Jackson to collect the restored car.

Compressed into that episode was the seed of truth that shaped my life. The lessons we learned in those months deeply affected us and the lives of our two children. Strong conviction, forged by experience, proved the words of King David, the sweet singer of Israel: "I love the Lord, because He has heard my voice and my supplication. Because He has inclined His ear to me, therefore, I will call on Him as long as I live."(2) Faith looks back on the past with assurance; Hope looks with confidence; "I will call upon Him as long as I live."

Chapter Thirty-Eight

ow does God speak? The apostles asserted that in those days of God's grace He would confirm His work with signs and wonders that He would make His ways known in dreams and visions.(1) As the months passed I gradually regained mobility and strength. The body cast was discarded and for another 3 months I wore a steel leg brace. Dr. Stewart released me to my ministry and we once more took up our itinerant preaching and teaching schedule.

In 1978 I had a dream. We were preaching in one of the cities on the great plains of West Texas, and on the Saturday night our hosts had organized a fellowship supper where we shared our testimony and talked about the great spiritual challenges facing South Africa.

In the dream I saw countless numbers of people of every tribe, nation and tongue. They were in huge groups, each cluster dressed in national costumes and holding out hands as though pleading for a gift.

In the dream I rushed hastily from group to group preaching to them, telling them the Good News of the Gospel. As I frenziedly tried to preach to each group, the voice of God spoke to me as clearly as I have ever heard anyone speak.

He said, "Do you love these people?"

I hurriedly replied, "Yes Lord, I love them!"

This happened three times. Each time the voice of the Lord interrupted me. Each time He said, "Do you love these people?" The answer each time was the same. "Yes Lord, you know that I love them." Between each question and answer I continued the urgent work of preaching, pleading with them to receive Christ.

Suddenly, among the crowds a man stood up. He was dirty, disheveled, repulsive to look at. I was startled and backed away.

Again I heard the voice of God, "Do you love this man?"

In the same hurried voice I replied, "Yes Lord, of course I love him!"

God responded, "Show him you love him. Put your arms around him and tell him you love him." In my dream, I saw myself walk to the man, and as I embraced him, I began to cry.

I didn't just cry. I began to weep and sob so bitterly that the bed in which we were sleeping began to shake. Ada woke up with a start and said, "What is wrong?"

I sat upright in the bed, shaking as I wept. My pillow was soaked with tears. Tears streamed down my face and ran like rivers down on my pajama top. I could not stop crying. As my shoulders heaved, and the tears flowed, I kept saying, "All those people…who will tell them about Jesus?"

God was touching my heart with *His* love. Breaking my heart so that I would see what Jesus saw, and feel what He felt when He saw the multitudes of harassed, broken down and lost people, and was moved with compassion.(2)

We were due to preach in the United Methodist Church that Sunday, and I wept unashamedly as I shared my dream. At the end of the service I gave an invitation to anyone who sincerely wanted to be a witness for Christ to come to the altar and make that commitment. Still weeping inconsolably, I prepared to walk to the altar to kneel there myself.

As I turned to speak to the congregation, *the man of my dream was suddenly standing in front of me!*

He was one of the most pitiful people I had ever seen. The man in my dream had looked repulsive, but I didn't know why. The dear man who stood before me was facially disfigured because cancer had devoured parts of his nose, one of his cheeks and his lips. This was no dream but the living picture of human suffering.

Again, the voice of God. Again the question: "Do you love this man?"

I said, "Yes Lord." And God said, "Show him you love him."

I stepped up to the man, put my arms around his shoulders, drew him to me and said; "Sir, I love you."

With that, we both broke down anew and were washed again with the tears of the kind of love that God has for us, and the kind of love we are to have for each other.

Later, in one of the most dramatic episodes of our ministry, I saw Ada demonstrate that same "God kind of love" in a church which we visited in the state of Massachusetts. At the close of a series of meetings that had tested our faith and our commitment to the extreme, Ada had a word spoken into her heart by the Holy Spirit.

One man in particular (an elder in the church) had been overtly opposed to our teaching on the Baptism of the Holy Spirit. By the conclusion of our eight-day mission, God had dramatically changed lives and empowered people through a gracious but very definite manifestation of His power. The husband of a young woman drove to the home where we were staying to thank us for the transformation he had seen in his wife in just one week.

But our antagonist was unmoved, despite such a visible witness of the effectiveness of the Word of God working by the power of the Holy Spirit. As we rested on the last Sunday afternoon of our mission, God spoke a word into Ada's heart.

The final gathering was to be a fellowship supper on Sunday night. When we had eaten and were coming to the close of the evening, Ada spoke up, saying she had a message from the Lord for the church. To everyone's surprise, she left the room for a moment and then returned—with a basin, a jug of water and a towel!

She then knelt down at the stubborn elder's feet and asked him to remove his shoes! She washed his feet, even as Jesus commanded His disciples to do. She then invited anyone else who was willing to come and have his or her feet washed also. People were so moved that many in the room were in tears. Ada's response of love to this man's bitter opposition was disarming, and a practical demonstration of love made visible. Many in that church declared that things would never be the same again. The Lord was magnified and His blessing lavished on our ministry.

Over the years we traveled thousands of miles by road and saw God's love expressed to us in many ways through loving and caring Christians. On one occasion our high mileage car had become a financial liability. A precious family in Florida, Jerry and Vickie Kumpf, instead of trading in their two-year old automobile, gave it to Ada and me as a love gift. We had been living on the edge, depending daily on the provision of our Father's loving care. Our testimony, wherever we had the opportunity, was to declare that God is both willing and able to keep the promises of His word.

One of the purest delights of our ministry occurred in the mountain resort of Ruidoso in New Mexico. Jenny, who was working as my secretary and as worship leader for young people in our missions, attended a music camp in the mountains. Captivated by the awesome majesty of the snow-capped Sierra Blanca and charmed by the Alpine-like village, she insisted we visit the quaint town. So, when we were invited to conduct an eight-day mission in the mountains, we accepted.

During the assignment we were introduced to Bobby and Sandy Alexander, a family with whom we became intertwined in friendship, love and ministry. Over the course of repeated visits to the region, I felt urged by the Holy Spirit to establish a church in Ruidoso. So, in fellowship with the Alexanders and numerous friends, what had been a Bible study group quickly escalated into an amazing church.

We hired a large house with rooms for services, children's meetings and Sunday school. Ada and I made our home in the main bedroom for six months and hosted a covered dish supper for 60 people every Wednesday night. I determined to establish a church based on the faithful preaching of God's Word, the vital expression of the Holy Spirit's presence and the true fellowship of believers as demonstrated in the book of Acts. In the space of two brief years we witnessed an exciting renewal. Contributing their time and talents, in one summer, the people themselves erected a striking building to accommodate their vibrant congregation. Men and women worked together on the project, side by side, like the Israelites of Nehemiah's day.(3)

Trinity Mountain Fellowship was a testimony to the power of God and the loving dedication of a motivated people. Based on the foundation of preaching the Word of God, and alive with the anointing of the Holy Spirit, the Church prospered mightily. The love and faithful friendship of Bobby and Sandy Alexander continued, and was one of the anchors to steady us in the storms which would threaten our ship as we sailed into the rough seas ahead of us.

Chapter Thirty-Nine

y 1993, seventeen summers had shone their warmth on us since our American odyssey had begun. They had been years in which, like the "sheep dogs" of Psalm 23, God's "goodness and mercy" had followed us. His goodness had supplied our needs, and His mercy had kept us in His love.(1)

We had traversed the length and breath of America the Beautiful, by road and by air. We had logged tens of thousands of miles in fulfillment of our commitment to the call of God. In the pursuit of obedience to the commission of Christ, we had, in the years of our ministry touched 48 of the States in the Union.

Now, came a testing of our faith, our courage and our endurance more monumental than anything we had ever experienced before the twin options of doubt and fear towered over us.

In September 1993, Dr. Brent Norman, confirming the diagnosis of Dr. Lean, had raised the dark specter of death, diagnosing the malignant tumor in Ada's left eye. Following the thunderous tolling of that somber bell, we returned to the condominium in Solana Beach to wait, and to pray.

Ada's birthday dawned three days later. That day we drove from Solana Beach to Riverside to visit Jay Self, a long-time friend of Bishop Adler of the CEC. It was an encounter with "angels unawares."(2) Jay and his wife Dottie received us with warmth and took us to lunch in one of the most unique restaurants in Riverside, opened by an African American gentleman who had been laid off from the General Motors plant in California. With members of his family he had begun the business and under their loving, personal supervision, the New Orleans-style restaurant had flourished and had become "the" place for lunch. Tipped off by our hosts, one of the family members asked if she might sing a special song for Ada during the meal.

In that crowded place, with all the noonday diners listening intently, she sang a song which brought a hush on the house and left us awash in tears. Tenderly, without accompaniment she sang; "May the good Lord bless and keep you." The entire song was powerful, wistful, with prophetic overtones.

> May the good Lord bless and keep you 'til we meet again.
> May your troubles all be small ones, and your blessings ten
>   times ten.
> May the good Lord bless and keep you 'til we meet again.

However, though we left the restaurant with warmed hearts, every waking moment was shadowed by the brooding awareness of the doctors' words, "You have cancer. You are going to die." But, in spite of the pending doom, we had invited our longstanding friends, Tony and Liz Louch with Bishop and Betty Adler to celebrate Ada's birthday with us at the condo in Solana Beach.

How could anyone be so bright, so vivacious and such a gracious hostess with so dark a cloud hovering over her? Only those who knew Ada would understand. She could cheer up any crowd by the sound of her spontaneous laughter. The social exchanges were joyous that birthday night, but a pervasive sense of threat ran just beneath the surface of our emotions. Like a barely visible mist, it brought the uneasy premonition of unwelcome change to the circle of friends.

Cautious lest we make rash decisions, we lived each day waiting for clear leading from the Lord. The Apostle Paul assures us that, as the children of God, "we are guided by the Spirit of God."(3) That guidance came to us through a phone call from one of Ada's close friends in El Paso, Nancy Lynch.

Pressured as we were to act and make the difficult choice between Radiation Plaque therapy and enucleation, our doctor's wife, Lyn Huss, had counseled, "Seek the opinion of a university hospital." We agreed in principle, but the question was, where? We were charting a course in unknown waters, and were strangers in this new world where every point of the compass pointed to the "C" word, cancer. Nancy asked Ada if she would be willing to go to the M.D. Anderson Cancer Center in Houston. Through personal friendship with the director of the center, Nancy was able to arrange an immediate consultation.

Another factor was at work, demonstrating the mystery of God's ways. His ways are not our ways and His thoughts are wholly other than ours. He assures us that His workings are always directed towards our good and the display of His glory.(4)

For nearly 4 years we had been trying to sell the house which we had bought and remodeled in El Paso. Who can anticipate the vagaries of the housing market or understand the boom and bust economy of the United States? But God, who knows the end from the beginning, had not allowed our house in El Paso to sell. With Nancy's aid, and the fact that we were homeowners in Texas, we were accorded the benefits granted to Texas residents by the M.D. Anderson Cancer Center which is one of the premier hospitals in the nation for the treatment of cancer.

Again with Nancy's help, plans were rapidly executed and we arrived in Houston on Monday, October 11, 1993. Ada was scheduled for admission the next morning at 7 a.m. Our friend Steve Ingraham spontaneously invited us to be guests in his home in Houston.

Unknown to us, he also arranged a spectacular dinner party at one of Houston's celebrated French restaurants. What a party! The restaurant was decorated with a breath-taking display of South Africa's National flower, the Protea. None of the other patrons in that restaurant would have guessed from the gaiety at our table that it would be followed by a pre-dawn journey into the unknown valleys of the cancer world.

In the grey of that Fall morning, we braced ourselves for the trauma, and began a two week saga of consultations, examinations and tests, punctuated by tense hours of waiting, waiting, and waiting some more. Part of the ordeal was the daily sight of hundreds of cancer patients silently moving down the corridors and filling the waiting rooms. We were face-to-face with the ravages of one of the body's arch-enemies. I was reminded of a sermon by the great English preacher, Charles Haddon Spurgeon. Commenting on 1 Cor. 15:26, the eloquent expositor had said, referring to death, "This is the work of an enemy."

As we waited in the lounges, my mind often drifted to a friend who had walked these same corridors, but was with us no more! Late in 1976, I had asked Jamie Buckingham to write my story. He had authored the autobiographies of many people, giving literary substance to personalities such as Katherine Kuhlman, David Wilkersen and Nicky Cruz. We were both speaking at a conference in Orlando, Florida, and Ada and I had just made the momentous decision to give away our earthly possessions and live trusting God to supply our every need.

Jamie had said to me, "You can tell a story as well as I can. You should write your book." I did. Now Ada and I walked the same corridors Jamie and Jackie had strolled during the days of his own battle with cancer. I thought much about Jamie and was grateful to have known a man of such openness, honesty, candor and humility. Jamie died in 1993.

We began our journey at the M. D. Anderson Cancer Center in the examining room of Dr. David Callender. We then saw other doctors. At M. D. Anderson, a physician's counsel is held once a week and each patient's case is reviewed. Ada was examined by no less than eight specialists. Our emotions traveled a roller coaster till we came to the day of reckoning. The collective opinion and final diagnosis was ocular melanoma: A malignant tumor in the left eye located perilously close to her optic nerve.

The prognosis was dire: "The cancer will spread to your lungs and your liver. We are not sure how long you will live, because this type of cancer may metastasize rapidly. The recommended treatment: immediate Radiation Plaque therapy or enucleation, removal of the eye." The final stanza in all the pronouncements was always the same: "Remove the eye and you remove the cancer....However, we do not know which course of action will afford you the greatest chance of survival."

They stood in a solemn circle around the examination chair where Ada was seated. Dr. Callender voiced the sentiment of the half dozen doctors and technicians when he said, "We are delighted to meet you, we are only sorry it is under such unfortunate circumstances."

There was, however, one dissonant note in this chorus. It came from Doctor Ha. In an almost forgotten moment he had spoken to us about a relatively new procedure called proton beam therapy. On the day he had discussed it with Ada, he had shown her how the patient is "masked" for the procedure.

That night, Ada had nightmares. She woke me up in the early hours and shared her dread of such a procedure and said she could not bear to think of going through such an ordeal. The grotesque mask was reminiscent of faces in horror movies. However, Dr. Ha contacted one of his colleagues in Boston, where the therapy was being pioneered. He obtained the name of the leading physician specialist, and advised us to make the journey to Massachusetts immediately.

We weighed the difference between radioactive plaque therapy and proton radiation therapy. In plaque therapy, the eye is lifted out its socket and a specially crafted gold plaque, charged with I 125 radioactive ions, is attached over the area of the tumor. After six or seven days, the eye is again loosened and the plaque removed. In Ada's case, because of the tumor's close proximity to the optic nerve, each of the physicians told us she would most definitely lose the sight of her left eye.

proton beam therapy, utilizing a recently developed form of radiation, is the technology by which a beam of radioactive particles is aimed at the tumor from outside the eye. This procedure also requires the eye to be removed by surgery. Minute stainless steel clips are attached to the back of the eye, precisely marking the boundaries of the tumor. In preparation for the radiation a mark is made on the patient's face. The exact position, size and shape of the tumor, as marked by the clips, is entered into a computer. This information determines the strength of, and depth to which, the radiated beam will penetrate the eye. The clips remain attached to the eye for the rest of the patient's life.

The Ingraham family, Steve and Ellen and their two children, Terri and Dereck, had been a strength, a comfort, a help without which we could not have survived the two weeks. In the love and goodness of God He sent these angels, ministers of His grace, to encourage, support and strengthen us.

Another gracious offer of friendship, love and support was expressed by long-distance. For many years we had enjoyed a special friendship with Dr. and Mrs Wilfred Kent. Wilf, as we affectionately called him, is a psychologist with an almost miraculous record of success is seeing restoration and healing of broken lives through a Biblically based counseling ministry. His wife Donna is a Registered Nurse. In numerous phone calls they encouraged us and prayed for us. I was taken aback when Donna said, "Peter if you say the word, I will fly immediately from Denver to be with you and to look after Ada."

Every opportunity we had, Ada chose to go to places of worship where she could be prayed for. In El Paso, prior to leaving for Houston, a group of friends had prayed for Ada at the altar of St. Clement's Episcopal Church. Ricky and Lou Ann Feuille, Tom and Marilyn La Nou and Alex and Jan Blomerth had gathered around Ada after Communion, and as they laid hands on her, she sank to the floor under the power of God's Spirit. It seemed incongruous to be lying on one's back in so sacred a spot. But then, when the Almighty moves so powerfully, who can dictate what shall occur?

In Houston, Steve and Terri took us to a Sunday morning service at Lakewood Church where John and Dodie Osteen exercise their God-blessed ministry. Pastor Osteen preached on the topic of "Don't limit God." After the message, Ada joined the people who surged to the front of the church for prayer. She determined she would not limit what God was able to do for her. Dodie Osteen prayed for Ada, and gave her a copy of her book *Healed of Cancer*.

Finally, the time for action had come. One option we were offered was a request from the physician at the Hermann Eye Clinic to enter a program designated The Ocular Melanoma Study Program. It is a national research program which people with Ada's rare form of eye cancer are invited to participate. Patients' names are entered into a computer database, and the computer then randomly decides which patients will receive radiation and which will be enucleated. Once the patient has undergone either of the procedures, they are "tracked" for the rest of their lives, to determine which of the two procedures is more successful in extending the life of the patient.

"You will be doing mankind a service if you enter the program," said the Director of the Eye Clinic. Ada retorted, "I have given my whole life to the service of mankind."

That was yet another hard choice offered by our situation. Daily, constantly, our lives were lived in an atmosphere of communion with our Heavenly Father. We walked softly, gently, prayerfully through every waking hour. Every morning and every night, I continued to anoint Ada's eye with oil, humbly obeying the direction of St. James. We prayed the prayer of faith. Eventually Ada said No. We would not enter the Ocular Melanoma Study Program. We would not give the power of choice to a computer.

I strongly believed we should continue to expect a miracle, and that we should leave the door open for God to move in His own way and time. Even as we prayed, God was orchestrating the circumstances which would break into our lives like a whirlwind.

> God moves in a mysterious way,
> His wonders to perform;
> He plants His footsteps in the sea,
> And rides upon the storm.
> Deep in unfathomable mines
> Of never-failing skill,
> He treasures up His bright-designs,
> And works His sovereign will.

Chapter Forty

We were in direct contact with many of our close and special friends. I had continued through the months to send our newsletter to the people on our small, but special mailing list. People from around the nation and in South Africa were praying for Ada. We valued the close ties which Ada had with her sisters and their families. Each of the three girls in South Africa—Garness, Aleanor (Pal) and Elaine, took Ada's plight to their respective church families for prayer.

A break in the stalemate came in one of my telephone conversations with Bishop Adler. I told him about Dr. Ha's suggestion that we fly to Boston. I also mentioned that there was one other hospital where proton radiation therapy is offered. The only two centers in the USA are in Boston and at Loma Linda in California.

Bishop Adler immediately responded with, "One of our members is a doctor in residence at Loma Linda. His name is Joseph Scoggins." My heartbeat quickened. I immediately phoned Dr. Scoggins' wife Kim. Within a short while she gave me the name of the specialist physician I should contact at Loma Linda. We prepared to leave Houston and fly back to El Paso, reorganize, and drive on to California.

It was Thursday, October 21, 1993. Our host, Stevie, as we had affectionately come to know him, organized a fabulous farewell lunch party for us. He invited some special friends, and together we enjoyed and celebrated in a meal which we will long remember. At the conclusion, we drifted out of the restaurant in ones and twos, with Steve going ahead. The cell phone in his car was ringing. It was his wife, Ellen. She had an urgent message for us. We were to call Dr. Ruiz at the Hermann Eye Center immediately.

The Hermann Eye Center is associated with the M. D. Anderson Cancer Center and performs all procedures and eye treatments on referral from M. D. Anderson. Ada had undergone extensive investigation at the Hermann Clinic, and any procedures recommended by M.D. Anderson would have been performed there. Dr. Ruiz, the Director, had examined Ada several times during our two weeks in Houston, and had performed the identical tests which had been done by Doctors Lean and Norman in California.

We were amazed. How had the surgeon at the Hermann Center reached us? The answer revealed the wonder of God's mysterious ways. On registering at the Hermann Eye Hospital, we had given, as our nearest relative, the name and office phone number of our son Dawson, in California. They had phoned Dawson who had taken the call and given the doctor's office Steve's home number. Ellen in turn called Steve on his cell phone.

The message conveyed to us was urgent. Mrs. Church was to contact Dr. Ruiz immediately. Seated in the back of the car, Ada took the phone after Steve had dialed the number. We could all hear both ends of the conversation as the car sped along the concrete freeway that circles Houston.

"Mrs. Church, this is Doctor Ruiz's office. Please hold the line for Dr. Ruiz."

I guessed that not many patients had personal calls from the Head of the Department. He said, "Mrs. Church, where are you?"

She replied, "We are on our way to the airport."

"Where are you going?"

"To California."

"Why California?"

"Dr. Ha at M. D. Anderson has suggested we investigate proton beam therapy."

Dr. Ruiz' voice was firm, insistent. "Mrs. Church, I don't think you should be going to California."

"Why?"

"We are not only concerned for your eye, we are concerned for your life!"

Silence. The party was over. Ada said, "Dr. Ruiz, you need to speak to my husband." The atmosphere in the car was electric. I took the phone, paused, took a deep breath and said, "Dr. Ruiz, what do you suggest?"

He said, "I would like to see your wife in my office tomorrow morning." I responded, "We'll be there." We canceled our flight to El Paso and put our plans for California on hold. Thankfully, our precious friend Nancy Lynch had bought tickets that could be changed at a moments notice.

On Friday morning we were again at the Hermann Eye Center. Again, Steve and his family rallied to make it possible. Dr. Ruiz reviewed Ada's chart. He looked again at the X-rays and the sonogram. He turned to us and said, "Mrs. Church, I think you should have the radioactive plaque therapy immediately."

We had decided, following all our prayers and waiting on the Lord, that we would follow the counsel of the physician. Ada had prayed, "Lord show these doctors what to do." We looked at each other, and Ada asked me, "What do you think?" I said, "I think we should do it." That put the wheels in motion, instantly!

Immediately, a problem arose. The doctor who would craft the gold plaque was not in his office. Dr. Ruiz gave the order, "Find him!" They eventually established contact with him, and Dr. Ruiz asked him if he could make the tiny gold plate *that weekend*. He said he could, but it would take a couple of days for the I 125 radioactive ions to "settle" in the plaque.

Dr. Ruiz asked if the plaque could be ready by Tuesday. He said he would try for Tuesday, but they agreed that if that were not possible, they would perform the surgery on Thursday. Dr. Ruiz asked if that was acceptable to us. We agreed. I began to do some mental calculations. We were looking at a minimum of 2 more weeks in Houston.

I prayed. Unknown to me, Ada was voicing the same prayer. "Lord, this is serious business. We *must* be sure they know exactly what they are doing." Through all the hours of examinations and tests, in the dim almost darkened consulting rooms, I had always sat quietly in the corner, observing, listening, praying. I felt the impact of every pronouncement of doom. I could not feel the same pain Ada felt, because those who suffer the pangs walk through the dark valley alone. All our most decisive battles are fought out in single combat. Our deepest emotions are endured alone.

But in the bond of true love there is an empathy, an understanding, that unites the heart and mind in a union that shares the hurt. My heart was torn. Were it possible, I would have borne Ada's pain. I could not, yet I suffered with her. I held her hand, steadied her, walked every step with her down those long lonesome corridors. When her eyes were moist, tears welled up in her eyes. We both sensed this was a moment of destiny.

My prayer was, "Lord, let the doctor look at the tumor one more time."

He was out of the examining room. Ada and I were alone in the dimly lighted room. There was nothing more to say, yet our hearts were one. Our silent prayer was one. There was a flurry of activity outside the room. The staff were booking surgery schedules and making arrangements. The door was ajar. Suddenly one of the staff stepped in and said, "Dr. Ruiz wants to take one last look at the tumor in Mrs. Church's eye."

We knew the routine so well by now. Eye drops, wait for the pupils to dilate, and then the probing, seeking search into the eye by the doctor's beam of light and magnifying scope. Dr. Ruiz went through the now-familiar routine. After an initial examination, he scooted his stool-on-wheels across to the counter where Ada's patient file was spread. He held color slides up to the light, measured sonogram pictures and then scooted back to Ada.

Another intensive search into the window of the soul. What did he see? Suddenly, he sat bolt upright, switched on the light in the darkened room turned to me and detonated what amounted to a verbal atomic bomb!

"I'm not convinced that Mrs. Church has melanoma!" he exclaimed.

Chapter Forty-One

His words left us speechless. When I recovered from the initial shock, my delayed reaction was to ask weakly, "What do you mean?"

"I'm not convinced now that Mrs. Church has a malignant tumor in her eye. There is something there, but I'm not sure it is a malignant melanoma." Another silence. My next question, "What do you suggest we do?"

"Go home, live a normal life, and let me see Mrs. Church in one year's time."

We had quietly gathered up our belongings, wandered out of the consulting area, and now stood in the foyer, facing the elevators, dazed. Everything seemed so otherworldly, trance-like. We were like two shell-shocked soldiers after an explosion. We were both elated, yet strangely quiet. Ripples of joy were flooding through us. We wanted to shout "Hallelujah!" right there in the hospital corridor. The shock had been so sudden, so totally unexpected, that our emotions were a blend of bemused wonder and hushed disbelief.

One minute we were preparing for surgery, with the words, "We are concerned for your life" hanging like a black cloud over our lives. Now, with breath-taking speed, the clouds had been swept away, the gates of our prison had burst open, and we were free!

Free! But where should we go!

What should we do?

Whom should we call?

How would we report this?

Finally, the shock wore off and I stepped to the pay phone in the foyer. My first, calls were to Jenny, to Dawson and to our Archbishop in San Clemente. Terri picked us up and drove us back to the Ingraham home. There we continued the task of calling everyone we knew who was bearing the burden with us.

The news spread like wild fire. Some even got the message in a garbled fashion. Passing information from person to person can be hazardous, but the word did get out and thousands rejoiced with us.

It was as though Springtime had come to us. We left Houston and headed west. Back in El Paso, I sat with J. O. Stewart, the man who had been my close friend and confidant for so many years. I respected his wisdom, his intellectual honesty, and his friendship. I told him the story, and concluded,

"J. O., I don't understand what has happened, if I had heard this story told about someone else, I would have been skeptical. All I can say is, it really has happened."

J. O.'s response was full of insight. "This is a miracle either way you view it. If indeed there has been a miracle of healing we are grateful to God. If we have to wait and see, then the miracle is that you did not let them take out Ada's eye as all the physicians urged as a first choice."

At the beginning of 1993 I had made the commitment to serve the Archbishop of the Charismatic Episcopal Church as his aide and assistant, and both Ada and I expressed our newfound sense of liberation as we gave ourselves whole-heartedly to the task. With the birth of this new movement, I had offered to serve Bishop Adler while trusting God to meet our financial needs.

Though we were rejoicing in the reprieve which Dr. Ruiz's words had brought, we struggled desperately through a year in which it became increasingly evident that I had erred in judgment. The financial support I had anticipated for my work with Bishop Adler did not materialize. Though we were living in the aftermath of the discovery of the cancer and the reprieve of Dr. Ruiz's diagnosis, donations to our ministry dropped dramatically. I was not engaged in an active preaching role. Although both M. D. Anderson and the Hermann Eye Hospitals gave us gracious and generous discounts, I began to accrue huge medical and other debts that I could not meet.

The sentiment which accompanied the lowest financial point in the history of our ministry was expressed by many: "If you are working for a denomination, they should pay your expenses and support you!" I could not continue, and in June of 1994, the House of Bishops of the CEC eliminated the position to which I had been appointed by the Archbishop. I had served for 16 months, paying most of the expenses incurred by my travel, devoting my time and talents, yet not receiving the income which Ada and I needed to meet the demands of daily living. It took a terrible toll on both of us.

The proverbial last straw to break the camel's back, was the loss of our home. For four years we had struggled valiantly to purchase the delightful house we had been occupying. We had discovered this abandoned gem on the fringe of the Texas-New Mexico border. Run down and dilapidated, on the very edge of the desert, a realtor had jokingly quipped, "Who would want to live in this place?"

Ada's response had been, "I would." For years we had labored with love, sweat and tears, and begun the transformation which made "this old house" a jewel which we cherished. In May, a wealthy Las Vegas entrepreneur laid cash on the barrel and bought our prize. It seemed like the knockout punch to all our dreams. Ada was broken in heart adding a further emotional conflict to her fight with cancer.

Over a span of twenty years we had been drawn back repeatedly to the charm of the Southwest. In the deserts of West Texas and New Mexico friendships had flourished and God had used our ministry there to touch the lives of thousands of people. We had planted churches, encouraged believers and used El Paso as a launching pad for many of our missionary and ministry excursions. We had seen the fulfillment of the prophet's word, "The desert shall rejoice and blossom as the rose."(1)

In the years 1992 to 1994 I had witnessed the blossoming of a strategic ministry among the pastors in El Paso. Together with Pastor J. R. Camfield we had sponsored the first March For Jesus in 1992: As part of a National celebration, the event brought the Christian community together in a display of unity and demonstrated the joy of our Faith. In song and dance thousands marched in harmony through the heart of the border city which had been born in violence and whose history was stained with blood and lawlessness.

That same year I had the pleasure of meeting the man God has used to bring the word of reconciliation to the Body of Christ and healing to communities. When I asked if he would come as God's messenger of peace to El Paso, John Dawson said, "I have wanted to come to El Paso for a long time, but I waited for a 'man of peace' to invite me." He came to El Paso and brought his message of hope and reconciliation to the Christian leaders.

Once a month I organized a prayer breakfast in which pastors and Christian leaders met for fellowship and prayer for the city. The Pastors' Prayer Fellowship was the foundation and basis, not only for the mutual encouragement of the Pastors, but the staging ground upon which these men and women could labor together in love to bring the Gospel of Christ to El Paso and its twin border city, Juarez.

I asked the Lord for the answer in seeking a common ground for fellowship and prayer. How could we bring fifty to one hundred individuals, of such varied persuasions and theologies together, and keep the focus and purpose of our gathering clear and centered on our mission? He reminded me of the acronym ACTS which I had learned years before. I used this as the framework for our hour-long prayer gatherings, and had a large banner made which accentuated the letters.

"A" was for Adoration. For thirty minutes we engaged in worship focused on the names of God using Scripture references to magnify the Person of Christ and the majesty of God. The pastors spontaneously joined in songs of praise and adoration.

"C" was for Confession. Knowing that when we see God in His splendor, we see ourselves in our unworthiness, thirty minutes were spent in confession and acknowledgment of our corporate shortcomings. It was a cleansing experience to receive the forgiveness of God and to see the healing of relationships.

"T" was for Thanksgiving. It was then time to thank God for all the bounty of His love and provision. The pastors recounted experiences of prayers answered. On one occasion a spontaneous love offering was taken to replace the roof of a mission church in Mexico.

"S" was for Supplication. For our prayer time we often broke into small groups. Having spent thirty minutes in each of the first three exercises, we were now ready to ask God for the provision we needed to accomplish His work. We prayed for each other, for the city and for any need mentioned. One morning a pastor slipped in late and shared with the group that he had just been diagnosed with cancer! We were able to console him and pray for his healing.

It was a gut-wrenching experience to leave those joys behind; home, friends, the work of God. But we knew that it was time for us to move on. So at the end of June 1994, with our faith continuing steadfast in the grace, goodness and ever-loving wisdom of our Heavenly Father, we placed our household of furniture in storage and headed west. Our son Dawson and his wife Brenda gave us the use of their cute cabin among the redwoods of Boulder Creek, south of San Francisco.

Earlier in the year, Ada's sisters urged her to return to South Africa for a season of renewed fellowship with her family and also to rest. They offered to pay her airfare. Ada's sister Eleanor (Pal) was married to the Rev. Edmund Roebert, pastor of the widely known and honored Hatfield Christian Church in Pretoria, South Africa. Ed and Pal were to be in the United States in July, and it was agreed that Ada should return with them to South Africa in August.

While there, Ada experienced the great joy of renewed friendships as well as prayer for others. Visiting my sister Hilda and her husband, Rev. Alan Butler, in Kuruman, the three of them traveled to African villages to minister the love of God. There, Ada felt the power and anointing of God as she prayed for the African women. Amid tears of joy as well as tears at parting, those brave women told her they would stand in faith for her, and hoped to see her again; if not on earth certainly in heaven. She returned to the States at the end of September refreshed, buoyed and bubbling with the blessing of God. It was now almost a year since Dr. Ruiz had offered his stunning diagnosis.

I met Ada in New York and we spent a nostalgic weekend with friends from our Darien days. Bert and Jan Bodnar hosted a reunion for us with friends from St. Paul's. Ada was invited by the new rector to share her story at a Sunday morning service. He good-humoredly quipped that since I had so often preached there in days gone by, it was now Ada's chance to bless the people. And she did, giving a glowing testimony to her shining faith and stead-fast trust in God. We also made a swing through the South and visited Dale, Jenny and our grand children. Then it was time for the long-awaited return to the Hermann Eye Center. The date was set; October 17, 1994.

We took our flight from Jacksonville and stopped in Houston for the appointment. For one whole year Ada had had little trouble with her eye, so we approached the coming consultation with mixed emotions. We were anticipating a good report, but there was that deep, dark chasm of uncertainty. It is always there when one is fac-ing a medical crisis with life and death as the issue.

Steve, our faithful and loving friend, together with another dear brother, Terry Scarborough, met us at the Houston International airport. Again, a battery of tests. We were apprehensive. Uncertain. At the final sonogram, Ada felt distinct discomfort. The probing hurt her eye. A student who was assisting the sonographer request-ed permission and was given an opportunity to take readings of the tumor. From that moment Ada began to feel a difference in her eye.

Then came the test for vision. The vision in the left eye was dramatically diminished. When all the tests were completed, we sat again in the examining room of Dr. Ruiz. The familiar routine, and the characteristic pushing back in the stool-on-wheels. The waiting; the tense pauses. Then, the chilling announcement. "Mrs. Church, the tumor in your eye is active. In the year since I first examined you the tumor has changed. This means it is definitely malignant."

We were plunged from day to night. From the warmth of spring to the cold of winter. Once more we asked, "What do you suggest?"

Now the answer was different; "I recommend immediate treat-ment. Again, you have two choices, enucleation or radioactive plaque therapy. We could schedule you for surgery on Tuesday or Thursday of next week. But you must decide immediately."

Silence was our only refuge. My eyes strained to hold back the stinging tears. Called upon to make such grave choices, cast so instantly into a dark valley of decision, there was one grace to sustain us. We echoed the words of the Psalmist, "Hear my cry, O God; listen to my prayer. From the ends of the earth I call to You; when my heart is overwhelmed, lead me to the Rock that is higher than I."(2)

Finally I spoke, "Dr. Ruiz, we deeply appreciate all you have done for us, but I do not feel we are in a position to make this decision now. We have asked God to guide us, in every decision we make, and now we need to go home and pray about this."

At the Houston International Airport on that fateful day of October 17th, after Steve had driven us from the Hermann Eye Hospital, I had finally, right there in one of the main corridors in full view of the scurrying throng, broken down and cried. I stood in full public view and unashamedly wept at the news my Beloved had just received. Our lives had been a roller coaster of emotional, spiritual and financial challenges. Yet, how deeply grateful we were for our years of reading, studying and hiding God's Word in our hearts. It is not presumption to say that, although we flinched, and were sometimes so brutally attacked by the enemy that we were, as St. Paul says, "Under great pressure, far beyond our ability to endure, so that we despaired even of life," yet we shared a confidence that God would see us through.(3)

Chapter Forty-Two

mid gathering signs of winter, we headed back to our retreat among the ancient, towering redwood trees of Boulder Creek. And there, again, God raised in our hearts the thought of taking an opinion at the University Hospital in Loma Linda. I went back to my file of a year before and found the name suggested to me by Dr. Scoggins. I phoned the number and made an appointment for Ada to see Doctor Eric Friedrichsen at the Inland Eye Institute.

Many years before I had memorized the words of the Psalmist, "I will instruct you and teach you in the way that you should go."(1) I earnestly, sincerely asked God to guide us. Through the years I had learned that God uses four influences to help us find and then walk in His will for our lives.

By His Word, by the inner witness of His Spirit, by our circumstances and also through the wise counsel of godly friends, the Lord leads us to the discovery of His plans and purposes. In these ways, we discover that in love, He says, "I know the thoughts that I think towards you. Thoughts of good and not of evil."(2) We were living daily in this expectation.

On November 11, we met Dr. Eric Friedrechsen. We were surprised to find such a large and progressive hospital in so remote a city, but we were immediately impressed by both the hospital and the institute. At every stage in the process of investigation we were treated with dignity, respect and cordiality. The floor in the foyer in the main entrance of the Hospital is embossed with an insignia which bears the words: "For the healing of the whole man, body, soul and spirit."

Ada knew, seeing that sign, she was in the place of God's choosing. Through the past months, the Lord had been revealing to her that His desire for her, indeed for all His people, was that they should be made whole in each of these realms of human experience. So many trials had assailed us, and we had been through so many traumatic experiences. It seemed as though our faith had been tested more severely in the past 24 months than in all the years that had gone before.

Ada had suffered through many "dark hours of the soul," but had never lost her joy! Even when she told of her dizzying contest with cancer, she recounted the darkest hours with a radiance that belied the depth of her suffering. In Loma Linda, Ada was again subjected to the rigors of the examinations she had undergone so many times. Dr. Fredrickson was a Seventh Day Adventist believer. We discovered he had been to South Africa as a missionary doctor, and we felt an instant sense of peace in knowing that God had led us to the best place, given us the best possible medical facility, and directed us to a man in whom we knew we could place our confidence.

Dr. Friedrichsen's diagnosis was decisive, and without equivocation; ocular melanoma. Ada unquestionably had a malignant tumor in her left eye, and it was active. That meant it was growing. Again, the ultimate question was asked and Dr. Friedrichsen's answer was kind, but firm: "We do not know what the chances of survival are, but if we do not treat the tumor, you will die very soon!"

The hard, sobering fact was that patients with this particular cancer have a maximum life expectancy of 5 years. Early detection and treatment by radiation determine the individual's prognosis and quality of life during that period.

Throughout the days of investigation, and the subsequent weeks of treatment, we were again had the pleasure of being able to stay in the condominium of our friends Wally and Betty Taber. Solana Beach was two hours drive from Loma Linda, but the quiet, peaceful serenity of the beach was like a soothing, healing balm. Ada walked each day on the beach. She gathered stones and sea shells and entered into a deeper fellowship of prayer and communion with Christ than she had ever known. Each evening she read to me from the delightful book *Parables of the Sea* by Phillip Keller. We continued also our twice-daily practice of reading from our favorite devotional book, *The Daily Light,* and praying together for each day's needs. And I anointed her eye morning and evening with oil.

We returned to Boulder Creek armed with all the information we had received about proton beam therapy. Dr. Friedrichsen was to present Ada's case to the Board which selects patients for the therapy, but he felt confident they would accept her. The weeks following were a time of planning, making arrangements and of waiting on the hospital for confirmation of schedules and dates.

One huge question had to be asked "How much would the procedure cost?" We knew, from our briefings at the hospital, that the procedure is enormously complicated and is administered in a facility larger than many hospitals. The protons are extracted in a machine called a synchrotron which is housed in a steel-reinforced walls 15 feet thick. The therapist can control the beam's depth so that the radiation can be focused on the tumor, reducing the effect on the surrounding normal tissue to a minimum.

Finally, the answer came back. Just the proton therapy, the five prescribed radiation treatments, would cost $26,000. I was dumb-struck! We were among the many in the US unable to afford medical insurance and these numbers were staggering. The supporting hospital expenses, such as doctor's fees, surgery fees, anesthesiologist fees, medications, CAT scans, and investigative procedures would all be extra. The Eye Institute charges would be over and above the Proton therapy and hospital costs. The figure for the entire procedure would eventually climb to about $40,000.

The mountainous sum seemed impossible. Ada and I were caught in the no-man's land between those who were homeless or destitute and qualified for welfare, and those who could afford the cost of medical insurance.

God gave me an idea. I spoke to Dr. Friedrichsen and asked him if he would intercede on our behalf for a reduction in all the fees and costs. All plans were suspended while the financial board weighed my request.

The answer came one morning in a phone call from the financial office; the hospital would grant us a reduction of 50%. Tears stung my eyes as I listened to the message conveyed by the lady who talked with me. With a catch in my voice I thanked her. Dr. Friedrichsen offered us a similar discounted fee.

I knew, in my heart, that, even with the proffered discount I was committing myself to a financial responsibility that might take me the rest of my life to honor, but I could do no less. Again, I wished that I could undergo the ordeal in my Ada's place. Knowing that was not possible, I rededicated myself to love, care for and provide for her to the best of my ability, with God's help.

We arrived back at the Loma Linda Hospital on December 19, 1994, to commence the treatment. In the coming months, we were to drive those long miles many times, and it is fitting to pay tribute to one of Ada's dear friends, who, obeying the still small voice of the Spirit's leading had, with unimagined love and generosity given Ada a new car, which in these times of hardship, had been like a heavenly carriage to convey us to these divinely directed appointments. That car was a chapel, a cathedral, a meeting place with God as we traveled the highways.

On December 20, Ada underwent the surgery to place the clips in her eye. These are minute markers that precisely indicate the boundaries of the tumor. Dr. Friedrichsen whimsically called them "Barbie Clips." An anesthesiologist administered a local anesthetic to Ada's eye and a white sheet was placed over her face with an opening through which the surgery was performed. In a two-hour procedure the eye was taken out, the clips were attached, and then the eye was replaced in its socket.

On December 23, with her eye still in trauma and terribly inflamed, Ada underwent a simulation of the treatment to come. In a simulation, the exact location of the tumor is entered into the data base of a computer. Over a two week period a program is developed which is then used to control the application of the proton beam.

Our son-in-law, Dale, calls that day, December 23, "Little Christmas Eve." By then, Ada was in physical distress. Her left eye was swathed in a large patch and the hospital provided dark eye shades for protection from the sunlight. Tired and traumatized, Ada wanted to hide away, and not be seen in public.

Dawson and Brenda had other ideas! They felt that the environment of home and the TLC of family life would lift our spirits during the Christmas season. With the energy characteristic of their vibrant, adventurous lives, they drove 300 miles from Northern California to be with us during Ada's surgery, then drove us all the way back to their home to celebrate Christmas with them and our two precious grandchildren, Lionel, aged six and a diminutive little cherub, Angela, who had just turned one.

We were comforted by the warmth of their concern even though the long drive and the large patch over her eye caused Ada personal fatigue and embarrassment. She sought what little anonymity she could find behind the dark eye shades. For one so meticulous about her personal appearance, this excursion into the light of public scrutiny was difficult to bear. She seemed but a shadow of her usual brightness.

Chapter Forty-Three

There is a mystery, a magical quality about the beginning of each new year. The breaking of 1995 dawned with emotions that hovered between bright hope and lurking uncertainty. It was like living in two worlds. The one was illuminated by the expectation of a miracle. The other shrouded in the mist of not knowing what lay before us.

We were due back in Loma Linda to commence the proton radiation therapy on January 5, so, with a few days grace between Christmas and the new year, we went back to the cabin in Boulder Creek. We had no fixed plans for celebrating on New Year's eve. Ada dreaded being seen in public with her eye red and inflamed from the surgery, and constantly wore her dark eye shades. However, there was one special thing we wanted to do; visit our friends, John and Sharne Price in Saratoga.

John is South African, Sharne is Australian. I phoned John a day or so before the close of the year and received his customary gracious invitation for us to have dinner with them on Sunday evening, New Year's Eve. Ever concerned for Ada, they, plus their two sparkling boys Jack and Alex, (and the poodle Bijou) gave us a rousing welcome. It was a tonic to be with them and together we welcomed the New Year.

One final blessing awaited us before we departed for Loma Linda. The experience of the years and the passage of time has served to teach me many precious truths. Among the simplest, yet most profound, was the value of true friends. This book, as expressed on the dedication page, honors those friends who have been the angels of God to encourage and help me in my journey towards the Refiner's goal; the purpose of God so eloquently, powerfully expressed in the lines:

When through fiery trials, thy pathway shall lie,
My Grace, all-sufficient, shall be thy supply.
The flame shall not hurt thee, I only design
Thy dross to consume and thy gold to refine.

True love, faithful friends and reliance on God's help are the stuff of life. Together these three ingredients provide the recipe that gives us the courage to overcome adversity and reach the heights to which we aspire.

The encouragement which gave us a feeling of security as we set out for the great unknown in Loma Linda was the pleasure of fellowship over a fabulous lunch with our friends, Jay and Pat Sindahl. Pat and Jay had served with us at St. Paul's in Darien. Through many trials, their love and support had strengthened us. When referring to them, we often spoke of them as our angel friends. Their grace, wisdom, and compassionate concern lighted many of our dark hours At the conclusion of our lunch at the fabled Chaminade Hotel in Santa Cruz, Jay presented us with a check. He said they had been blessed and wanted to share their blessing with us. The gift was to help with the expenses of Ada's treatment.

Through the testing times of the past eighteen months, I had often been brought to tears. Sometimes by grief, sometimes by my own sense of inadequacy, sometimes as a relief from emotional strain, and then, sometimes in humble appreciation I had sighed or cried. The shortest verse in the Bible is "Jesus wept."(1) It is also one of the most profound.

One of the most notable evidences of a life touched by the Holy Spirit is the reproducing of His character in the heart of a believer. As Jesus had wept at the tomb of his friend Lazarus, I too was deeply moved by the love of my friends. I wept again.

Neither Ada nor I were adequately prepared for the trial we faced when she underwent the first treatment. We had viewed an instructional video, and the doctors had given us verbal descriptions, but none of these could adequately convey the tortuous path that lay ahead. There were to be five treatments, spread over seven days, each session requiring Ada to be encased in the grotesque mask with her head bolted to the back of a high-back chair. Once bolted in position she was unable to move her head. With a bite block clamped in her mouth she was unable to swallow, and her breathing was labored and difficult because of the constrictions. She had to hold this position for about an hour while staring steadily up to the left at a red pinpoint of light.

The reason for having to strain the eye to look in that direction is that, at the time of irradiation, the beam is focused directly on the tumor. To make her task even more un-nerving, it was the area in which the vision in her left eye was most impaired. Her constant prayer was, "Lord help me to look at the light." Her prayer was a metaphor for her life!

The beam is directed by data that has been programmed into the computer. The patient has to keep the eye fixed on the critical spot for the 60 seconds during which the proton beam is carrying the radiation to the base of the tumor. All this has to be accomplished with the discomfort, not only of the mask and the bite block, but also with the eyelids clipped open and taped back to prevent the radiation from affecting the tissue of the eyelids.

While all this is in progress I have to watch as Ada is subjected to the harrowing experience. Then finally comes a moment when the patient is literally alone. Just before the proton beam is engaged, everyone but the patient leaves the treatment room. The patient has a heavy lead apron draped over her shoulders, around the neck and covering the upper body; another discomfort to be endured.

For one brief minute, the proton beam is activated.

I watched the TV monitor intently because I could see the tiny clips on the screen, and I could see exactly where the beam was going to be aimed. My prayer was, "Lord, You control the sun, the moon and the stars in their orbit. You rule the universe by Your power; Father, please help these fallible humans to aim the beam exactly at that microscopic point at the base of the tumor." Success depends upon the precision of the intricate procedure. It is incredibly complex. And so much depends upon Ada being able to keep her vision fixed on that one tiny spot of light.

When the hourlong procedure was over, Ada could barely be lifted out of the chair. She was unsteady, disoriented, shaking. How my heart ached for her. So brave, so bright, and yet so frail.

The procedure was repeated on five successive days. Then it was over. We retreated to our haven, the Taber's condominium at Solana Beach. For several days, Ada rested. Even when we thought it time return to Boulder Creek, Ada seemed unable to face the task of packing up and taking the long drive north.

During the preceding weeks, we had often visited our friends, Tony and Liz Louch who were staying in San Clemente. Tony, ever wise, advised me not to be in haste, but to allow Ada a week or two to recover from the strain of the previous week. We stayed on in Solana Beach, and Ada was able to enjoy the therapy of the beach with its gentle breezes and refreshing air. Then, on January 17th, a calamity shattered our calm in Southern California and called us back to Boulder Creek.

Chapter Forty-Four

fter years of drought, the hills and valleys of California were dry and dusty, baked hard by seven seasons of sun and wind. The earth on the mountain slopes had become like dried out sponge.

In November of 1994 it began to rain. The first showers brought blessed relief to the parched land and to the people who had endured the lean years of water shortages and restrictions. But the sighs of pleasure gave way to concern as the heavens opened and the rain poured down in torrents. Unstable because of the years of drought, the mountainsides began to give way as the waterlogged soil turned to mud and slid down the slopes like oil slicks. Torrential rains deluged California at the beginning of 1995.

Brenda phoned us with the news that, because of the unceasing downpour, a mudslide had swept away part of the hillside next to the cabin. The slide had also taken out the footings of the deck, and from what the neighbors reported, the house itself was threatened.

It was time to go home. We packed up and headed north to Boulder Creek. The sight that greeted us on our arrival was alarming. The house, like almost every house in those mountains, is built on a steep slope. As the torrents of rain gushed down the inclines, the gathering streams turned into a rushing river that swept down our driveway.

Surging fiercely around the corner of the house, the tide swept all before it. Much of the bank next to the house had flowed as a seething river of mud into the yard and onto the patio of the dwellers below us. Three redwood trees, with roots exposed, clung precariously to the washed-out hillside. They could have fallen, at any instant, endangering the houses and occupants below.

The power of the floodwater was awesome. A huge redwood trunk that had served as a retaining wall at the bottom of the slope had been swept aside like a matchstick causing the soil behind it to give way. As the whole mud bath surged down the hill, it carried the foundations of our deck with it. Posts were hanging in midair like the disjointed limbs of a scarecrow. It was a war zone in which the elements had done battle with the houses and left the wounded and dead littered across the hillside. The flood had come close to undermining the foundations at the corner of the house, threatening to sweep it down the hillside. To avert this disaster, the neighbors had installed a temporary culvert and drain.

What a homecoming! And it was still raining.

Endless rounds of consultations followed. I sought help from the city, the County and the State but no one would assume responsibility. As the rains continued to fall I enlisted the help of neighbors and packed sand bags around the house to keep the rushing waters at bay. The basement flooded, the roof sprang a leak and in one week of severe rainstorms, I was up every night keeping the makeshift drain clear of debris and mud that continued to flow down the incline.

A record rainfall of 100 inches was recorded in our area making it impossible to carry out permanent repairs. Reconstruction would have to wait for the summer, the season when the California countryside takes on a warm golden sheen. Finally, the rains did cease and the summer sun smiled on us once again. Hidden away among the tall trees and the misty privacy of Boulder Creek, we spent the summer in a time of special closeness encapsulating the essence of all our years together.

Ada expanded the range of her artistic interests and developed a craft to enrich the lives of many people with a touch of love and beauty. She made gift baskets for friends and other women to whom she wished to offer an expression of love. More than a hundred of these decorated baskets with shells, flowers, and ribbons emerged from her sun-filled little workshop. She labeled them *A Bath Odyssey By Ada*. They were filled with exotic bath products, perfumes, towels and other objects of beauty. She used every dollar she could find and every bargain she could strike to fill her baskets with love.

On Super Bowl Sunday, though hampered by limited vision, the trauma of treatment and the flood, her irrepressible spontaneity found expression in an unusual way. She overheard me telling Jenny about a couple who had just brought their newborn baby home to a single room in the basement of a hillside cabin. The windowless space was no bigger than 8'x 10'. The cramped dark hole held one bed, a minute cooking space and one tattered sofa.

I had gone to visit the family and had found the infant cradled in a towel slung between the foot of the bed and the kitchen sink. As I drew the word-picture for Jenny, who was in Florida, Ada was instantly stirred. As I replaced the telephone on its cradle, Ada said, "Do you remember the crib we saw at the Goodwill store on our way home from Church?" Of course I remembered! We ourselves were living off the stuff we had picked up for pennies at that Goodwill.

"Well," said Ada firmly, "we are going to get that bassinet, fix it up and take it to that family." Then she added, "Why didn't you tell me about this family?" I had deliberately not told her because

I did not want her to take on another burden. Ada would take the concerns and distresses of others to heart, and grieve deeply over anyone in need.

That was the end of the Super Bowl for me. No TV! We spent the afternoon repairing and cleaning the crib. In addition, Ada made me stop at a quaint gift shop where she negotiated the purchase of a beautiful blanket for the baby. All we had between us was a $20 bill. The blanket was quite a bit more but she explained the situation to the owner and struck a deal by asking the lady to help contribute to the family in need.

She also decorated a gorgeous gift basket for the mother, filling it with powders, perfumes, soaps, candles and towels. As I witnessed those impulses of grace and love, acted out so spontaneously, in spite of her own struggles, the words of Jesus took on new meaning for me: "Because you did it to one of the lowliest of these, you did it to me."(1)

Another delight which occupied Ada's days was the building of two miniature Victorian model homes. With painstaking care and patience (plus technical assistance from her husband), she crafted two gorgeous doll houses and selected colors for the miniatures from her book on Victorian Homes. She wanted her granddaughters in both families (Dawson's and Jenny's) to each have one, lovingly expressing both the heritage and the aspirations of her own heart.

What was her secret defense against the spirit of discouragement, doubt, darkness and despair? She lived in a faith and love relationship with Jesus! Years before she had decided to read the entire Bible through from cover to cover every year. Faithful to that commitment, and using the Bible Reading Chart that we had produced, she had read the Bible through eighteen times.

For her, it was not merely an exercise of habit. It was a daily delight. She would record the special promises of God in her daily diary, and then share with me the truths she gleaned. By these she gained strength and courage and learned the secrets of a life built upon a rock. The influence of the word of God upon her was vibrantly evident.

With sincere devotion, and in her longing to worship God, Ada discovered a quaint church in the redwoods, St. Andrew's Episcopal Church. Whenever possible we attended Sunday worship there together. One afternoon Ada invited the rector and his wife, Colville and Sylvia Smythe, to an English-style "high tea," with home-baked scones and whipped cream. Ada shared with the secret of her strength and faith, reading the Bible through each year. Sylvia asked Ada to show her the chart. She was genuinely interested, and took a copy to use herself.

However, within a few months, the Smythes received an invitation to pastor another church and prepared to leave Boulder Creek. Ada was deeply disappointed to see them leave, feeling the all too familiar twinge of sorrow at another parting. At their farewell, Sylvia honored Ada with the compliment, "The greatest legacy you have left me is helping me to read the Bible. I have never before read it, but I now read it every day and I am learning so much and enjoying the blessing."

For us too the cloud of God's leading was lifting, and in August of 1995, we left our sanctuary in the redwoods. Many years before we had bought a house in Atlantic Beach, Florida, and had always thought of it as one day being our retirement haven. We had had a succession of tenants in the house, and it now needed renovating. We returned to Florida, somewhat uncertain, but not through a lack of faith or confidence. Factored into this uncertainty was the knowledge that Ada would need to return to Loma Linda in California every six months for follow-up consultations.

Dr. Friedrichsen had told us that ideally, the tumor would shrink slowly. The slower the shrinkage of the tumor, the greater would be the expectation of success. The prognosis was always uncertain, and every visit to the Radiation Therapy Center was tinged with a degree of uneasiness.

In the summer, after we had been in Florida a year, Ada made the journey back to California on her own. We did not have the funds for both of us to go, so for the first time she faced the ordeal solo. Dawson met her in San Francisco and drove her to San Clemente, where Bishop and Mrs. Adler graciously provided an escort to the hospital, and hosted her throughout her stay in Southern California.

Her visit to the Eye Institute was an unnerving experience. Dr. Friedrichsen had relinquished his duties to devote himself to research, and a physician unknown to Ada conducted the initial investigations. Lacking the grace and reassuring manner of Dr. Friedrichsen, the stranger alarmed her with negative suggestions, which later proved to be unfounded. Dr. Laredo at the Proton therapy Center put Ada through the usual tests of probing her abdomen and searching for any sign that the cancer might have metastasized. Later, sonograms and other readings confirmed that the tumor was indeed shrinking. Something else of great significance occurred during that trip. It marked a high water mark in Ada's walk, witness and work for God.

Chapter Forty-Five

For a number of years, since the birth of March for Jesus, Ada had never missed being with Jenny at the annual march in Jacksonville. As the organizer for Jacksonville, Jenny had consistently been used by God to draw the pastors of the city together and bring thousands of people into the streets to participate in the celebration of praise, joy, dance and enthusiastic witness for Christ. But in May 1996 Ada was not there. She was in Boulder Creek. And there, Ada marched for Jesus carrying a homemade banner that proclaimed simply "Jesus."

Coincidentally, that weekend Boulder Creek was hosting a huge event, the annual Festival of Arts. The one intersection in town was a tangle, with police attempting to control bumper-to-bumper traffic that backed up for a mile. Amidst the thousands thronging the one and only main street, a solitary witness in a sea of merry-makers, Ada marched up and down, attracting the amazed stares of passers-by.

Reactions to this beautiful blonde woman with the banner ranged from the comical to the bizarre. Two boys approached her. One asked, "What does that mean?" She replied, "It means that Jesus loves you. He gave His life to be your Savior and one day He is coming back to this earth to be the King." One of the boys responded, "Oh!" The other said, "You don't look like Jesus!" A biker in his black leather, riding slowly past on a Harley Davidson shouted, "Right on man. Hallelujah!" God does have a sense of humor.

As Ada marched by the site where a rock concert was to happen, she found the performance was delayed by an electrical hitch. The noisy crowd was restive. Walking down to the very front of the amphitheater, Ada stood in front of the empty stage and held her banner high. She got some hoots, a few howls, and a number of people waved at her.

Following what may have been the most unusual March For Jesus in the world, Ada said she would never again be afraid to be a witness for Christ! It had given her boldness beyond anything she had known before. Exhilarated by the event she penned the poem "A March for Jesus," in the afterglow of her one-woman march.

Returning to Florida, in July she embarked on one of the most ambitious projects of her life. Anyone who knew Ada knew the greatest thrill of her life was to redecorate homes. Through all our married days, over the more than forty years, we had lived in so many different houses that she compared her life to the wanderings of Israel. How well I remember a day in 1961 when she promised to walk with me in all the ways by which God would lead me. In an Apostolic ministry of preaching, teaching, planting churches and offering guidance and help to the church, she had never broken that pledge.

Our journeys had called us sometimes to live in difficult, even poor circumstances, but she could, contrary to the proverb, "Make a silk purse out of a sow's ear." Her skill transformed the dingiest of places into dwellings of peace, beauty and harmony. In this summer of '96 she worked a charming transformation on Dale and Jenny's home in Jacksonville. For two months, working days, and often nights, she brought together a collage of colors, fabrics and finishes to create a masterpiece. Her reward came the night Jenny returned from summer vacation and Ada welcomed her at the door of a home transformed by a loving and skilled touch. Jenny squealed with delight then wept for joy, blown away by the change Ada had effected throughout her home.

At Dale's invitation, I had taken on, first a consulting, and later a pastoral and discipling role at Church of the Messiah. One of the priests in the church is also a family physician. Ada consulted Dr. Miguel Rosada, who took her under his personal care. He became an angel of God, caring for Ada in the months to come. With tenderness and compassion, and always available to us, he undertook the task of watching over her medical, physical and emotional well-being.

The last days of that year were the most poignant. We were living in the house we thought might one day be our retirement home. Our grandchildren dubbed it The Beach House. One block from the shore, it was their delight to visit "Granny's house," shed their city clothes and rush down to the waters edge to romp on white sands and bathe in the rippling waves of the Atlantic Ocean. And, of course there was always the promise of an English tea with Ada's home baked scones complete with strawberry jam and fresh whipped cream.

In November Ada decided to spruce up, of all things, the garage! She cleaned it thoroughly, painted the old cabinets, and even the floor! Wall paper was hung against two walls, and the opposite wall decoupaged with pages from *Victoria* magazine. She began to serve tea to guests in her self-styled tea room. In this recreated garage, with its stenciled borders and chair rail (installed by me at her cajoling), she prepared for two major events. Our son Dawson's 40th birthday celebration, and the fulfillment of a long-cherished dream.

For years she had imagined having a truly family Christmas with all her children and grand children together for a reunion. We had been in America twenty years and had never had the entire family together at one place in one moment of time. We were not only the proud parents of Dawson and Jenny; but our family was extended by Dale and Brenda. Dale and Jenny had four children; Jessica, Peter, Bethany and Ruthie. Dawson and Brenda had Lionel and Angela.

This was to be the year. Ada dreamed of it as the ultimate celebration, a gathering of all her children for a Christmas to beat every other celebration in the world. The investment was not to be in material things but in fulfillment of a mother's dream.

However, there would be a cloud emptying rain on the parade. On the morning Dawson and Brenda flew out of San Francisco, Brenda's father suffered a fatal heart attack. They learned of the tragedy only when they arrived on the East Coast. Brenda stayed through the Christmas season, and then went back West to be with her family.

One of my personal joys that Christmas was to take all six of my grand children on the ferry across the St. John's River and treat them to hot chocolate in the fairy-land atmosphere of the Ritz Carlton Hotel on Amelia Island.

Chapter Forty-Six

ow strangely, mysteriously, silently God moves in our lives. An old hymn poignantly describes the changing scenes and seasons of life:

In shady, green pastures,
So rich and so sweet,
God leads His dear children along;
Where the water's cool flow,
Bathes the weary one's feet,
God leads His dear children along.

Sometimes on the mount,
Where the sun shines so bright,
God leads His dear children along;
Sometimes in the valley,
In the darkest of night,
God leads His dear children along.

Some through the waters,
Some through the flood,
Some through the fire,
But all through the blood;

Some through great sorrow,
But God gives a song,
In the night season
And all the day long.

Circumstances, directed so evidently by the hand of the God who knows the end from the beginning, conspired together, and on January 10, 1997, Ada and I moved from the Beach House. We signed a lease-purchase contract with a family eager to start their children in school in January, and went to stay with Dale and Jenny.

I don't know that any of us realized the significance of so ordinary an event. Yet, somehow, deep within us there was a sense of Divine destiny. We intended our stay with Dale and Jenny to be brief while we located a place of our own. Ada dreamed of opening a Bed and Breakfast; she chose the name The Queen Victoria Inn for her dream house.

It had been two years since the proton radiation therapy, and she was due for the second annual check-up at Loma Linda. However, I simply did not have the financial resources for both of us to fly to California and pay for the costly tests. I decided that we should ask our friends Dr. and Mrs. Jim Gills if they would conduct the tests at their clinic in Tarpon Springs, Florida. Ever gracious, they welcomed us, and in February I took Ada to St. Luke's. Exhaustive tests all proved favorable. Dr. Gills and the other specialists concurred that indeed the tumor was inactive and that it was shrinking. We were happy with the results and quietly hopeful for the future.

As usual, the eye examinations were followed by a physical. For previous examinations Ada had been seen at Loma Linda by Dr. Lilia Loredo. These tests had always been negative. This year we returned to our mentor, Dr. Rosada, in Jacksonville, approaching the examination with greater confidence than we had previously felt. Hoever, when he probed Ada's abdomen, she winced with pain. It had never been that way before. He immediately referred Ada to a diagnostic imaging center for a CAT Scan.

As we prepared for the appointment, the hours took on a surrealistic aura. We knew we were living in the now, but an inexplicable sense of remoteness seemed to pervade the present. We arrived at the hospital at 7 a.m. on February 11. As we pulled to the curb in front of the hospital, we were moved to tears. Jenny, with her flowing blonde hair and wrapped in a long blue coat Ada had given her, was standing at the curbside to meet us. Though the procedure was not accompanied by physical pain, the emotional and mental pressure was intense. Throughout the hours of the procedure, Ada retained her air of calm and serenity.

That night Dr. Rosada tried to contact us, but we were having dinner with a couple who had recently visited the Church. Wednesday morning early Dr. Rosada's office called again; he wanted to see us immediately. An ominous cloud engulfed us as we hurriedly readied ourselves for the consultation. We were not harassed by fear or anxiety. Ada dressed with her usual care but a premonition of something urgently threatening had invaded our space.

Dr. Rosada's report was sobering. The CAT Scan showed five spots on Ada's liver, indicating an abnormality. He was sending us at once to an oncologist. On our arrival the oncologist studied the pictures and ordered a biopsy of the liver.

The procedure was performed on Thursday and again our beloved Jenny was there waiting to walk through the trauma with us. This was more serious than anything we had experienced since the surgery and Proton therapy two years before. Though an outpatient procedure, we spent the whole day waiting. When we rejoined Ada in the recovery room she was serene. An otherworldly aura of tranquility seemed to surround her.

We had to wait five days for the results. Then, once again we were in the consulting room of the oncologist. His manner was professional, detached, almost aloof. "Mrs. Church," he said, "The biopsy is positive. The melanoma has metastasized (spread) to your liver."

I have never been on a battle field. I have never seen men and women called to perform heroic deeds. But that day I saw courage. Calm, strong, yet gentle courage. The doctor asked Ada, "Do you have a living will?" Ada replied levelly, "No: I don't have a living will, but I do have a will to live!" In answer to our questions about possible treatments, the oncologist offered the option of chemotherapy or other supplemental radiation therapies.

Prior to our visit, Ada and I had discussed what our choice would be in event the spots did indeed indicate that cancer had spread to her liver. Now, in the face of it, she asked the doctor what success the proffered radiation therapies promised. His answer was a grave reminder that Ada's cancer was of a rare type. He could offer less than a ten percent chance of success. Solemnly he told us that all one could hope for was a slim possibility of extending her life by one year. The chemotherapy would cause hair loss, nausea and could dramatically reduce the quality of her life. All with no guarantee of success!

Ada spoke gently but firmly. "Doctor, I have decided I do not wish to undergo chemotherapy. I am going to trust God with my life. I am not afraid of dying; if I have to die, I want to die with dignity."

I expressed my desire and intention, "I want us to return to the hospital in California and consult with the doctors who performed the original procedures two years ago."

We left the oncologist's office quietly. I took Ada to the car and excused myself for a few minutes. I phoned Jenny and Dale who were waiting at the Church for my report, but when I made the connection, I could not speak. Choked with emotion I was weeping as I tried to speak into the mouthpiece of the telephone. Jenny simply asked, "Daddy is it good or bad?" All I could manage to say was, "Bad." She said, "We are here for you. Come to the church right away."

We did. The meeting was tearful and distressing. There seemed so little to say. It was difficult to give even the simple facts. The strongest among us was Ada. She reiterated her statement; "I am not afraid to die, but if I am to die, I want to die with dignity."

The moment of truth had come. The years of waiting, of faith and hope, of patient endurance, now focused on that scene in Dale's office. Speculation had given way to the sober reality of the first doctors' prediction: "This disease will cause your demise."

I determined that we would go back to Loma Linda at the earliest possible moment and, in addition, would seek out a nutritional therapist who could provide the best possible alternative remedies for Ada's condition. I realized it would be of utmost importance to find a program of diet and supplemental nutrition that could give Ada the maximum opportunity to build her immune system and the optimum chance for her body to fight the cancer.

We arrived at the John Wayne Airport in Orange County on Tuesday, March 3rd. Bishop Adler had dispatched his niece Sheila to meet us, and they provided us with a vehicle to drive to our appointments at the Loma Linda University Medical Center. Dr. Blaharski, at the Inland Eye Institute, was considerate and kindly. Dr. Loredo at the Proton Therapy Center was equally gracious, but their findings only confirmed the diagnosis. The melanoma had metastasized to Ada's liver.

Questions raced through my mind. Had the proton beam therapy not been successful? Why had we incurred this trauma, and what of the expense? We had suffered and sacrificed. It would take years to pay off the medical bills which had swelled to $40,000. My heart cried out, "Why God? Why!"

I asked Dr. Blaharski for some explanation of the dilemma in which we found ourselves. We had submitted to the treatment, incurred the expense and done all we could. His answer was mystifying, confusing. He said, "The cat was probably out of the bag before we began the proton therapy."

We were faced with the inscrutable mysteries of the unpredictable behavior of the relentless reaper—cancer! Dr. Loredo arranged a consultation with an oncologist at the Inland Eye Institute. That Tuesday evening we repeated what had become a staple of our visits to Loma Linda. We had a wonderful dinner date with our Riverside friends, Fred and Ruth Waugh, and staying the night in the suite which had become our regular "pad" at the Campus Crusade Hotel at Arrowhead Springs. The next day we headed for Palm Springs where our friends Doctor Bernie Huss and his wife Lyn were waiting for us. There seemed to be a tacit consensus that our visit would be one of fellowship and friendship. We did not discuss Ada's diagnosis, but rather enjoyed an evening of pleasure at a favorite eating place.

On Thursday, minutes before we left Palm Springs, Ada made a quick call across the street to visit a gentleman she had met and ministered to on her previous visit six months before. Ever concerned for others, she took the time to enquire how he was. She returned to the Huss's house feeling weary and ill. While I was completing my preparations to leave, she lay down on the bed and fell asleep.

After a short nap she awoke rather suddenly and stood up. As she moved towards the door, she stumbled and fell headlong into the passageway, slamming her face into the wall. I heard the crash and rushed to the hallway to find her lying bruised and scraped on the floor. A cry of anguish burst from my lips as she just lay there. She could not get up. I struggled to lift her and help her back on to the bed. A smudge of lipstick and a spot of blood marked the wall where she struck her face.

Later, when I phoned Lyn, she asked. "Do you think it was her vision, or could she have lost her balance due to a problem in the brain?" The consultation at Loma Linda was like a "last straw" for Ada. Again, she was offered the option of chemotherapy. The picture was grim. The oncologist said it would be "hell." The doctor said she would have to live within one hour's distance of the hospital, and the chances of success were slight.

The cost? The oncologist estimated $20,000 for the initial treatments, and then additional charges *if* the chemo seemed to be helping.

Again, Ada's decision was "No." It was a quiet, but firm response. And so we set out on our quest for an alternative. Back in San Clemente we had a joyous, surprising visit from Ada's nephew Paul Dixon and his South African wife Vivienne. Bishop and Mrs. Adler were our gracious hosts; Tony and Liz, as usual, entertained us lavishly and Dawson drove down from Northern California to take us back to their home in Santa Rosa. Soon after our arrival there, Ada had a most distressing night. Her entire body shook uncontrollably for hours. I held her and tried to calm her, but she quivered throughout the night.

The next day we faced one of the most crucial challenges of our spiritual pilgrimage. Throughout nearly four years since discovering the tumor in Ada's eye, she had been hounded by the accusing thought, "You have brought this affliction on yourself. It is *your* fault. If you would only do certain things, *then* you will be healed." She searched her heart for any clue which might lead to a confession which would release her from the voice which inwardly accused her.

The final battle with that dark enemy was fought in the living room of Dawson's home. Ada was physically weary from the night of shaking, and her faith was under assault from the Deceiver, the Enemy. In a passionate outpouring I reviewed for her the time-tested truths upon which our lives, our ministry, out past and our future were built. I went back over the years of preaching and teaching. Reaching even further back, I reminded her of the great preaching of the anointed men who had molded our faith in the days of our youth and courtship.

I sat down on the sofa next to her, took her hand and said, "I love you. I have given myself to you, and now I am asking you to believe me; believe what we have stood *for* and stood *on* all the years of our lives. The ultimate truth is this: we stand on the unfailing promises of God. Our faith and our confidence are in the Person and the Promises of the One who said, 'I am the Lord! I do not change.'(1) You have made every honest attempt to be right in the sight of God. I too have confessed every sin I know and have dealt with every shortcoming I am aware of. I know I am not perfect, but I trust in the love and forgiving Grace of God. Together we have followed the Biblical principle, 'If we confess our sins, He is faithful and just to forgive us our sins!'(2) Now is the time to rest in the Truth for which we have given our lives."

I then reminded her that we are not accepted by God because we are good nor because we do good things. He accepts us because of the merits of Jesus Christ and makes us worthy in His sight because we place our trust in the truth: "We are reconciled to God by the death of His Son, and—we are saved by His life"(3) and because "The blood of Jesus Christ cleanses us from all sin."(4)

It was a spiritual battle. A fight for the very foundation of Ada's faith. Would she believe the lies of the Devil and the opinions of people, or would she find rest and security in the Sovereignty of the God we had served together for 42 years? I saw a gentle peace come over Ada. And, with a quiet voice she said, "Is it true?" I said "Yes!" She then said, "I believe it." We never had to fight that demon of doubt and discouragement again. That battle was won.

My search for a nutritionist finally settled on a lady in San Antonio who had been highly recommended by our colleague Malcolm Smith. Before leaving California, we took the time to visit with our "angel" friends Pat and Jay Sindahl and with special people from the Darien, Connecticut days: Margo Elliott and Tony and Judith Wilson. It was like walking through a dream come true. The years spent with Terry and Ruth Fullam at St. Paul's seemed now rich and fruitful as we fellowshipped with these saints who had dispersed to the proverbial "four corners" and were serving the Lord so fruitfully in new and very exciting fields of endeavor. Ada was overjoyed to see these dear ones, all "walking in truth."(5)

On our journey Eastward, we made a stop in El Paso. Strangely, mysteriously, drawn back so often to El Paso, we were received as ever with warmth and love by J. O. and Marlene Stewart, and visited a number of our close, long time friends. Ada returned to the Garden Club where she had spent so many happy days, and called on Anita Carter, a lady she had taken under her care when we lived in El Paso. She renewed her relationship and friendship with the Women's Bible study group at St. Clement's Church, and we broke the bread of fellowship with our dear friends Wally and Betty Taber.

In El Paso, the man who had been our attorney for many years, Ricky Feuille, prepared a Living Will for Ada, so her decision that, if the worst came, she did not want her days agonizingly prolonged by the intervention of artificial life support systems. It seemed unreal to be signing such a document. But it needed to be done.

I don't know how, but miraculously, Ada experienced an anointing of energy and power to participate with me in one of the most incredible services we ever conducted. Our faithful, loving friends and partners in the Gospel, Jack and Sharon Brock, invited us to preach at the three services of Christ Community Church in Alamogordo, New Mexico, on Palm Sunday. On Sunday night Ada spoke to the congregation and read her poem *Easter.* The effect was electrifying. Later, we received a letter from one of the members of the congregation.

It read, "Dear Peter and Ada. Thank you for all you shared with us at Christ Community Church. I have always been blessed by your testimonies, your messages and your great peaceful yet awe-inspiring way of speaking about our wonderful Lord. How I appreciate His goodness in allowing the gifts He's invested in you to be shared with all of us! Thank you! Thank you for proclaiming Him as Magnificent and Wonderful, a God of unchanging character and limitless love!"

It was then on to San Antonio. On Friday, March 28th, Ada met and was instantly drawn to Dr. Nancy Reed of Wellspring International. Following an extensive consultation, Dr. Reed prescribed a diet and a program of natural and herbal supplements for Ada.

I noticed then how tired, how weary my beloved Ada appeared. She simply lay on the couch at Dr. Reed's office and expressed exhaustion and fatigue from the travel. Earlier, while we had been at Dawson's home, I had been secretly alarmed one afternoon when I went to wake her up for a drive through the beautiful hills and valleys of the wine country. I could not rouse her from her afternoon nap.

We arrived back in Jacksonville on Good Friday, March 28, 1997, and celebrated the significance of that Easter Season with a deeper appreciation of the eternal truths upon which our faith is built. During the weeks in California we had been shaken and tried, but I thanked God that we had come to rest on the solid foundation of the wonderful words of His covenant-love. The Passion of our

Lord Jesus Christ and the Power of His resurrection, were our hope for time and for eternity.

Chapter Forty-Seven

wice in my life I have looked into the inscrutable depths of what the apostle Paul calls "the last enemy."(1) Twice I have felt I was facing the final hours of my life. In the heat of life's most serious battles we rarely realize that these fierce trials are a preparation for the conflicts which lie in wait down the road of life.

My first face-off with the 'grim reaper' was in the palpable blackness of that granite tomb in 1950. The cold finger of death touched my body in the dank, musty depths of a gold mine.

My second encounter in the arena of life and death occurred in 1988.

"Dad your posture is so bad!" Standing behind me in our bathroom, Dawson volunteered the observation with compassion and concern.

That was in 1984. I consulted Dr. William Reed in Tampa, who, through the Fellowship of Christian Physicians, referred me to Dr. James Hughes in Jackson, Mississippi. Over a period of 4 years, Dr. Hughes and his wife Virginia ministered to both Ada and me, and guided us to an orthopedic surgeon who performed a complex procedure to relieve, among other complications, a condition called spinal stenosis which was causing me unspeakable physical agony.

My physical condition had deteriorated to the point where, because of the excruciating pain, I was unable, even with effort, to stand upright. The pain was chronic and constant because the nerve roots extending from the vertebrae in my lower back were being pinched in the way a garden hose is flattened when one parks a car on it. That was Dr. Hughes's analogy. A practical, understandable picture of a complex medical condition.

The delicate procedure was to be performed by Doctor Henry Bohlman in Cleveland, Ohio, reputed to be among the finest surgeons performing almost unbelievable feats of restoration in surgeries of the spine. Dawson came from California to be with us and stayed with Ada in the hotel. Our friend J. O. Stewart flew from El Paso to offer close support for Ada.

The crisis peaked between the fifth and seventh days following the surgery. Several factors joined forces to bring me to a point of mental and spiritual despair. The pain suppressant Demerol was causing me to hallucinate. As evenings came on everything in the room took on grotesque demonic forms, writhing and crawling like hordes of insects and snakes. The clock on the wall opposite my bed presented itself as the hideous face of a gargoyle leering at me in the gathering gloom. Where walls joined the ceilings, the angles began to crawl with spiders weaving thick, drooping webs.

I said to Dawson, "You should tell them to dust this room, it is full of cobwebs." He chuckled, "Okay, I'll let them know."

One night I awakened to see a huge insect crawling from the vase of flowers on my night stand. In terror, I fought off the monster with a wild swing of my arm. I swept the vase and telephone off the bedside table. Everything went crashing to the floor with a nerve-shattering clatter. Waking up later, I saw a continuous stream of figures playing on my ceiling like a movie film. They were like living images of people dressed in national costumes from all over the world. They marched and moved across the ceiling in an endless, eerie parade.

What no one in my family realized was that I had lost an excessive amount of blood during the 6 hour operation. Before surgery, I had donated my own blood for transfusion. I learned a new word. By definition I had become an "autologous" blood donor. However, that bank had been used up during surgery and we had decided, ahead of time, that because of the risk of receiving contaminated blood, I would not accept any unknown donors. Without sufficient resources to renew its blood supply, my body was failing. Without enough blood to feed my brain, my consciousness was slipping away. My near-death experience happened at the lowest ebb of my body's natural resources.

For five days I was as ill as anyone could be and still live. Because all the muscles in my lower back had been severed in the operation, I was unable to roll myself over in the bed. I was like a beached whale. I had strained both shoulders in attempts to move my wasted frame from side-to-side in the bed. I was nauseated by the pain medications, and both hips had developed swollen lumps from repeated injections. There was no way I could be comfortable, and I was constantly wet from perspiration, making the soggy sheets cling to my back.

Somewhere in that dark, delirious, pain-filled night I rang the call bell for the nurse. She never came. I knew I was slipping into oblivion, but I was helpless. I rang again and again, all to no avail. As the blackness of pain and despair engulfed me, it felt as though I was sinking deeper and deeper into a bottomless pit. There came a point when I was so distraught, and my body so racked with pain, that I could not even pray. My breathing became shallow, just as it had when I was trapped under the rock in the gold mine. All I could manage to do was suck little gasps of air into my lungs.

I could not even panic; I had no strength left to either struggle or call. Nothingness slowly sucked me in. Each breath might be my last. With each panting exhalation, the only thing I could do was utter the name, "Jesus, Jesus, Jesus."

It was the lowest point of my life. I touched bedrock, the beginning and the ending of life. All my human resources exhausted, I rested on the reality of the Person of Jesus Christ, and experienced the comfort of God's Word: "Underneath are the everlasting arms."(2)

Toward daybreak, a nurse came in, discovered me unconscious, and the hospital staff performed an emergency blood transfusion. This saved my life, and gradually I came back from the edge.

Over months of recovery, I proved again that the Christian life is an ever-ongoing opportunity to trust in God. Faith is not a one-time experience, it is a lifestyle. True faith, as described by the apostle Peter, is a continuing, persevering possession.(3) Life's fiery trials reveal whether we are founded on the unmovable foundation of an indestructible faith or on the unstable, shifting sands of earthly values, human philosophies, and temporal things.

Chapter Forty-Eight

wo extremities, the miracle of birth and the mystery of death, are presented by the concepts of *first days* and *last days*. Ada and I were slowly slipping into the twilight zone that separates beginnings and endings.

There was also a subtle shift in our roles. In the years now fading into the mists of memory, Ada had been the "strong" partner in our union. I had often referred to our relationship as a perfect example of St. Peter's words: "Husbands...live with your wives in an understanding way, as with a weaker vessel...."(1) The Apostle means the words "weaker vessel" in the sense that the wife is to be treasured as a rare and precious work of art, and esteemed as an object that must be cared for with tenderness. In our relationship, Ada had been the "weaker" and yet the stronger of the two of us.

Because of my physical disability, Ada had cheerfully performed many menial and practical tasks which made my living and ministry possible. She was, in many ways, far stronger than I. She had demonstrated endurance as we traveled thousands of miles. When necessity required it she carried our luggage, and when our itinerary took us by road, she did most of the driving to spare me the acute pain and discomfort caused by the constant strain to my back and legs. Now, I watched her wilt like a flower in the heat as we almost imperceptibly slipped into a "changing of the guard."

In 1996 Ada had organized the rollicking fortieth birthday party for Dawson. He flew from California to be with us, and Ada's energy seemed boundless as she turned the backyard into a tropical paradise with palm fronds, branches, picnic tables and a buffet complete with a traditional English trifle dessert. We ended the hilarity with a soiree on the beach as Dawson entertained us with Scottish songs, amid great hilarity. Ada seemed borne along by a gentle but irresistible force. It was *her* enthusiasm, which like a river of joy carried us all through the memorable holiday period of that year.

The dawn of 1997 had heralded the mystifying changes in her. She navigated the events of February and March with quiet grace. It was now April and there was a serenity about Ada's demeanor as we took another turn in a road we had never traveled before. Somewhere, Ada lost her appetite. She was no longer eating the meals regularly prepared for the family. Armed with the herbal extracts, vitamins and the special recipes Dr. Reed had prescribed, I began the daily routine of preparing smoothies with fruit, juices and nutritional supplements.

It also became necessary to prepare supplementary, very light, delicate meals for Ada. Caring for her became the primary concern. The closeness in which we had lived for so many years now mellowed even more into a relationship that demonstrated the poignantly reciprocal virtues of mutual commitment and loving trust.

Ada became almost childlike in looking to me to be there when she needed things. She a rose every morning, and without fail, took a bath, dressed immaculately, curled her hair and put on her makeup. It was almost unbelievable, but those rituals of spring revealed the inner person that made Ada the joyful, cheerful elegant "daughter of the King" that she had reflected so elegantly.(2)

April 16th marked our 42nd wedding anniversary. It was the most subdued celebration we had held in all the years of our marriage. Wayne and Wallis Brooks gathered a few friends at their home for the occasion, and again, although she was not as animated as usual, the guests commented on Ada's bright countenance and cheerful presence.

An event of great moment took place over the weekend of May 4th. Jessica, our granddaughter, was to compete in the United States National Rhythmic Gymnastics Championships in Houston. In all the years that Jessica had been involved in gymnastics, Ada had lovingly, positively supported her. Now, the biggest challenge of Jessica's 13 years stood before her. For years she had spent six days a week, five hours a day, working out and training at the gym. She had worked and dreamed through all those hours of gaining a place on the United States Rhythmic Gymnastics National Team. It would be one step closer to her ultimate goal, to represent the United States at the Olympic Games. When she was ten years old, Jessica had written an essay. Her dream and commitment had found expression in her own words. "When my Grand Daddy was young, he wanted to go to the Olympic Games, but a mine fell on him. Now I want to go to the Olympic Games for him."

The question that faced us now was this: Could Ada make the demanding round trip by air to Houston; and would she be able to sit through the hours of competition? I have seldom been so torn over a decision. Ada wanted to go. It was a dream come true for her, as it was for Jessica. But could she stand the rigors of the trip? She had weakened noticeably over the past weeks, yet I felt it was a "now or never" opportunity. We decided we would make the journey together.

What a weekend! On Friday night, our ever-loving, ever-faithful friend Stevie Ingraham organized a dinner party in Ada's honor at one of Houston's most delightful French restaurants. Ada could hardly eat more than a taste, but her firm faith and quiet show of strength and endurance touched us all. To Ada's delight, Jessica realized her dream. She won a place on the national team.

May 11th was Mother's Day. Forty-two years before, on that exact day in far-away South Africa, we had commenced our ministry as two young adventurers, very much in love. That Mother's Day, at Church of the Messiah, in Jacksonville, Florida, we would be together for the last time as lovers, parents and partners in the House of God.

On Monday, two important events occurred. It was Dale's birthday and Ada had an appointment with Dr. Rosada. Late in the afternoon, in Dr. Rosada's office, we quietly discussed heart-searching issues. It must have been apparent to Dr. Rosada that I was carrying a great load of responsibility by caring for Ada day and night. He raised the question of hospice care for Ada. Without objection Ada agreed that it would be good to have someone help me.

I was surprised at how easily Ada handled this development. It had the potential to cause anxiety, but she maintained an air of dignity and calm. During the week, Ada received loving, encouraging, uplifting calls from a number of close friends. She talked at length to Dawson. Her sister Pal called from South Africa. And each morning she rose, groomed herself and dressed for the day.

Every evening, as we had done through forty-two years of partnership, I sat by her side on the bed and read to her from the Bible. She had always loved that. On the rare occasions when I had asked her to read, she had almost invariably said, "No, I like you to read to me." There were evenings also when I would read poetry to her. She gently steered me away from poems that spoke of parting, or death, disappointed love, or broken dreams.

For several weeks Jenny and I had noticed occasional signs of mental confusion. The week before, Ada and I had been babysitting the grandchildren in the downstairs den. I had risen from the sofa and walked down the hallway to prepare her bed. The children had gone upstairs. I felt an urge to return to the den, and as I rounded the corner of the hallway, I saw Ada lying stretched out on the floor in front of the fireplace. She had tried to stand up but had fallen and struck her arm and head on the hearth. I yelled for Jessica who rushed down the stairs and helped me lift Ada back into bed.

Dr. Rosada suspected that the cancer had spread to other areas of her body. On May 16th, the admitting nurse of Hospice North East arrived at Jenny's home to discuss Ada's needs and how the organization could help with home care.

Jenny was my representative in the consultation. I simply could not face it. My beloved daughter sat on the bed with her mother, and for two hours the foursome discussed the ultimate issues of life. On that memorable day in 1993, when Dr. Brent Norman had solemnly told Ada, "This will cause your demise," she had said, "I am not afraid of dying." When she had been offered the slim chance of an extension of life through chemotherapy, she had replied, "I am not afraid of dying, but if I am to die, I want to die with dignity."

I was proud of her.

The Hospice team had come at Dr. Rosada's request. I was so impressed with their sincerity, their thoroughness and the service they promised. One of these was the procurement of a hospital bed. I thought the very mention would evoke a negative response in Ada. But with a calm that amazed me, she agreed that an adjustable bed would be a good idea.

That afternoon, the Hospice aide arrived to help Ada with her shower. Just two days before Ada had told me she could no longer lift herself out of the bathtub, and so Jenny had helped by giving her "Mommy," whom she now loving referred to as "my baby," a shower.

On Saturday, amid a flurry of activity, a hospital bed was delivered through the generous help of the Red Cross. I shall always be grateful to men like Dr. Rosada, Dr. Huss and Dr. Gillis, and for the services provided by Hospice and the Red Cross, who, knowing our need, were willing to donate their time and talents to serve us, even knowing that we had no medical insurance and no means to pay.

Saturday May 17th night marked another milestone in Ada's journey. She was strangely confused. On Sunday morning, I had arranged for someone to sit with her, but Jenny felt very strongly that either she or I must be with Ada. I had something of great importance I wanted to share with the congregation, so Jenny decided to stay with her "Baby" and I would go to church. The urgent word which I had in my heart was the challenge to the church to be, in the spiritual realm, what the Hospice service promised in the medical realm. There was a compelling drive in me to tell the people of God: "We *must* obey the commandment of Christ to love one another."(3)

Dale was on an overseas ministry trip, and when I spoke to the Dean, Jacob Danner, who was officiating at the service, I also explained why Jenny was not present in her accustomed role as Worship Leader. I told him I had a word for the congregation, and that Jenny was at home caring for Ada.

For the first time in all the long months of our journey into this unknown world, I spoke the somber words to Jacob, "Ada could die at any moment now." While I was at Church, Jenny, prompted by the Spirit of the Lord, phoned Dawson and urged him to come from California immediately.

That afternoon, Jenny invited Dale's mother and father to visit Ada. It was a most remarkable occasion. Ada had been sleeping all morning following the visit by the Hospice nurse and aide. For the first time in the months of my personal care, Ada did not drink her specially prepared smoothie. But when Jesse and Bonita Howard arrived, she sat up in the hospital bed and engaged in an animated conversation with them.

It must have appeared bizarre. Jenny and I were nonplussed. We knew Ada was gravely ill. The doctor's predictions, the Hospice team, the noticeable change in Ada's condition; all the signs were there. But with the Howards, and then later when her sister Pal phoned from South Africa, Ada was able to have an almost cheerful conversation.

Throughout the two weeks prior to this, all Ada's close family had phoned. Garness from Cape Town, Elaine from Johannesburg. They were mystified by my reports, and the apparent contradictions of the situation. What they were unaware of was that Ada was always within earshot of my conversations. I didn't want Ada to hear me describe her condition as grave. I maintained a positive attitude whenever I talked to her or in her hearing.

A heart-breaking moment had occurred during those two weeks. One day, with the gentle spirit she always displayed, she had very simply asked me, "Am I dying?" My response was an honest, "I am not even thinking of dying. I am doing everything we know to get you well." She accepted my word. And that was the attitude I focused on in all my conversations with family and friends.

Sunday, May 18th, 6:00 p.m. The day is almost over. Dawson phoned to say he had missed his flight from San Francisco, but was being re-routed so that he and Lionel could be with us by Monday morning. Jenny and I seat Ada on the edge of her bed ready to take her to the bathroom. Instead of standing up, Ada begins to speak. "You need to rearrange this room. The sofa is in the wrong place; it should be across the corner. And the tables should be against the walls with the flowers on them." But this is the bedroom. There is no sofa. Jenny, trying to be lighthearted says, "Mommy, Jesus has gone to Heaven to prepare your mansion. When you get there, you can tell God how to decorate it." We take her to the bathroom, but on the way back, she makes a detour to my room, where I have been sleeping. She lies down on my bed and says, "Let me show you how to decorate this room." Jenny and I don't know whether to laugh or cry, but we finally lead her back to her bed.

10:00 p.m. It's time to get Ada ready for the night. We try and get her out of the bed, but she has become weak, and all she can do is slump into the bedside chair Hospice has provided. We can barely hold her upright on the chair, and we struggle to get her back to bed. We notice that her breathing has become very labored. Jenny tries to give her a drink of water, but Ada can barely swallow a few drops from the drinking straw. Jenny phones Dr. Rosada.

11:00 p.m. Dr. Rosada arrives. He expresses concern over her breathing. She has, just this afternoon, begun to take morphine in tablet form, and Dr. Rosada thinks this may have added to the drowsiness and heavy breathing. He instructs us in how to determine Ada's condition by her breathing. He leaves. Jenny goes to bed.

12:00 p.m. I leave Ada's bedside and go to my room.

Monday, May 19th, 1:00 a.m. I look at Ada, she is apparently asleep but still breathing heavily.

4:00 a.m. I look in on Ada again. Her breathing pattern seems much the same.

6:00 a.m. I awaken and go immediately into Ada's room. The warning signs have begun. The irregular breathing pattern described by Dr. Rosada has set in. I hurry upstairs, look in on Jenny, but she is sound asleep. I don't want to waken her because she is so weary. I hurry to the kitchen and phone the Hospice nurse. One of their promises is to be on 24 hour call. She asks me if I can put the telephone to Ada's mouth so she can hear her breathing pattern. Jenny appears in the kitchen; my movement and my talking on the phone has awakened her. We rush downstairs to Ada's room, and as we walk in Jenny sees Ada, she cries out, "O God, Mommy's dying."

6:20 a.m. The hospice nurse arrives, followed closely by Dr. Rosada.

The Monday morning of May 19th was overcast. For nearly two hours, our dear Dr. Rosada and the nurse gently, lovingly ministered to Ada. At the first sight of Ada's final battle, Jenny had spoken words of strength to her beloved Mother. She had said, Mommy, "Hold on. Be strong."

But when she saw that the battle for life was vain, and the distress in her mother's eyes, Jenny spoke with tender loving compassion and said, "Mommy you must go now; Jesus is here to take you home." Sensing that Ada might be in distress about the burdens she carried on her heart, Jenny promised, "Mommy, we will take care of each other. I promise you I will take care of Daddy." Knowing that Ada was ever concerned for her children, Jenny said, "Mommy I have this wonderful home which you fixed up so beautifully for me. Dawson has a house and we will give Daddy a home. We will love each other and take care of each other. Mommy, you can go Home now." As Jenny coaxed her cherished "Mommy" home, I read to her from the Book we both had loved so long; The Bible. I prayed for her as she struggled to draw her final breaths. I read some of her favorite Psalms. I read from the Gospel of John, and then as I began to read from the Book of Revelation, the sun, for one brief shining moment burst through the clouds and flooded into the room.

Ada saw the light. She raised her head from the bed, looked at the ray of golden sunlight and sank back on her pillow.

At 7:55 a.m. she drew her final breath.

The Sun of Righteousness had risen, with healing in His Wings.
(4)

I have never cried so deeply, so agonizingly, or with such utter abandon. The words, "Why, Why, Why?" were wrung from my broken heart.

Father Lou Caron, one of our priests, met Dawson and Lionel at the airport, and when he arrived at the house and I wept on his big, broad shoulders; all I could force from my brokenness were the words, "My son, My son, My son; your mother is dead."

Around me plans were being made, people came and went like shadows in a mist. Dr. Rosada remained with us in the room until the storm of first shock subsided.

Jenny arranged for each of her four children to come quietly into the room to say Goodbye to their Granny. Lionel too was there in those sacred moments. Each child paused to gaze on the face they had loved so dearly. Each one lingered a while.

Little Ruthie, with the innocence of the very young, sat on my lap and said, "Is Granny in there?" I answered, "No." She replied, "I want to talk to Granny." I said, "Granny is with Jesus." With the simplicity of childlike faith this diminutive four year old said, "Then let me talk to Jesus about Granny."

The pain we all felt was again expressed by those lisping lips. Referring back to a terrible accident which had befallen her just a year ago, Ruthie spoke for all of us when she said, "I miss Granny so much. It hurts even more than when boiling water falls on you."

I fought one of the hardest battles of my life on that Monday morning when the morticians arrived to take my Beloved's body away. That final struggle was more than I could bear. I said, "No! You can not take her away from me." Finally under the gracious ministry of Dr. Rosada, and at Jenny's urging, I allowed Dawson to take me for a drive in Ada's car. While we were away from the house, the earthly temple of grace and beauty which had been Ada's dwelling place was taken away to be prepared for her final rest in this vale of tears.

The emotional pain and the gaping, dark feeling of emptiness that engulfed me was eased by the presence of loved ones and friends. Suddenly, as if by a divine transportation, my dear friend J. O. Stewart from El Paso appeared at my side. The next day he drove me to the quiet elegance and beauty of the Ponte Vedra area south of Jacksonville and allowed me time to reminisce in the tranquil atmosphere of the places Ada and I had loved to visit. The entire staff of Church of the Messiah rallied to our side. Our family was overwhelmed by the kindness and demonstration of Christian love and care showered upon us by the pastors and people of the Church. As never before I experienced an outpouring of true Christian care as Jenny's friends, the women of the Church, literally took over the control of every detail of our stricken lives. They prepared all our meals, manned the telephones and stayed in the house in shifts twenty-four hours a day.

On Friday, May 23rd, a service of tender triumph was held at Church of the Messiah. My son-in-law, Dale, conducted the service; Francis McNutt spoke to our hearts as he comforted us with the assurance that grief, expressed in tears, is part of the process of healing. Terry Fullam, in his inimitable manner preached a message from Psalm 31:14, 15 which focused my heart on the truth that our "times are in God's Hand."

We laid Ada to rest in the Arlington Park Memorial Gardens and chose as the inscription for her headstone the words which I believe gave expression to her whole life: "Blessed is she that believed; for there shall be a fulfillment of those things which were told her from the Lord."(5)

In the letter announcing Ada's passing to our wide circle of friends, I requested that in lieu of flowers, people would donate gifts toward a fund set up for the purpose of helping Jessica on the road to realizing her Olympic dream.

On May 31st, Jenny and I traveled to San Clemente, California where Archbishop Adler celebrated a memorial service in Ada's honor. Again, I was overcome by the expressions of love, respect and appreciation which the people of St. Michael's Church and other areas of California demonstrated in their tributes to Ada. At the service, our friend and colleague, Jay Sindahl spoke with power and compassion on the theme of "Going Home." My faithful friend Tony Louch led the congregation in expressions of loving remembrance and dramatized the power of Ada's legacy when he read her masterful poem, *Easter*.

Even though we mourned so deeply, there was an air of quiet triumph in all the remembrances, eulogies and expressions of loss. As she had lived, so she died, and so she was laid to rest, "In sure and certain hope of the resurrection...to an inheritance which is imperishable, which is pure, undefiled, which will never pass away; reserved in heaven for her."(6)

The secrets of our life together, and the mystery of Ada's death, lie in the truth and comfort of the words: "We do not sorrow as those who have no hope."(7) With full confidence we can say, "I know that my Redeemer lives and at the last day He will stand upon the earth; in my flesh I shall see God...and my eyes shall behold Him."(8) Scripture gives us the answers to live by when those we love are taken from us, such as these favorite passages:

"The trumpet shall sound, the dead in Christ shall rise first, then we which are alive and remain shall be caught up together with them in the clouds to meet the Lord in the air. So shall we ever be (together) with the Lord."(9)

"Jesus said, 'I am the resurrection and the life; he that believes in me though he were dead, yet shall he live, and whoever lives and believes in me shall never die, and I will raise him up at the last day.'"(10)

Chapter Forty-Eight

"Then shall come to pass the saying, Death is swallowed up in victory."(11)

"Wherefore comfort one another with these words."(12)

"Even so, come, Lord Jesus."(13)

Epilogue

"Weeping may endure for a night but joy comes in the morning," according to Psalm 30:5. There have been many bright mornings for me since Ada's death, now many years in the past. This chronicle of God's goodness would not be complete without mentioning some of them.

In the letter that my granddaughter Jessica wrote as an assignment for school when she was 10 years old, she said, "When my Granddaddy was young he wanted to go to the Olympic Games, but a mine fell on him and he was paralyzed. Now I want to go to the Olympic Games for him."

In 1997, as a 13-year-old fledgling rhythmic gymnast, she won a place on the USA Junior National Team. At 15, she became the youngest gymnast ever to win the title of National Senior Rhythmic Gymnastics Champion. With a sweet grace and a winsome witness for Christ, she represented the United States with distinction and made her mark on the international scene before retiring from gymnastics. Today she has a successful career coaching ballet dancers and serves on the board of USA Gymnastics. For many years she had a poster in her bathroom proclaiming: "God gives the talent. We must give the effort." We are not all athletes, but we all, every one of us, has a special gift, a talent from God. It is what we do with the talent that counts.

As the Congregational Pastor at Church of the Messiah in Jacksonville for many years, one of my duties was the responsibility of ensuring visitors to the church were suitably welcomed. In order for a church to grow, it must have the same formula that makes for a successful restaurant. A flourishing restaurant will provide 3 elements. They are friendly service, a pleasant atmosphere and good food. Applied to the church, that translates into how we receive people, how comfortable they feel in our services, and whether or not we meet their spiritual needs.

On the first Sunday in November 1997, a lovely visitor named Suzanne attended our church on crutches. I welcomed her and identified with her injury, which was a broken foot. I invited her to our Newcomers' Class. She not only joined the church, but instantly made a remarkable impression with the freshness of her witness and her bright presence.

We grew closer, and on December 12, 1998, Suzanne and I were married at Church of the Messiah in a magnificent ceremony. Surrounded by hundreds of friends and family, and in the presence of bishops and priests, Archbishop Randolph Adler and my son-in-law Bishop Dale Howard performed a glorious ceremony. Suzanne said it was like being crowned Queen. Dale announced, "Suzanne loved the church so much, she married it!"

Since then we have remained in a wonderful partnership and ministry which has touched the lives of many people and helped shape the life of the church in significant ways. The lesson? God gives us the capacity to expand our ability to love. Bishop Adler made the comment that our love for a departed partner does not diminish. It never dies, but God gives us the capacity to love again. It is a love that does not replace, but is added to the love we have known before.

The Charismatic Episcopal Church (CEC) was an exciting movement in the early days when I was involved with it. Dale left the Episcopal church to become a priest and eventually a Bishop in the CEC. For a time it was the fastest-growing denomination in the USA. However, the CEC soon became riven with power struggles and conflicts. Many of the founding bishops and priests eventually split from the church, resigned, or like Archbishop Adler, retired. In one of those power struggles Dale was abruptly ousted. He and Jenny went on to start their own independent church in Jacksonville.

Their four children continued to do well, with Ruth graduating from Juilliard School in New York as a professional ballerina, Peter finding his place as an entrepreneur, and Bethany collaborating with Jenny and Dale in their ventures. Dawson and Brenda parted amicably soon after Ada's death. After graduating from university Lionel became an online marketing manager while Angela discovered a love of mathematics and computer science. Dawson eventually met and married Christine, who the whole family has come to love as a "living angel." He founded the National Institute for Integrative Healthcare to research and train professionals in promising new therapies, and manages Energy Psychology Group, one of the largest alternative medicine businesses on the web.

One of my favorite stories is called *The Mystery of Hard Times*. It was written by an anonymous author, and it goes like this:

"A man found the cocoon of a butterfly. One day a small opening appeared in the envelope. He sat and watched for several hours as the butterfly struggled to force its body through that little hole. Then, it stopped making progress. It seemed as though it was stuck and could go no farther. So the man decided to help the butterfly. He took a pair of scissors and snipped off the remaining bit of the cocoon. The butterfly then emerged easily, but it had a swollen body and small shriveled wings. The man continued to watch the butterfly, expecting that the body would shrink and the wings would expand to support the body, enabling the creature to fly.

"It never happened! Sadly, the butterfly spent the rest of its life crawling around with a swollen body and shriveled wings. What the man in his mistaken kindness did not understand was that the restricting cocoon and the struggle required for the butterfly to press through the tiny opening were God's way of forcing fluid from the body of the butterfly into its wings so that they could expand for flight once it achieved its freedom from the cocoon.

"The difficulties and struggles of life are God's way of making us strong. If He allowed us to go through life without challenges and obstacles, we would never become strong. We would never be able to fly."

As I look back, I am overwhelmed by the grace and love of God, so evident in my life despite all the tragedies and setbacks that accompanied breaking out of the cocoon. I shall never forget hearing the great Bible expositor Dr. Martin Lloyd-Jones preach on the words of St. Paul in which the Apostle out weighs the "light affliction" of our trials with the "weight of glory" that is the reward of our faith.(1) The bottom line of *all* testing, trials, sufferings and afflictions is that, compared with the reward that God promises, the adversity that seems so heavy and endless will one day seem fleeting and trivial "at the appearing of our Lord Jesus Christ."(2) My hope is that as you have shared these sorrows and glories with me, you will have found meaning in the trials of your own life, and that you will find the courage to bear them easily, graciously and joyfully.

Scripture References

Chapter 18

1. Proverbs 16:9
2. Proverbs 16:33
3. Matthew 6:19, 21
4. II Timothy 2:2
5. Ephesians 3:20
6. Isaiah 50:10
7. I Peter 1:5
8. II Corinthians 12:9
9. II Timothy 4:8

Chapter 19

1. I Corinthians 4:6
2. Philippians 4:19

Chapter 20

1. II Corinthians 5:6–8
2. Philippians 1:23
3. Psalm 36:5,6

Chapter 23

1. Micah 7:6
2. Matthew 10:36

Chapter 24

1. Matthew 25:21

Chapter 25

1. Psalm 118:9
2. I Samuel 17:47 (Living Bible)

Chapter 28

1. Ecclesiastes 1:2
2. Isaiah 42:6
3. Isaiah 43:10, 11
4. Isaiah 40:28–31
5. Isaiah 41:10, 13, 15
6. II Corinthians 5:7
7. Acts 4:31, 3
8. Isaiah 43:19
9. Psalm 46:10

Chapter 30

1. Proverbs 20:24
2. Proverbs 23:17, 18 (Living Bible)

Part 2

Prelude

1. Revelation 3:20
2. 1 Corinthians 3:6
3. 1 Corinthians 4:2
4. Job 23:10

Chapter 31

1. Revelation 3:16
2. Acts 1:8
3. Proverbs 23:17,18
4. Hebrews 4:16; 13:5

Chapter 32

1. 1 1Timothy 1:12
2. Proverbs 18:24

Chapter 33

1. Thessalonians 5:7
2. Psalm 23:4
3. Deuteronomy 31:6, 8
4. James 5:14

Chapter 34

1. John 12:24
2. Luke 3:16; 24:49
3. Acts 1:5; 2:1–4 and 15–18
4. Daniel 12:3; Proverbs 11:3

Chapter 35

1. 1 Corinthians 12:8–11, 28–30
2. Matthew 3:11; Acts 1:5

Chapter 36

1. John 13:33, 34
2. Acts 20:24

Chapter 37

1. Job 23:10
2. Psalm 116:1, 2
3. Psalm 41:9

Chapter 38

1. Philippians 1:3, 4
2. Psalm 41:9

3. Job 19:19

4. Psalm 73:16, 17

5. Psalm 73:23, 24

Chapter 39

1. Psalm 23:6

2. Romans 8:14

3. Isaiah 55:8, 9

4. Jeremiah 29:11 with Romans 8:28

Chapter 40

1. Isaiah 35:1

2. Psalm 61:1, 2

3. 11 Corinthians 1:8, 9; 4:7, 8; 6:4–10; 11:23–28

Chapter 41

1. Psalm 32:8

2. Jeremiah 29:10, 11

3. II Corinthians 1:3, 4

Chapter 42

1. John 11:35

Chapter 45

1. Malachi 3:6

2. 1 John 1:8, 9

3. 1 John 1:7

4. 11 John 4

Chapter 46

1. 1 Peter 3:7

2. Psalm 45:13

3. John 13:34, 35

4. Malachi 4:2

5. Luke 1:45

Chapter 47

1. 1 Thessalonians 4:13

2. Deuteronomy 33:27

3. 1 Peter 3:7

Chapter 48

1. 1 Peter 1:4

2. Psalm 45:13

3. John 11:25, 26; 6:40

4. Malachi 4:2

5. Luke 1:45

6. *Book of Common Prayer*

7. 1 Thessalonians 4:13

8. Job 19:25, 26; 6:40

9. 1 Thessalonians 4:16, 17

10. John 11:35

11. 1 Corinthians 15:51–55

12. 1 Thessalonians 5:18

13. Revelation 22:20

Epilogue

1. 1 Corinthians 15:51–55

2. Revelation 22:20

www.ingramcontent.com/pod-product-compliance
Lightning Source LLC
Chambersburg PA
CBHW020520100426
42813CB00030B/3306/J